CONSUMER GUIDE®

Fix It, Clean It, Store It

Publications International, Ltd.

Contents

CHAPTER 1 ▪ CLEANING
5

CHAPTER 2 ▪ CLOTHES CARE
67

CHAPTER 3 ▪ FOOD
110

CHAPTER 4 ▪ MAINTENANCE AND REPAIR
173

CHAPTER 5 ▪ ORGANIZING YOUR HOME
221

CHAPTER 6 ▪ PAINT AND WALLCOVERINGS
239

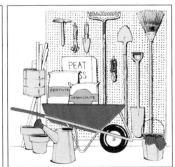

CHAPTER 7 ■ HOME SAFETY
AND SECURITY
262

CHAPTER 8 ■ CHILD CARE
273

CHAPTER 9 ■ MOVING
287

CHAPTER 10 ■ PERSONAL GROOMING
297

CHAPTER 11 ■ PET CARE
305

INDEX
312

Cleaning

To minimize the drudgery while maximizing your cleaning power, you'll need the right tools, reliable cleaning products, and an efficient cleaning strategy that accommodates your personal and household needs. Your cleaning schedule for both regular and seasonal care should be comfortable for you. You may want to clean for an hour every morning, two hours after work, or all Saturday morning. As long as you have a schedule that leaves room for the occasional change of plans, you'll stay ahead of housework.

YOUR CLEANING CLOSET

CREATING A CLEANING CENTER

You will be more likely to start your cleaning chores and to finish the task if you have everything you need on hand and in one place. A cleaning center that saves you time and steps is the efficient beginning to quick and easy cleaning methods.

■ Make sure the closet is equipped to store all the cleaning tools and products you buy or make. If you can't fit them all into one place, you'll waste time digging around

under the sink for the cleanser and going out to the garage for the mop and bucket.

■ Put up a pegboard or hooks to hang brushes and mops. They'll not only be easier to find, but they'll last longer if they are hung.

■ Install plenty of shelves to hold bottles and cartons. This will get dangerous cleaning products out of the reach of children and give you space to store a complete array of cleaning supplies.

■ If you need to make room in your closet, store bathroom cleaning supplies in a secure storage area in the bathroom. If you have more than one bathroom, duplicate your supplies so you don't have to carry them around.

TOOLS OF THE TRADE

You'll want to make sure you stock your cleaning closet with most of the following items:

■ Baskets for carrying supplies from one room to another.

■ Broom, dustpan, and dust mop for quick cleanups.

■ Brushes in an assortment of sizes: a hard-bristle scrub brush, toilet brushes, and other soft- and medium-bristle brushes for scrubbing and dusting.

■ Buckets with double compartments to hold both your cleaning solution and rinse water. Use red fingernail polish to plainly mark pint, quart, and gallon levels inside the bucket.

■ Nothing absorbs water better than soft leather, so a chamois is perfect for drying washed cars and windows. After you use it, wash your chamois in detergent and water, rinse thoroughly, squeeze out the water, stretch it to full size, and place it on a flat surface to dry.

■ Cleaning agents. Whether you make your own or purchase commercial products, make sure you know how to use them.

■ Cleaning cloths can be made from old clothes, sheets, and towels. Light colors and natural fabrics, like cotton and linen, make the best cleaning cloths.

■ Long-handle dust mop for cleaning ceilings and cobwebs.

■ Mops with detachable heads.

■ Rubber gloves protect your hands whenever you work with cleaning solutions. Don't forget to put them on.

■ Scouring pads, made of both synthetics and steel wool.

■ Sponges in various sizes. These should be tossed out as soon as they start to shred.

■ Squeegees speed window washing. If you don't have one, an old

GLOSSARY OF CLEANING AGENTS

■ All-purpose cleaners remove grease and grimy dirt.

■ Ammonia is available in clear or sudsy form. It is a good grease cutter, wax stripper, window cleaner, and general soil remover. If you object to the strong odor of ammonia, buy a scented product. Scented ammonia is not suitable for stain removal.

■ Baking soda is one of the most versatile cleaning products available. Used by itself in dry form, it acts as a very mild scouring powder that will not scratch even the most delicate surfaces. Add water to make a paste, and use it to scour dirty surfaces. Combined with other ingredients, it makes a very good cleaning and deodorizing solution.

■ Bleach helps remove stains and whiten laundry; it's also good for cleaning toilets.

■ Dishwashing liquid detergents are used for many cleaning tasks in addition to doing dishes.

windshield wiper is a good stand-in for a commercial squeegee.

■ Vacuum cleaner. Uprights are especially good for wall-to-wall carpets and large rugs and areas with heavy traffic. Because of their portability, canisters are superior for cleaning walls, woodwork, shelves, and furniture.

■ Waxes, polishes, and oils for wood, leather, brass, chrome, silver, glass, and all the other surfaces that you'll want to shine.

BATHROOMS

The average person can tolerate a growing collection of dust balls under the bed or a drawer full of tarnished flatware in the sideboard. But a grimy bathroom is another story. The bathroom should be cleaned once a week, and even more frequently if it gets heavy use from a large family. Fortunately, most bathrooms are made of materials that are easy to keep clean. Tile and porcelain surfaces are stain-resistant if dirt and scum are not allowed to build up on them. Make it a firm rule in your home to rinse out the tub or shower stall immediately after you use it. Spray water from the shower head on all interior surfaces, then lather soap onto a damp sponge, swish it around the tub or stall, and rinse.

COUNTERTOPS AND BASINS

Bathroom countertops are sloshed, splotched, and splattered with everything from hair spray to shoe polish. In most homes, countertops are made of materials that can stand up to the assault: ceramic tile, plastic laminate, and cultured marble. These materials are durable and easy to clean.

CULTURED MARBLE

Cultured marble resembles real marble, but it is a lot more versatile and much easier to care for. Avoid using abrasive cleaners and steel-wool pads, because they will scratch the surface, making it difficult to keep clean.

PLASTIC LAMINATE

Plastic laminate is made of thin layers of plastic superimposed on craft paper and overlaid on particle board or plywood. The color of most plastic laminate is only in the top layer. The glossy, matte, or textured surface is also laid on. A light application of furniture wax will protect and brighten laminate surfaces.

■ To clean plastic laminate, use a two-sided scrubbing pad with fiber on one side and a sponge on the other. Moistened slightly with water, the fiber side is just abrasive enough to loosen greasy smears

SUBSTITUTE TOOLS

■ An automobile snow brush is perfect for cleaning under a refrigerator.

■ Use an old shaving brush or baby's hairbrush to avoid harming delicate fabric or pleated lamp shades when dusting.

■ Paintbrushes make excellent dusters for small or hard-to-reach areas. Flick them along door jambs, around windows, and into corners where dust cloths won't fit.

■ Instead of buying dust cloths chemically treated to "attract" dust, make your own from cheesecloth. Dip the cloth in a solution of 2 cups water and ¼ cup lemon oil, and allow it to dry before using.

■ An old nylon stocking rolled into a ball becomes a non-scratch scrub pad for cleaning the sink and tub.

■ Dust and other debris often collect behind large appliances. Clean out these hard-to-reach areas by making a yardstick "duster"—just cover the end with a sock, secured with rubber bands, or fasten a small sponge to the end of the yardstick with staples or rubber bands.

and other soil. Turning the scrubber over, use the sponge side to wipe the surface clean.

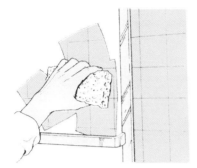

■ When a spot or stain persists, sprinkle baking soda on the spot and scrub gently. If this doesn't take care of the problem, apply a polishing cleanser with a wet sponge.

MIRRORS

To clean mirrors, use a clean, dry cloth and one of the following solutions:

1. Mix ⅓ cup clear ammonia in 1 gallon warm water. Apply it with a sponge or pour the solution into a spray container, and spray it directly on the mirror. Buff with a lint-free cloth, chamois, or paper towel. Vinegar may be substituted for ammonia.

2. Pour vinegar into a shallow bowl or pan, then crumple a sheet of newspaper, dip it in the vinegar, and apply to the mirror. Wipe the glass several times with the same newspaper until the mirror is almost dry.

Then shine it with a clean, soft cloth or dry newspaper.

3. Mix 2 cups isopropyl rubbing alcohol (70 percent solution), 2 tablespoons liquid dishwashing detergent, and 2 cups water. Stir until thoroughly mixed, and then pour into a spray bottle. Spray directly on the mirror. Buff with a lint-free cloth, chamois, or paper towel.

SHOWER STALLS

Shower enclosures are a chore to keep clean—but they can be less of a problem if you follow these suggestions:

■ Keep mildew from taking hold by wiping shower walls with a towel after each shower.

■ If the shower area is subject to mildew, periodically spray it with a mildew inhibitor and disinfectant.

■ Leave the shower door slightly open to allow air to circulate; this will discourage the growth of mildew.

■ Remove hard-water deposits on shower enclosures with a solution of white vinegar and water.

■ Glass shower doors will sparkle when you clean them with a sponge dipped in white vinegar.

■ Add 1 cup liquid fabric softener to 1 quart warm water, and use to loosen and clean soap scum from shower doors.

■ Mix 1 part mineral oil with 4 parts water in a clean, empty spray bottle. Spray on soap scum and dirt in your shower or tub. Wipe off with a sponge.

■ Remove water spots on the metal frames around shower doors and enclosures with lemon oil.

■ If the grout or caulking in your shower breaks away where the walls join the tub or shower floor, recaulk immediately to prevent water damage.

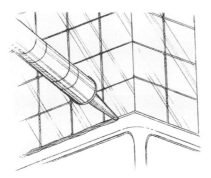

■ When tile walls need a thorough cleaning, run the shower water at its hottest temperature so the steam will loosen the dirt. Then, using a sponge mop, clean with a mixture of ½ cup vinegar, 1 cup clear ammonia, and ¼ cup baking soda in 1 gallon of warm water. After cleaning, rinse with clear water. Note: Never use harsh abrasive powders or steel-wool pads.

■ Coat the tile walls of your shower with furniture polish to prevent soap scum buildup and water spots.

■ Clean mineral deposits from a shower head by removing the head, taking it apart, and soaking it in vinegar. Then brush deposits loose with an old toothbrush. Clean the holes by poking them with a wire, pin, toothpick, or ice pick.

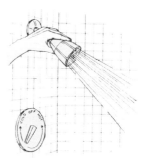

SHOWER STALL CLEANER

Mix ½ cup vinegar, 1 cup ammonia, ¼ cup baking soda, and 1 gallon hot water. Caution: Wear rubber gloves and work in a well-ventilated area when using this powerful solution. Apply it to the walls of the shower with a sponge, scrubbing with a brush, if necessary, to remove all the scum. Rinse well with clear water, and wipe dry.

BATHTUBS

Most bathtubs are made of porcelain. If the fixtures are older, chances are the material is porcelain on cast iron. These fixtures may not be as acid- and alkaline-resistant as newer porcelain-on-steel tubs. Fiberglass and acrylic tubs, which are lighter and easier to install than steel tubs, are used in new construction and remodeling, but they are not as durable as porcelain-coated steel. If you have a fiberglass tub, you will have to be especially careful when you clean it to avoid scratching the surface.

■ Porcelain tubs should be cleaned with nonabrasive powder or liquid cleanser. Sprinkle powder on a damp sponge and apply it to the porcelain surface of the tub or basin. Use a synthetic scouring pad on stubborn soil. Rinse well.

■ When you clean the bathtub, also remove hair from the traps in the drains to prevent clogging.

■ Fiberglass tubs should be cleaned with a commercial fiberglass-cleaning product or nonabrasive liquid cleanser. Apply either product with a damp sponge, and rinse with clear water.

■ Commercial rust removers are very effective in removing rust stains. Wear rubber gloves when you work with these products because they contain acid. You can also clean discolored porcelain fixtures with a paste made of cream of tartar moistened with hydrogen peroxide or a paste made of borax moistened with lemon juice. Scrub the paste into lightly stained areas with a brush, and rinse well.

■ A ring around the tub can be rubbed away without cleaners using a nylon net ball or pad.

BASIC BATHROOM CLEANER

Mix 3 tablespoons baking soda, ½ cup ammonia, and 2 cups warm water and use for everyday cleaning. Be sure to wear rubber gloves and use in a well-ventilated area. For a bathroom cleaner without the ammonia, mix 16 ounces baking soda, 4 tablespoons dishwashing liquid, and 1 cup warm water.

■ Cover a stubborn bathtub ring with a paste of cream of tartar and hydrogen peroxide. When the paste dries, wipe it off.

■ To remove discoloration from a yellowed bathtub, rub the tub with a solution of salt and turpentine. Rinse well. Caution: Wear rubber gloves when you work with this solution.

SHOWER CURTAINS AND BATH MATS

Like tubs and enclosures, shower curtains and bath mats are subject to mildew. Fortunately, they're easy to clean. The following tips should help make this chore a breeze:

■ Keep a new shower curtain looking fresh by using the old shower curtain as a liner. Hang the new curtain on the same hooks in front of the old curtain. The old curtain will take the beating from water

CLEANING SCHEDULE

EVERY DAY

Remove surface litter from carpets and bare floors with a canister vacuum or broom.

Wash dishes, wipe countertops and cooking appliances.

Empty wastebaskets and kitchen garbage.

Wipe basins and bathtubs.

Make beds and straighten rooms.

EVERY WEEK OR TWO

Vacuum carpets and bare floors thoroughly with your vacuum cleaner.

Vacuum upholstery and drapes with the upholstery tool, using the crevice tool in the seams of furniture coverings.

Dust and polish furniture.

Clean the range, and wipe out the refrigerator.

Wash kitchen and bathroom floors.

Clean toilets, fixtures, and bathroom mirrors.

Change bed linens.

SEASONAL OR AS NEEDED

Clean rugs and carpets using a carpet-cleaning solution or an absorbent powder.

Remove old wax, apply new wax, and buff bare floors.

Shampoo upholstered furniture.

Wash lamp shades, walls, and woodwork.

Dust books, pictures, and lamps.

Clean mirrors, TVs, picture frames, and art objects.

Clean oven, microwave, refrigerator, freezer, and other appliances.

Wash bath mats and shower curtain.

Organize closets.

Turn mattresses, wash pads and pillow covers, and air or wash pillows.

YEARLY

Vacuum rug pads and the backs of rugs.

Shampoo carpets and clean rugs. Turn rugs to equalize wear.

Wash windows, curtains, blinds, and shades. Clean draperies.

Wash or dry-clean bedspreads, blankets, and slipcovers.

---

and soap scum while the new one stays clean.

■ To prevent shower curtains from wrinkling, put them in the washing machine with ½ cup of detergent and ½ cup of baking soda, along with two large bath towels. Add a cup of vinegar to the rinse cycle; hang the curtains up immediately after washing, and let them air-dry.

■ When you clean a plastic shower curtain, keep it soft and flexible by adding a few drops of mineral oil to the rinse water. Maintain its softness by wiping it occasionally with a solution of warm water and mineral oil.

■ Eliminate mildew by spraying newly washed shower curtains with a disinfectant.

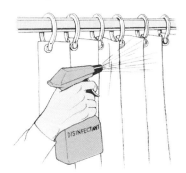

■ Clean a rubber or vinyl bath mat by tossing it into the washer with bath towels. The terry cloth scrubs the mat, and everything comes out clean.

TOILETS

Cleaning the toilet is one of those chores that you want to get through as quickly as possible. Many toilet-bowl cleaners and deodorizers claim that they'll help you do this. Some

CLOGGED DRAIN OPENER

Moderately clogged drains can sometimes be opened by pouring ½ cup baking soda, followed by ½ cup vinegar, down the drain. Caution: The interaction of these two ingredients creates foaming and fumes, so replace the drain cover loosely. Flush the drain with clear water after about three hours.

products are truly helpful, some are not. Toilet bowls and tanks are usually made of vitreous china, which is nonporous and easy to clean. Before you clean your toilet, read the label on your cleaning product to learn its exact chemical makeup and how it should be used. Be especially careful never to mix products that contain chlorine bleach with ammonia-base products. Always wear rubber gloves when you work with toilet cleaners. Be careful not to allow cleaners to remain in the toilet or to touch other bathroom surfaces.

TOILET-BOWL CLEANERS

Clean and disinfect your toilet bowl with ½ cup chlorine bleach. Pour it into the bowl, and let it stand for ten minutes. Then scrub with the toilet brush and flush.

UNCLOGGING DRAINS

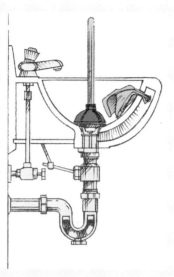

In many homes, the bathroom sink doubles as a dressing table, and everyone in the family shampoos in the shower. Hair and soap are washed into bathroom drains day and night, and the cruddy mess can quickly jam up the plumbing. Regular clearing of the traps saves your plumbing, and it also cuts down on cleaning time—water that flows out of the tub quickly doesn't allow dirt to settle on these surfaces.

If clearing the trap doesn't clear the drain, you'll have to take stronger measures. First plunge the drain. Before you use the plunger in the bathroom basin, plug the overflow opening. This allows the plunger to exercise its maximum suction effect on the clogged drain.

If plunging does not open the drain, use a chemical drain opener. These products must be handled with special care because they are caustic and harmful to skin and eyes. Use them in a well-ventilated area, and follow the manufacturer's instructions. Chemical drain openers will damage porcelain enamel and should not be allowed to remain on the surface of your fixtures for any length of time.

If the first type of chemical drain opener you use does not work, do not use a different chemical drain cleaner unless the initial cleaner has been totally flushed away. Never use a plunger or a pressurized drain opener after using a chemical cleaner; it may cause dangerous chemicals to splash on you. Also, be sure to tell your plumber what you have put into the drain before he or she starts to work. The combination of ammonia and other household cleaners with chemical drain openers produces hazardous gases.

■ Keep a long-handle brush for cleaning toilet bowls.

■ Disposable toilet brushes contain toilet cleaner and can make the job much faster.

■ Sprinkle ¼ cup of sodium bisulfate (sodium acid sulfate) into a wet toilet bowl for a single scrubbing and flushing. Wear rubber gloves. Let it stand for 15 minutes and then scrub and flush as usual. Caution: Never combine bleach with toilet-bowl cleaners; the mix can release toxic gases.

■ Give your toilet an overnight cleaning by putting ¼ cup borax in the bowl and letting it sit overnight. In the morning, scrub stains away.

■ You can achieve the same effect overnight by putting 2 denture cleanser tablets in the toilet and letting them sit overnight. Scrub the toilet in the morning.

■ Rust stains under a toilet-bowl rim sometimes yield to laundry

bleach—be sure to protect your hands with rubber gloves. Rub off truly stubborn stains with extra-fine steel wool or with wet-dry sandpaper (available at hardware stores).

■ Chemical toilet-bowl cleaners should never be used to clean the bathtub or sink; the chemicals will ruin the finish.

BEDDING

All bedding should be cleaned on a regular basis. The key to successful cleaning is to do it before the soil is heavy and to know the fabrics involved in order to use the right cleaning procedures. Keep a file of manufacturers' care labels, and follow their directions when cleaning is necessary.

BEDSPREADS

Bedspreads are made from different kinds of fabric, many of which are washable. Bedspreads should be washed before they become heavily soiled. Treat spots and stains with a spray prewash product. Before you clean your bedspread, dip a corner in the detergent solution to check for colorfastness. If the color bleeds, have your bedspread dry-cleaned.

■ Use a large commercial washing machine for oversize bedspreads.

An overcrowded washer won't clean very well, and the wet weight can be hard on your washer.

■ Dry bedspreads on a clothesline or in a large, commercial dryer.

BLANKETS

Although blankets are made of many different fibers and blends, most of them are washable by hand or machine. Even some wool blankets can be machine-washed.

■ Vacuum blankets occasionally to remove dust and lint.

■ Air blankets on a clothesline periodically to freshen them.

■ Before you wash a blanket, mend or replace bindings and treat spots and stains.

■ Electric blankets should always be washed, not dry-cleaned, since cleaning solvents can damage the wiring. Mothproofing is harmful to the wiring, too.

DOWN-FILLED COMFORTERS AND QUILTS

The down filling in comforters and quilts is held in place by tufts of yarn or by stitched-through patterns. Most down-filled comforters and quilts are washable, but some older ones are too fragile to be cleaned at home.

Test comforters and quilts for colorfastness by wetting an inconspicuous spot with the detergent solution you plan to use and blotting the area with a white blotter.

■ If comforters or quilts are in good condition, machine-wash and dry them. Use cold water and an all-purpose detergent.

■ Fragile down comforters and quilts should be hand-washed in the bathtub or a deep laundry tub.

■ Drape a wet comforter or quilt over several clotheslines to allow excess moisture to drip out; reposition periodically.

■ If the comforter or quilt is strong enough to be dried in a clothes dryer, use a low temperature setting and include a pair of clean, dry tennis shoes to help fluff the down. The dryer can also be set on air-dry (no heat) to dry the quilt.

COMFORTERS AND QUILTS

Padded bed coverings may be filled with wool, cotton batting, or polyester fiber. The filling is held in place by tufts of yarn or by stitched-through patterns. Most cotton- or polyester-filled comforters and quilts are washable, but some older ones are too delicate to be cleaned at home. Check the manufacturer's instructions where possible.

■ Clean patchwork quilts with the method that is appropriate for the most delicate fabric in the quilt.

■ Never attempt to wash silk- or velvet-covered quilts and comforters. Unless a wool batting or covering is marked washable, do not wash it.

■ For large quilts, use a commercial washer. Let quilts and comforters soak in the machine for about ten minutes before starting them through a gentle washing cycle.

■ Hand-wash and line-dry old or fragile quilts and all quilts with cotton batting. Machine-washing is too harsh and can cause the batting to bunch up. Use a bathtub or deep laundry tub, and allow the soap or detergent to dissolve in the water before adding the quilt.

MATTRESSES AND BOX SPRINGS

Mattresses are usually made from foam or springs and casing; some older mattresses are made of hair, and futon mattresses are filled with cotton. All mattresses benefit from routine care.

■ Every month, turn the mattress over and around end to end to ensure even wear.

■ Cover mattresses with quilted or rubberized covers to prevent soiling.

■ Remove spots and stains promptly, but do not allow the mattress to become excessively wet when you clean it. Do not make the bed until the mattress is fully dry.

PILLOWS

Pillowcases are routinely replaced when soiled bed linens are changed, but the pillow itself also requires regular cleaning. Know the pillow's filling—down, feather, foam, polyester, or kapok—so that you use the appropriate cleaning method. For polyester-filled pillows, read the care instruction tags; some polyester-filled pillows are washable, while others are not. Kapok is the silky covering of seeds from the ceiba tree; pillows with this stuffing need frequent airing but cannot be washed.

■ Protect each pillow with a zip-on cotton or polyester cover.

■ Refresh pillows once a month by airing them near an open window or hanging them on a clothesline.

■ Fluff feather and down pillows daily to get rid of dust and to redistribute the filling.

■ Before you wash feather or down pillows, make sure there are no holes or ripped seams. Machine- or

TIME-SAVERS

■ Each week, give special attention to one room in the house. This will save you time on fall and spring cleaning, because you've been cleaning more thoroughly throughout the year.

■ Make an efficient cleaning apron from a compartmented shoe bag by attaching strings and filling the pockets with rags, polishes, brushes, and other objects.

■ Put small decorative items into a basket and out of harm's way. Put the dirty items that you want to clean in a separate box or basket, and take them to the kitchen. Don't redistribute anything until you have finished cleaning the room.

■ Pull all furniture away from the walls. Turn back rugs at the edges, and take up small rugs to make vacuuming the floor easier.

■ Dust settles downward, so avoid dirtying what you have just cleaned by working from top to bottom. Clean the floor last.

■ Sweep, vacuum, and dust before cleaning with a liquid cleaning solution to avoid making mud.

■ Go easy on cleaners. Soap or wax used sparingly cleans and beautifies surfaces. If you use too much, you will have to spend time removing the buildup.

■ When you are cleaning something up high, don't stand on tiptoe. Grab a stepladder. If you are cleaning down low, sit on the floor. Straining up or down is tiring, inefficient, and bad for your back.

■ Concentrate on one room at a time; don't run all over your house or apartment pushing dirt around.

■ To clean your radiators, hang a damp cloth or damp newspapers behind the radiator. Blow on the radiator with a hair dryer to force hidden dirt and dust onto the damp cloth.

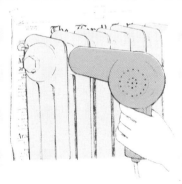

■ To clean a dust mop without making a mess, slip a large paper bag over the head of the mop, secure the top, and shake so the dust falls into the bag.

hand-wash feather and down pillows in cool water with a light-duty detergent. Wash two pillows at a time, or add a couple of bath towels to balance the load.

■ Dry down and feather pillows in the dryer on the low-heat setting. Including a pair of clean, dry tennis shoes in the dryer will help distribute the down as it dries.

■ Hand-wash and line-dry foam pillows. Change the hanging position hourly to dry the filling evenly. Never put a foam pillow in the dryer.

■ Machine- or hand-wash polyester-filled pillows in warm water with an all-purpose detergent. Dry the pillows in the dryer on a moderate heat setting.

SLEEPING BAGS

■ Pretreat spots and stains on the bag cover with liquid detergent.

■ Wash down-filled sleeping bags in cool water with mild detergent.

■ Wash polyester-filled sleeping bags in warm water with an all-purpose detergent.

■ If your sleeping bag can be machine-dried, tumble it with a clean, dry tennis shoe to prevent matting and a clean, dry bath towel to absorb excess moisture.

■ If you line-dry the sleeping bag, unzip it before drying.

CARPETING

ROUTINE CARPET CLEANING

Carpets need to be vacuumed once a week and more often in areas of heavy traffic. Frequent vacuuming prolongs the life of your carpet by preventing a buildup of gritty particles that can cut carpet fibers. Every few weeks, take a little extra time and use your crevice tool for cleaning around baseboards and radiators and in other hard-to-reach places.

■ To vacuum wall-to-wall carpeting, divide the floor into quadrants and vacuum an entire quadrant before moving on to the next.

■ Take your time when you vacuum a carpet, especially a plush carpet

continued on page 22

CARPET FRESHENER

1 cup crushed, dried herbs (rosemary, southernwood, and lavender are good choices)
1 teaspoon ground cloves
1 teaspoon cinnamon
1 teaspoon baking soda
Combine ingredients, and sprinkle over carpet. Allow to sit for a few minutes, then vacuum.

TREATING SPECIFIC CARPET STAINS

- Acid stains: Acid spills, such as drain cleaner or vinegar, demand quick action. Dilute them immediately with baking soda and water or with club soda. Then apply a solution of ammonia (1 part) and water (10 parts). Rinse with cold water, let dry, and vacuum gently.

- Alcoholic beverages: Quickly dilute the spot with cold water. Absorb the excess liquid. Then mix 1 teaspoon mild detergent, 1 teaspoon white vinegar, and 1 quart warm water. Apply the solution to the spot, and let the carpet dry. Vacuum gently.

- Blood: Absorb as much of the blood as you can. Then mix 1 teaspoon mild detergent, 1 teaspoon white vinegar, and 1 quart warm water. Apply the solution to the spot, and let dry. Apply dry-cleaning fluid. Vacuum gently after the carpet is dry.

- Butter: Scrape up as much of the butter as you can. Apply dry-cleaning fluid, and let the carpet dry. If the spot remains, repeat the procedure. Vacuum gently.

- Candle wax: Press an ice cube against the wax stain. The wax will harden and can then be pulled off.

- Catsup: Sponge a mixture of 1 cup vinegar and 2 cups water into rug. Frequently wring out sponge until stain is gone.

- Chewing gum: Chewing gum can be a sticky mess, so harden it by pressing an ice cube against the blob of gum. Once hardened, the gum can be pulled off.

- Chocolate: Immediately scrape the chocolate from the carpet. Mix 1 teaspoon mild detergent, 1 teaspoon white vinegar, and 1 quart warm water. Apply the solution to the spot. Rinse well. Vacuum gently.

- Coffee: Blot spilled coffee immediately. Then mix 1 teaspoon mild detergent, 1 teaspoon white vinegar, and 1 quart warm water. Apply the solution to the spot, and let dry. Apply dry-cleaning fluid. Vacuum gently after the carpet is dry.

- Crayon: Scrape away excess crayon or remove it by placing a blotter over the crayon stain and pressing it with a warm iron until the blotter absorbs the melted crayon. Move the blotter frequently so that it doesn't get oversaturated. Apply dry-cleaning fluid, and let the carpet dry. Vacuum gently.

■ Fruit: Fruit stains can be very hard to remove if they are allowed to set, but if you act quickly this method usually prevents a permanent stain. Scrape up spilled fruit, and absorb fruit juice. Mix 1 teaspoon mild detergent, 1 teaspoon white vinegar, and 1 quart warm water. Apply the solution to the spot, and let the carpet dry. If the spot remains, repeat the procedure. Vacuum gently.

■ Gravy: Wipe up as much of the spilled gravy as possible. Mix 1 teaspoon mild detergent, 1 teaspoon white vinegar, and 1 quart warm water. Apply the solution to the spot. Let the carpet dry. Apply dry-cleaning fluid, and let the carpet dry. Vacuum.

■ Mud: Allow the mud to dry completely and then brush or scrape off as much as possible. Mix 1 teaspoon mild detergent, 1 teaspoon white vinegar, and 1 quart warm water. Apply the solution to the spot. Let the carpet dry. If the stain remains, apply dry-cleaning fluid and blot dry. When the spot is completely dry, vacuum gently.

■ Salad dressing: Absorb as much salad dressing as you can. Mix 1 teaspoon mild detergent, 1 teaspoon white vinegar, and 1 quart warm water. Apply the solution to the spot. Let the carpet dry. If the spot remains, repeat the procedure. Vacuum gently.

■ Soft drinks: The carbonation in soft drinks will help you clean spilled drinks quickly, but act fast because some of the dyes in the drinks can permanently stain your carpet. Blot up the spilled drink. Mix 1 teaspoon mild detergent, 1 teaspoon white vinegar, and 1 quart warm water. Apply the solution to the spot. Let the carpet dry. If the spot remains, repeat the procedure. Vacuum gently.

■ Urine: Mix 1 teaspoon mild detergent, 1 teaspoon white vinegar, and 1 quart warm water. Apply the solution to the spot. Let the carpet dry. If the spot remains, repeat the procedure. Vacuum gently.

■ Vomit: Treat vomit quickly. Blot up as much as possible, then dilute immediately with baking soda and water or with club soda. Apply a solution of 1 part ammonia and 10 parts water. Rinse with cold water, let dry, and then vacuum.

■ Wine: When red wine is spilled on your carpet, dilute it with white wine, then clean the spot with cold water and cover with table salt. Wait ten minutes, then vacuum up the salt.

CARPET FRESHENER VARIATIONS

Mix 1 small box baking soda with your favorite potpourri oil, using just a few drops, and sprinkle on as carpet freshener. Leave on a carpet 10 to 20 minutes, then vacuum.

Use 1 cup baking soda, 1 cup cornstarch, and 15 drops essential oil fragrance. Leave on carpet 10 to 20 minutes, then vacuum. Store mixture in a glass jar or airtight container.

continued from page 19

in which dirt is sure to be deeply embedded. One pass with a high-powered upright is not enough. Go over each section of carpeting several times, and work slowly to allow the suction to remove all the ground-in dust and dirt.

■ Pay special attention to the areas where people sit and move their feet. Vacuum these areas of heavy traffic with a crisscross pattern of overlapping strokes.

■ Soil retardants can be applied to new carpets or to newly cleaned carpets. Follow manufacturers' advice. Apply soil retardants only with professional equipment using the recommended application techniques.

■ Add baking soda to the bag in your vacuum to fight odors.

CLEANING SPOTS AND SPILLS

Clean spots and spills immediately. If you catch the spill when it's fresh, you've got a good chance of removing it totally.

■ Carefully blot or scrape the entire area before applying any cleaning solution. Remove as much of the spill as possible.

■ Before using any cleaning solution, test your carpet in an inconspicuous area to make sure the cleaner won't damage or discolor it. Test the cleaning agents that you keep on hand before you have to use them to make sure they will not harm your carpet.

■ Do not rub the spill—that might spread the problem to a larger area.

■ When you apply spot cleaner, work from the outside of the stain toward the inside to avoid spreading the stain. After applying a cleaning solution, blot up all the moisture.

SPECIAL CARPET PROBLEMS

When your carpet is burned, stained, or discolored, you could simply move a big chair over the spot and forget about it. Or you can use one of the following simple methods to restore your carpet to its original good looks.

■ If the spot remover you use alters the color of your carpet, try touching up small places with artists' acrylic paint. If acrylic paint doesn't work, try using a felt-tip marker or a permanent-ink marker of the appropriate color. Go slowly, and blend the color into the fibers.

■ To raise depressions left in a carpet by heavy furniture, try steaming. Hold a steam iron close enough for steam to reach the carpet, but don't let the iron touch the fibers, especially if they are synthetic, because they could melt. Lift the fibers by scraping them with the edge of a coin or spoon.

■ If a carpet thread is loose, snip it level with the pile. If you try to pull out the thread, you risk unraveling part of the carpet.

■ To repair a large burned area, cut out the damaged area and substitute a patch of identical size and shape. Secure the new piece of carpeting with double-sided carpet tape or a latex adhesive.

■ To repair a small area burned down to the carpet backing, snip off the charred fibers and put white glue in the opening. Then snip fibers from a scrap of carpet or an inconspicuous part of the carpet (perhaps in a closet). When the glue gets tacky, poke the fibers into place. If the burn isn't all the way down to the backing, just snip off the charred tips of the fibers with scissors. The slightly shorter length of a few carpet fibers will never be noticed.

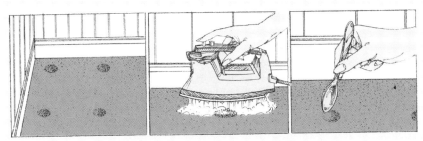

Depressions in carpets can be raised by steaming (center), then by scraping the fibers with the edge of a spoon (right).

■ A clean white bath towel is unsurpassed for drying carpet and brushing the nap back up to a standing position.

■ If you feel that there is still too much moisture after blotting the carpet, place a ¾-inch-thick stack of white towels over the spot and weigh them down with a heavy object.

DEEP-CLEANING CARPETS

There comes a time in the life of every carpet when vacuuming can no longer restore its clean appearance. There are four major indicators of the need for a deep-cleaning job: the carpet is matted and feels sticky; the carpet is no longer the same color as the remnant you saved when the carpet was new; the carpet has grimy circles around the chairs; or the carpet releases a dust storm when you run across the room.

If any of these descriptions fit your carpet, then it is time to deep-clean it. Unless you have the time and strength to do a thorough cleaning job, it's time to call in the professionals. The only method for cleaning carpeting down to the backing is to agitate it with a shampooer and rinse with an extractor.

■ Before cleaning your carpet, test for colorfastness. Moisten a white towel with the cleaning solution that you are going to use, and apply it to an inconspicuous area. If the towel does not pick up any color from the carpet, it is probably safe to use the solution on the entire carpet.

■ Remove as much furniture from the room as possible, and place foil or plastic film under the legs and bases of the remaining furniture to prevent stains.

■ Vacuum the carpet thoroughly, then spot-clean and pretreat stains before shampooing the carpet.

■ Follow the instructions printed on the carpet cleaner.

■ Use single strokes over the carpet surface.

■ Do not apply heavy pressure with the machine.

■ Wipe cleaning solutions and foam from furniture legs and woodwork immediately to prevent damage.

■ Fluff damp fibers against the nap after shampooing to aid drying.

■ Make sure the room is well-ventilated after cleaning to speed drying.

■ Try not to walk on carpets until they are completely dry.

FIREPLACES

Your fireplace needs regular care and cleaning to assure a safe and efficient fire. Creosote, a flammable tarlike substance that accumulates in the chimney and flue, should be removed by a professional, eliminating the worry of at least one potential fire hazard. Give your fireplace and its accessories routine cleaning throughout the wood-burning season to eliminate an accumulation of soot, ashes, and creosote tars.

■ Vacuum or dust the hearth area weekly to prevent dust and soot buildup. Do not sweep or vacuum until all the embers have been extinguished for at least 12 hours.

■ Burn only seasoned, well-dried wood to minimize dangerous creosote buildup.

■ Inspect the firebox, flue, and chimney annually for creosote accumulation.

■ Do not use water to drown a fire unless there is an emergency. It will make a paste of the ashes, which is difficult to remove.

■ Never use an abrasive cleanser inside the fireplace. Many leave a flammable residue.

FIREBOX

The firebox is the area that contains the fire; it is commonly constructed of either metal sheeting or firebrick. Since the heat of the fire keeps the firebox clean, very little upkeep is required.

■ Gently scrub the walls of the firebox opening with a stiff-bristle brush (not a wire brush) only to the height of the lintel (the heavy steel brace that supports the masonry above the fireplace opening).

■ Be gentle with firebrick because it crumbles easily. Be careful not to bend any edges on a metal firebox where it joins the flue. Bent edges leave openings to the wall stud or supports where fire could spread.

■ If your fireplace does not have an ash pit or box, shovel the bulk of the ashes into a bag and vacuum the remaining lightweight ashes.

■ When cleaning your fireplace, sprinkle damp coffee grounds over the cooled ashes to keep down the dust.

FIRE SCREEN

Most fire screens are black painted metal, but if your screen is brass-plate, clean it as you would other brass objects.

CLEANING PAINTED FIRE SCREENS

Mix ½ cup vinegar and 1 gallon warm water. Add 1 teaspoon ammonia. Dip a cloth into the solution, and wipe down both sides of the screen. Rinse with a cloth dipped in clear, warm water.

GLASS ENCLOSURES

Glass enclosures for the fireplace are constructed of tempered glass. To clean the glass and metal edging facing the room, see "Windows and Window Coverings." Clean the glass facing the fire after every other fire to remove the residue of soot. For baked-on soot, scrape the glass very carefully with a glass scraper to avoid scratching the surface.

GRATE AND CAST-IRON TOOLS

The grate is usually made from cast iron and can accumulate a buildup of creosote tars or sap from burning green wood. Cast-iron tools may be cleaned in the same way as grates. To remove buildup, take the grate or tool outside and hose it down. Sprinkle an abrasive cleanser on the surface, and scrub with a stiff-bristle brush or steel-wool soap pad.

CLEANING GLASS FIREPLACE ENCLOSURES

To remove smoke stains, mix ½ cup vinegar with 1 gallon clear, warm water. Add 1 tablespoon clear ammonia. Either spray this solution on the glass or wipe it on with a cloth dipped in the solution. Rinse with clear, warm water, and dry with a clean cloth.

ANDIRONS AND BRASS OR BRASS-PLATE TOOLS

There are many products that can restore brass fireplace tools to their original beauty with a little time and effort. To make your own, use the recipe "Cleaning Fireplace Tools."

CLEANING FIREPLACE TOOLS

Clean the grime and soot from fireplace tools or andirons by dipping fine-grade (000) steel wool in vegetable oil and rubbing gently. Apply a polish to bring up the shine.

FLOORS

Dirt from the street collects on feet and gets tracked into your house dozens of times a day. The little dumps, spills, and heel marks of daily living accumulate with startling speed. And unless your home has only one kind of floor throughout, you will have to deal with cleaning different kinds of hard-surface floors. The first step toward efficient floor cleaning is to know what your floor is made of. The cleaning method that works for one surface may ruin another.

ASPHALT TILE

Asphalt tile floor won't retain the footprints when you replace your favorite old TV chair in the family room with a new one. Although asphalt is resilient, grease, oil, solvents (such as kerosene, gasoline, naphtha, and turpentine), harsh cleaning preparations, strong soaps, and scouring can damage the surface. If you take the time to damp-mop your asphalt floor every week, you will not have to wash it and apply polish as often as if you allow dirt to build up. Make sure that the cleaner you use can withstand damp-mopping. If it can't, you will have to reapply it anyway. A cup of fabric softener in ½ pail of water will help keep the floor's shine.

■ Don't flood the floor with water; excess water can seep into the seams and loosen adhesives that hold down the tiles.

■ Remove heel marks by dipping fine-grade (000) steel wool in liquid floor wax and rubbing the spot. Wipe with a damp cloth.

BRICK

Caring for a porous brick floor is a lot of work no matter what you do. If you use a solvent-base wax on the floor, you have to seal it. If you use a water-base polish, you'll occasionally have to strip the wax buildup. The best way to care for your brick floor is to keep it sealed and waxed. You'll need to use a commercial sealer for brick; neither varnish nor lacquer will do.

■ Damp-mopping after vacuuming will prevent dirt from building up on your brick floor. Try putting 1 cup of vinegar in the water; the floor will shine without being polished—a real time-saver.

■ Use a solvent-base wax, so that you don't have to strip your floor. A solvent-base polish can be applied over a water-base polish, but a water-base polish cannot be applied over a solvent-base polish. The solvents in the wax dissolve the layer of wax that is on the floor during each application, so there is no wax buildup.

■ Remove wax buildup by applying a wax-stripping product with a scrub brush or floor-scrubbing machine that has a brush attachment. Rinse the floor thoroughly after applying the stripper. Do not clean your brick floor with acids, strong soaps, or abrasives.

QUICK CARE FOR A BRICK FLOOR

While the following method of caring for a brick floor is not as effective as treatment with a stripper, sealer, and paste wax, it is quick and inexpensive. Since this homemade solution contains ammonia, the floor is stripped every time you wash it, eliminating wax buildup. Most acrylic liquid waxes are self-sealing, allowing you to skip the application of a sealer. Clean and strip the floor with a solution of ¼ cup low-sudsing, all-purpose cleaner; 1 cup clear ammonia; and ½ gallon cool or cold water. Caution: Wear rubber gloves, and work in a well-ventilated area when using this powerful solution. Apply the solution to the floor with a sponge mop, using pressure for heavily soiled areas; rinse with cool, clear water for spotless results. Then apply two thin coats of an acrylic floor wax.

CERAMIC TILE

Glazed (shiny) ceramic tile is virtually stainproof, but unglazed (matte) ceramic tile is porous and must be sealed to resist stains. A new unglazed ceramic-tile floor needs to be sealed with a commercial sealer and a water-base wax. Both types of tile are installed with grout.

■ Never use harsh abrasive cleaners that might scratch the glaze.

■ Do not clean unglazed ceramic tiles with acids, strong soaps, or abrasives.

■ Damp-mop ceramic tile with an all-purpose cleaner. Dry the floor with a soft cloth to avoid streaks.

■ Sparkle your ceramic tile walls and countertops by rubbing the tile with car wax. Buff after ten minutes.

■ About once a year, strip the wax buildup on your unglazed tile floor and rewax. Rinse the floor thoroughly with clear water after applying the stripper.

CONCRETE

Concrete is very porous and soaks up stains quickly. While few of us are so fastidious that we seal or paint our garage floors, sealing a cement floor inside your home with a commercial sealer will save time in the long run, because the sealed floor will require little cleaning.

For an unsealed concrete floor, sweep up the loose surface dirt, and then wash it with either a strong all-purpose cleaning solution or the following homemade cleaning solution.

HEAVY-DUTY FLOOR CLEANER

Mix ¼ cup low-sudsing, all-purpose cleaner; 1 cup ammonia; and ½ gallon cool or cold water. Caution: Wear rubber gloves, and work in a well-ventilated area when using this powerful solution. Apply the solution to the floor with a sponge mop, using pressure for heavily soiled areas; rinse with cool, clear water for spotless results. Dry with a soft cloth. This solution can be used on asphalt, glazed or unglazed ceramic tile, concrete, flagstone, and slate floors.

FLAGSTONE AND SLATE

These natural-stone flooring materials are similar; they have rough, porous surfaces and are set into grout. Flagstone and slate floors must be sealed with a commercial sealer, not lacquer or varnish.

■ The best way to seal a flagstone or slate floor is with a commercial sealer for terrazzo and slate. After the sealer dries, apply two thin coats of an acrylic floor finish with a long-handle wax applicator fitted with a lamb's wool pad, or apply paste wax with a floor-polishing machine. To do this, use a spatula to spread a small amount of paste wax directly on the brushes of the polisher. Slowly operate the polisher back and forth to apply a thin coat of wax. When dry, buff the floor.

■ A self-polishing liquid will build up on your floor, and you'll occasionally have to strip the wax buildup and rewax. After applying the stripper according to the manufacturer's directions, rinse the floor thoroughly with clear water, then apply wax.

■ Damp-mop flagstone or slate floors using either clear water, an all-purpose cleaning solution in warm water, or water to which fabric softener has been added. Wring the mop until it doesn't drip, and apply it to the floor in slow, even strokes. If the freshly mopped floor dries with a luster-dulling film, you can mop it again with water containing a cup of white vinegar; the floor will glisten.

LINOLEUM

To shine and resist foot traffic, linoleum must be waxed. But once it is waxed, the only regular maintenance linoleum floors need is vacuuming and an occasional swipe with a damp mop.

■ A cup of vinegar in the mop water will bring up the shine on the floor, so you can delay rewaxing until it's really necessary.

■ Remove heel marks from linoleum by dipping fine-grade (000) steel wool in liquid floor wax. Rub the spot gently, and wipe with a damp cloth.

■ Solvent-base products can soften and damage linoleum. Scouring the floor, flooding it with water, or using very hot water is also bad for linoleum floors.

■ The fastest way to clean a linoleum floor is with a one-step cleaner or polish, but the best way to clean the floor is to mop it with an all-purpose cleaner. Dissolve the cleaner in warm water, rinse, and apply two thin coats of self-polishing liquid.

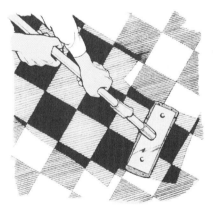

MARBLE

Marble can be used throughout the house—on floors, countertops, and even bathroom walls. It is available in a variety of colors, with a polished or nonpolished finish, and in an array of thicknesses and shapes. Nonpolished marble is very porous, stains easily, and must be sealed with a commercial sealer. Do not use varnish or lacquer to seal marble; it quickly peels off. Polished marble is less porous but can still be stained; a commercial marble sealer is also recommended for this finish.

■ Marble floors look great after being damp-mopped using either clear water, an all-purpose cleaning solution in warm water, or a mixture of 1 cup fabric softener and ½ gallon water.

■ Self-polishing liquid wax is a fast, shiny finish for marble. Occasionally, you'll have to strip the wax buildup and rewax. After applying the stripper according to the manufacturer's directions, rinse the floor thoroughly, then apply wax.

■ Use either a water-base self-polishing wax or a paste wax. If you use a paste wax, test it in a corner to see if it will discolor the flooring. If a solvent-base paste wax is used, rewax to strip the old wax and to renew the shine.

QUARRY TILE

Like brick, quarry tile looks durable, but this unglazed clay tile is very porous and readily soaks up stains. Quarry-tile floors have to be sealed with as many as three coats of sealer and further protected by wax.

CLEANING THE GARAGE FLOOR

The garage floor is the biggest cleaning challenge: Cement floors soak up oil and grease stains, gather piles of litter, and collect road dirt. But not many people spend much time in the garage, so you don't need to attack the mess very often. As strange as it seems, kitty litter can be a big help in the garage. Spread some around to absorb oil and grease. Also, keep the garage door closed so that leaves and other windblown debris don't collect in your garage.

When it comes time to clean the garage floor, sweep out the dirt and dust, and spread kitty litter with a stiff broom, working from the back of the garage to the front. Then get out the garden hose and flush the floor with clear water. You can scour tough globs of dirt with your stiff broom or blast them with a jet of water.

After you have gotten rid of the loose surface dirt, use the Heavy-Duty Floor Cleaner (recipe on page 29). It works as well as a commercial heavy-duty cleaner, and it's much cheaper. Apply to the concrete floor with a sponge mop, using pressure for heavily soiled areas; rinse with cool, clear water for spotless results. Let the floor dry.

■ Seal a quarry-tile floor with a commercial sealer for terrazzo and slate. After the sealer dries, apply two thin coats of an acrylic floor finish. Use a wax applicator fitted with a lamb's wool pad or apply paste wax with a floor-polishing machine. To do this, use a spatula to spread a small amount of paste wax directly on the brushes of the polisher. Slowly operate the polisher back and forth to apply an even, thin coat of wax. When the wax is dry, buff the floor.

■ To keep your sealed and waxed quarry-tile floor looking new, all you have to do is damp-mop it occasionally after you vacuum. If the mopped floor dries with a luster-dulling film, restore the shine by mopping it again with water containing a cup of white vinegar.

CARING FOR A WOOD FLOOR

The sight of a glimmering wood floor speaks to us of glamour, good living, and very hard work on somebody's part. It's true that you have to take care of a wood floor, but you don't have to break your back to do so if you take care of it on a regular basis.

The product used to seal a wood floor determines how it can be cared for. Varnish, shellac, polyurethane, or lacquer are used to finish floors, but only polyurethane requires no further treatment. The integrity and beauty of wood floors with varnish, shellac, or lacquer finishes can be maintained only by using solvent-base cleaners and polishes. Water should never be used on wood floors, except those treated with polyurethane. They can be damp-mopped.

The fastest way to clean a lacquered, varnished, or shellacked floor is with a one-step cleaner/polish. After vacuuming, pour the liquid on a small area and rub lightly with a wax applicator. Working on a small section at a time, stroke the floor in the direction of the grain. Blot up any excess liquid with a clean cloth.

The best way to clean a wood floor is not the fastest but will result in a long-lasting shine. After vacuuming the floor, apply a liquid wood-floor cleaner with a dry wax applicator on a small area at a time. Let it soak for a few minutes, and wipe up the excess. When the floor is dry, buff with a floor polisher. Caution: This is a combustible mixture; use only in a well-ventilated area.

■ Apply a commercial wax-stripping product with a floor-scrubbing machine that has a brush attachment. After applying the stripper according to the manufacturer's directions, rinse the floor thoroughly with clear water. Use a nonabrasive powder and a synthetic scouring pad for stubborn spots.

■ If you use a paste wax, you will never have to strip the floor. Test the wax in a corner first to see if it will discolor the tile.

RUBBER TILE

Rubber tile provides an antistatic surface that is ideal for home offices and rooms with computers. Careful care of rubber flooring is necessary because it can be damaged by exposure to strong cleaners.

■ Make a rubber-tile floor look freshly waxed by adding 1 cup of fabric softener to ½ pail of water.

■ The quickest way to clean a rubber-tile floor is to use an all-purpose cleaning solution. Read the product label for precautionary measures, and test it in a corner before using it on the entire floor.

■ Occasionally remove wax buildup with a cleaner or wax stripper. Follow stripping with two thin coats of self-polishing wax; allow to dry between coats.

■ Remove heel marks from rubber tile by dipping fine-grade (000) steel wool in liquid floor wax. Rub the spot gently, and wipe with a damp cloth.

■ Solvent-base products can soften and damage a rubber-tile floor. Also, keep scouring pads, strong soaps, and hot water away from rubber tile.

■ Flooding the floor with water will cause big problems; excess water can loosen the adhesives that hold down the flooring.

TERRAZZO

Terrazzo is a very durable floor commonly used in bathrooms and halls. This flooring is made of marble chips set in cement. After it cures, terrazzo is ground and polished.

■ The best way to seal a terrazzo floor is with a commercial sealer for terrazzo and slate. After the sealer dries, apply two thin coats of an acrylic floor finish. When the wax is dry, buff the floor.

■ All a terrazzo floor needs to keep it looking good is a quick going-over with a damp mop, using either clear water, an all-purpose cleaner in warm water, or a mixture of 1 cup fabric softener and ½ gallon water. If your mopped floor dries with a film, mop it again with water containing a cup of white vinegar, and the floor will glisten.

■ To strip the wax buildup on your floor, apply a wax-stripping product with a floor-scrubbing machine that has a brush attachment. After applying the stripper according to the manufacturer's directions, rinse the floor thoroughly with water.

VINYL

A no-wax vinyl floor is a breeze to maintain. All you have to do is keep it clean.

■ Wipe up spills with a sponge dipped in dishwashing liquid.

■ Scrub off heel marks with a synthetic scouring pad.

■ To wash the floor, use an all-purpose cleaning solution. Test any cleaner in a corner before using it on the entire floor.

■ Sometimes a no-wax floor dries with a film. Don't panic; just mop it again with water containing 1 cup of white vinegar, and the floor will glisten like new.

■ Do not scour the tile or flood with water. Water can seep into the seams and loosen the adhesives that hold the flooring down.

■ If your vinyl floor is old or not a no-wax variety, clean it with an all-purpose cleaner dissolved in water. After you have cleaned the floor, rinse the tile with clear water. When the floor is dry, apply two thin coats of a self-polishing floor finish, allowing the floor to dry between coats.

FURNISHINGS

BOOKS AND COMPACT DISCS

Books and CDs rarely require heavy cleaning, but they appreciate a dusting now and then.

■ If you arrange books at the front of shelves, air will be able to circulate around the books to prevent mustiness.

■ Protect books from direct sunlight, which will fade the bindings and cause them to deteriorate.

■ Leather-bound books should be treated periodically with a light oil so that the leather won't crack.

■ To remove grease stains from books, rub the affected areas with soft white bread crumbs.

■ Dry out the moisture in a damp book by sprinkling the pages with cornstarch. Let it sit overnight, then brush the cornstarch out.

■ Dust your CD, DVD, cassette, or record collection and stereo equipment regularly.

■ Avoid exposing compact discs to direct sunlight or extreme heat.

■ To clean grease or oil spots from a CD, use a soft cloth dipped in ethyl alcohol, then wipe dry. Always wipe from the center of the disc outward.

■ Dust, dirt, or fingerprints can cause CDs to skip. Blow lightly on the disc to remove any dust, then wipe lightly with a soft cloth to clean.

LAMP SHADES

Lamp shades are made of many different materials; some are washable and some are not. Keep all the care information from the manufacturer so you know the proper cleaning procedure.

■ Vacuum lamp shades regularly with the brush attachment.

■ Dry-clean shades that are glued to their frames. Remove spots from nonwashable fabric shades with a spot remover.

WASHING LAMP SHADES

Using the bathtub or a large laundry sink, make a sudsy warm-water solution with liquid dishwashing detergent. Dip the shade in and out of the solution, making sure that the shade is completely covered, and then rinse it in lukewarm water, following the same dipping procedure. Rinse until the water is clear. Take the shade outside and swing it vigorously in a circle to get rid of excess moisture, and then dry it quickly in the sun or with an electric fan or hair dryer.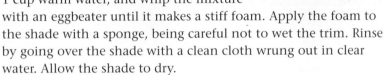

If the lamp shade is washable but has a glued-on trim that prevents immersing it in water, use the following method for cleaning. Mix ¼ cup dishwashing liquid with 1 cup warm water, and whip the mixture with an eggbeater until it makes a stiff foam. Apply the foam to the shade with a sponge, being careful not to wet the trim. Rinse by going over the shade with a clean cloth wrung out in clear water. Allow the shade to dry.

■ Wash silk, nylon, and rayon shades only if they are sewn to the frame.

■ Plastic and fiberglass shades only need to be wiped occasionally with a cloth to remove soil.

METALS

BRASS

Strip cracked and peeling lacquer from coated brass objects with a solution of 1 cup baking soda in 2 gallons boiling water. Let the article stand in the water until it cools, then peel off the lacquer.

PEWTER

■ Pewter can be cleaned with the outer leaves from a head of cabbage. Rub a leaf over the surface, and then buff it with a soft cloth.

■ Since pewter stains easily, wash pewter food containers and flatware immediately after use. Acidic foods, salt, and salad dressing are likely to blacken pewter.

PIANOS

A piano should be treated with respect and care. Have it tuned by a licensed piano tuner approximately

CLEANING CHANDELIERS

A chandelier can be cleaned without taking it down. Vacuum chandeliers thoroughly on a regular basis and before cleaning. In a drinking glass, mix a solution of ¼ cup denatured alcohol and ¾ cup water. Cover the floor or table under the chandelier with newspaper or plastic, and set up a ladder so that you can reach the pendants. Submerge the crystals in the glass for a few seconds, swishing them back and forth, and then let them air-dry.

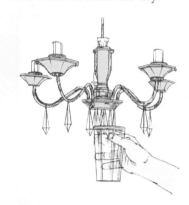

BRASS CLEANER

Make a paste from 1 tablespoon salt, 1 tablespoon flour, and 1 tablespoon vinegar. Apply the paste with a soft cloth and rub. You may also dip a cut lemon in salt and rub it on the brass. Wash the object in warm soapy water, and buff to bring up the shine.

GOLD CLEANER

Mix 1 teaspoon of ash with enough water to form a paste. Rub the paste on the surface of the gold with a soft cloth, rinse, and buff with a chamois. Baking soda can be substituted for ash.

four times the first year for a new piano, semiannually for an older model, and whenever the piano is moved from one location to another.

■ Dust the piano case regularly with a soft cloth.

■ Use a nonsilicone furniture polish or wax on the case of a piano that has a varnish or lacquer finish.

■ A piano that has a high-gloss polyester epoxy finish can be cleaned with a cloth and buffed; it should never be waxed or rubbed with furniture polish.

■ Remove stubborn stains from ivory or plastic keys with a cloth dipped in baking soda, being careful not to let the soda fall between the keys. Wipe the keys with another cloth and buff.

SILVER TARNISH REMOVERS

1. Place tarnished silver in a glass dish, add a piece of aluminum foil, and cover with 1 quart of hot water mixed with 1 tablespoon baking soda. A reaction between the foil and the silver will remove any tarnish. Don't use this process on raised designs; you will lose the dark accents of the pattern.

2. Make a paste of 3 parts baking soda to 1 part water. Using a soft cloth, rub the paste gently on the silver. Tarnish will disappear rapidly. After rinsing, buff the silver with a soft cloth.

3. Make a paste by mixing powdered white chalk with just enough ammonia to moisten. Rub the paste gently on the silver with a soft cloth. Rinse and buff to bring up the shine.

COPPER CLEANERS

1. Make a paste of 1 tablespoon salt, 1 tablespoon flour, and 1 tablespoon vinegar. Rub it over the surface, then wash the copper object in hot soapy water. Rinse and buff for a shiny finish.

2. Mix 2 tablespoons vinegar and 1 tablespoon salt to make a copper cleaner. Wash, rinse, and dry the item after this treatment. A cut lemon dipped in salt will also clean copper.

PICTURES AND DECORATIVE OBJECTS

FABRIC FLOWERS

Delicate fabric blossoms collect dust and eventually look dingy unless you clean them regularly. Read and follow the manufacturer's instructions for the care of fabric flowers; some are washable, but many are not.

■ Remove dust with a vacuum cleaner set at low suction.

■ Wipe silk flowers with a sponge; don't wash them.

■ Dip washable flowers into a mild solution of dishwashing detergent only when other methods have failed. Hang the flowers by the stems to dry, or use a hair dryer.

■ Perk up slightly wilted flowers with steam from a tea kettle or an iron.

■ Some sturdy fabric flowers may be freshened when shaken in a paper bag with dry cut oats, cornmeal, or salt.

PAINTINGS

Paintings, whether oil, acrylic, or watercolor, require a minimum amount of care. If the painting becomes damaged, it should not be repaired or cleaned at home.

■ Vacuum the painting, frame, and glass regularly using the brush attachment.

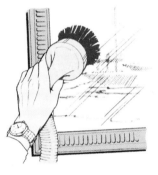

■ When you clean the glass over a painting, do not allow any moisture to get behind the glass.

■ Do not spray furniture polish directly on picture frames. Spray it on a cloth and then carefully apply the polish to the frame only.

■ To make a tarnished gilt frame gleam again, wipe it with a rag dampened with turpentine.

REMOVING WAX FROM CANDLESTICKS

One problem common to all candlesticks is caused by dripped wax. Remove a hardened wax drip by gently pushing it off the candlestick with the balls of your fingers or by using a fingernail that has been covered with a thin cloth to prevent scratching the surface. If the wax resists these methods, dip the candlestick in warm water to soften the wax for removal, or if the candlestick cannot be immersed, the wax can be softened with warm air from a hair dryer. Silver candlesticks that have wax dripped on them can be cleaned unharmed if you put them in the freezer first. After the wax freezes, it will peel off easily.

ALABASTER

Alabaster looks like marble and is made into vases, statues, lamp bases, and other ornamental objects. It is fine grained but soft enough to be scratched with a fingernail. Alabaster is easily broken, soiled, and weathered and must be handled with care.

■ Dust alabaster frequently with a soft untreated cloth.

■ An oil polish or soft wax will probably discolor alabaster, and abrasive cleaners will scratch it. It can be cleaned with commercial

CLEANING ALABASTER AND MARBLE

Clean alabaster and marble with borax; it is mild enough not to scratch the surface. Dip a moistened cloth into a small amount of dry borax, and rub it on the object. Rinse with warm water, and buff-dry with a soft cloth.

products that clean marble. Caution: Work in a well-ventilated area to avoid breathing fumes from these products.

BONE AND IVORY

Many useful and decorative objects are made of bone, including sword and knife handles and miniature carvings. Like ivory, it is an animal product and must be treated with special care. Ivory, an animal dentine, is used for ornamental objects and piano keys. Most "ivory" objects manufactured today are synthetic, because most countries ban the

BRIGHTENING YELLOWED IVORY

When ivory begins to yellow, treat it with a lemon and salt mixture. Cut a lemon in half, dip it in salt, and rub it over the ivory surface. Let it dry, wipe the object with a cloth, and buff for a bright finish.

importation of ivory to protect endangered elephants. To clean bone and real ivory:

■ Dust frequently with a soft cloth or the brush attachment of your vacuum cleaner.

■ Occasionally wash bone and ivory objects in mild soapsuds; rinse and buff.

■ Do not allow bone or ivory pieces that are cemented together to soak in water; the adhesive will loosen.

■ Never wash knives with bone or ivory handles in the dishwasher.

■ Keep ivory objects where light will reach them; continual darkness causes ivory to yellow.

JADE

Jade is a beautiful stone that is used to make lamp bases, vases, carved ornaments, and jewelry. The color of jade ranges from white to dark green with occasional tints of brown, mauve, blue, yellow, red, gray, or black. Because jade is hard and not porous, very little care is required. Dust it regularly, and buff it with a soft cloth when it begins to look dull.

MARBLE

Marble is a beautiful polished form of limestone that is used for tabletops, floors, countertops, walls, steps, fireplace facings, and statuary. It comes in a variety of colors and has either a shiny or a matte finish. Marble used for floors, tabletops, countertops, and steps should be sealed with a special stone sealer to reduce its porosity.

- Protect marble tabletops with coasters, and wipe up acidic food spills immediately to prevent permanent surface etching.

- Wipe marble surfaces with a sponge to remove light soil. Do not use an abrasive or caustic cleaner on marble. Do not use oil polish or soft wax, because they will discolor the marble.

- Commercial polishes, some of which are flammable, are available for cleaning marble. Read and follow the manufacturer's directions.

PORCELAIN

Porcelain and other types of clay are fashioned into many kinds of art objects, including vases, lamp bases, candlesticks, and statuary.

- Dust porcelain regularly with the brush attachment of your vacuum cleaner or a clean, soft cloth.

- If a porcelain object becomes dirty, wash it in mild soapsuds, using warm water.

WOOD FURNITURE

Whether your wood furniture is oiled, painted, or polished affects how it is cleaned. It's obvious when wood is painted, but be sure that you know the surface before you clean it. For example, some wood furniture is lightly lacquered and will not absorb oil, while other woods, particularly teak and rosewood, have no finish and benefit from a yearly application of furniture oil.

OILED WOOD

Oiled wood surfaces have a warm, soft glow and require only an occasional application of furniture oil to keep them looking nice.

- Be careful never to wax an oil finish. Wax blocks the pores of the wood, causing it to dry out and become brittle.

OIL FINISH FOR WOOD

Pour equal parts of turpentine and boiled linseed oil into a jar, tighten the lid, and shake to blend. Caution: Wear rubber gloves. Pour a small amount of the mixture on a soft cloth, and rub the surface of the furniture following the grain of the wood. The wood will appear oily, but within an hour the polish will be completely absorbed, leaving a lovely soft sheen.

■ To remove white spots on oil-finish furniture, such as those left by wet drinking glasses, rub them with toothpaste on a cloth. Or rub the white spots with a mild abrasive and oil. Appropriate abrasives are ash, salt, baking soda, or pumice; oils include olive oil, petroleum jelly, or cooking oil.

PAINTED WOOD

For painted wood furniture, the best care is probably the least since some polishes and waxes can damage the color and decoration.

■ Vacuum the furniture regularly with a brush attachment; wipe occasionally with a sponge to remove smudges and finger marks.

■ If you feel you must wax, use a hard paste wax only once a year.

POLISHED WOOD

This kind of furniture is finished with varnish, lacquer, or wax. Any commercial polish will clean wood surfaces quickly. Choose a product that is appropriate for the finish of your furniture. Paste wax gives a harder, longer-lasting finish than spray or liquid polish and is recommended for antiques.

■ If you wear cotton gloves while you wax furniture, you will not leave fingerprints.

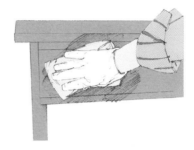

■ Sprinkle cornstarch over the surface of recently polished furniture, and rub it to a high gloss. Cornstarch absorbs excess oil or wax and leaves a glistening surface that is free of fingerprints.

■ Wipe polished wood furniture with a cloth dipped in tea, then buff.

■ Apply mayonnaise to the white rings or spots on your wood furniture, let it sit for an hour, then wipe off with a soft cloth and polish.

SPECIALTY WOODS

The specialty woods used for furniture are wicker, rattan, bamboo, cane, and rush. They usually have a natural finish, but some pieces may have a varnish or shellac coating.

■ Vacuum regularly with the brush attachment.

BASIC FURNITURE POLISH

Mix ½ teaspoon light olive oil and ¼ cup white vinegar in a small bowl. Pour mixture into clean, resealable jar, and label clearly. When ready to use, shake well, then apply polish liberally to wood surfaces with a soft cloth. Wipe away excess.

■ With the exception of rush chair seats that are damaged by moisture, occasionally rinse specialty woods with water to restore moisture to the fibers.

■ Wetting cane seats tightens them; spray the unvarnished side with water, and allow it to dry naturally.

UPHOLSTERY

The vast majority of furniture is upholstered in fabric, leather, or vinyl. Most furniture upholstered in fabric can be shampooed safely at home; the exception to this is fabric marked "Dry-clean only." Spot-clean this kind of fabric with a solvent or try the recipe for Upholstery Shampoo.

Leather must be cleaned with pure soap products (no detergents) and benefits from applying conditioner occasionally to restore moisture and bring up the sheen.

Vinyl upholstery can be cleaned in the same way as leather or with a commercial cleaner developed especially for cleaning vinyl. Never use oil; it will harden the upholstery.

VINYL UPHOLSTERY CLEANER

The best way to clean vinyl upholstery is with baking soda on a cloth, followed by a light washing with dishwashing liquid.

UPHOLSTERY SHAMPOO

Mix ¼ cup of dishwashing liquid with 1 cup of warm water, and whip the solution with an eggbeater. Apply the foam to the upholstery, a small section at a time, with a clean, soft-bristled brush. Shake off any excess water. Rinse the upholstery by gently rubbing the fabric with a moist, clean cloth; rinse the cloth as necessary.

LEATHER UPHOLSTERY CLEANER

A sudsy solution of dishwashing liquid and warm water is one of the best ways to clean leather upholstery. Apply the suds only, scrubbing gently with a soft-bristled brush; wipe clean with a damp sponge.

INTERIOR SURFACES

Light, routine cleaning of your walls and ceilings will keep them looking fresh and delay the need for a major cleaning. Generally, walls and ceilings are painted with either latex or alkyd paint. Latex, a water-base paint, is easy to wash after it has "cured" or set for a period of time. Alkyd, or oil-base paint, is durable and washable. Both types come in four finishes: flat (for walls and ceiling), satin (for doors and trim), semigloss (for walls), and gloss (for kitchen and bathroom walls and woodwork). You can clean painted walls with all-purpose cleaners.

CEILINGS

Most painted ceiling surfaces are washable, but some ceilings, especially the acoustic type, need special treatment. Remove cobwebs from all ceilings monthly, or as needed, with a vacuum brush attachment or a long-handle mop. Wash or clean ceilings first if you are cleaning the whole room. Do not allow drips to run down walls. Protect furniture and floors with drop cloths or newspaper while you clean. Use a sponge mop to clean ceilings so you won't need a ladder.

ACOUSTIC FINISH

This rough sound-absorbing finish is often used in new construction and remodeling. While it is relatively cheap and quick to apply, spray-on acoustic finishes cannot be cleaned. When the ceiling becomes dirty, the best thing to do is to vacuum it using a brush attachment, and then respray it.

CEILING TILE

Vinyl-coated ceiling tile can be cleaned with an all-purpose cleaning solution. Nonwashable tiles can be spot-cleaned with special products available at hardware stores. When an overall cleaning is needed, the tiles may be painted. There's no need for special paint.

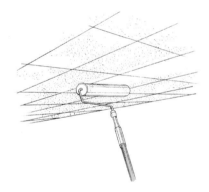

PLASTER

Decorative plaster ceilings, as opposed to flat, painted plaster ceilings, are really not cleanable because of the unpainted surface and deep texture. When a plaster ceiling becomes dirty, the best treatment is to vacuum it carefully, using a brush attachment.

CLEANING PAINTED WALLS AND CEILINGS

Mix ½ cup vinegar, 1 cup clear ammonia, ¼ cup baking soda, and 1 gallon warm water. Caution: Wear rubber gloves, and work in a well-ventilated area when using this powerful solution. Apply to the wall with a sponge, and rinse with clear water. If your walls have a rough texture, use old nylon stockings or socks rather than a sponge because they won't tear and leave difficult-to-remove bits on the surface.

WALLS

Walls require more routine cleaning than ceilings, mainly because it's a lot easier for fingerprints, crayon marks, and scuff marks to land on them. Using a brush attachment, vacuum walls when you clean the room. Go behind pictures and mirrors with the small brush attachment. Remove cobwebs monthly or as needed. When you vacuum, be careful not to press cobwebs against the wall. When you're ready to wash the wall, use an all-purpose cleaner for cleaning washable walls. Test the product to make sure it does not harm your wall covering by washing an inconspicuous place first.

■ Wash walls from the bottom to the top, overlapping the cleaned areas to prevent streaks.

■ To prevent water from running down your arm when washing walls, make a bracelet from a sponge or washcloth held in place with a thick rubber band.

■ Lift crayon marks off a painted wall by rubbing them carefully with a cloth or sponge dampened with mineral spirits or lighter fluid. Remove any shine by sponging lightly with hot water.

CLEANING A BRICK WALL

A brick wall requires little attention. A solution of hot water and all-purpose cleaner can be used to clean accumulated dirt and stains from the surface. If the mortar between the bricks is especially dirty, add chlorine bleach to the cleaning solution.

■ To remove transparent tape from a wall without marring the paint or wallpaper, use a warm iron. Through a protective cloth, press the tape to soften and loosen its adhesive backing.

■ Remove smudges while they are fresh, but do not scrub with much pressure or use synthetic scouring pads or abrasive cleansers.

■ To clean textured walls, old nylon stockings are better than sponges or cloths because they won't tear and leave difficult-to-remove bits and pieces on the surface.

■ Slight smoke stains above a fireplace opening are quickly removed with abrasive cleanser. Scrub the powder into the moistened brick and then rinse well with clear water to make sure that no white residue remains.

■ If cleaning changes the color of the brick, even out the color by rubbing another brick of the same color over the discolored surface.

■ If the brick wall is especially dirty, use a commercial brick cleaner and a stiff brush. Rinse with clean, hot water and wipe dry. Caution: Wear rubber gloves, and store this and other dangerous chemicals out of the reach of children.

WALLCOVERINGS

Paper wallcoverings are considered nonwashable and require special cleaning techniques. Many wallcoverings are made of washable vinyl. Some manufacturers caution against using ammonia on these products, so be sure to check the instructions or test the cleaning product you plan to use in an inconspicuous area or on a leftover piece.

■ Sponge washable wallcoverings and some vinyl coverings with a mild detergent. To find out how

RECIPES FOR CLEANING VINYL WALLCOVERINGS

1. Mix ½ cup vinegar and 1 quart water, and gently apply to the surface with a sponge. Caution: Wear rubber gloves. Don't use too much moisture; it could seep under the seams and loosen the backing.

2. Make a detergent to clean vinyl wallcoverings with a minimum of moisture. Mix ¼ cup dishwashing liquid with 1 cup warm water in a mixing bowl, and beat the mixture to a stiff foam with an eggbeater. Working in a small area, dip a sponge into the foam and apply it to the wall to loosen dirt. Rinse the detergent with a sponge dipped in clear water and squeezed dry.

CLEANING SPECIAL WALL TILES

DECORATOR TILE

Self-sticking decorator tiles, which are often vinyl-coated, are grease- and stain-resistant. A quick wipe with a sponge dipped in an all-purpose cleaning solution is usually all that is needed to keep them fresh and bright.

METAL TILE

Metal tile can be wiped clean with a cloth dampened in an all-purpose cleaner and then buffed with a soft cloth.

MIRROR TILE

These wall tiles, whether clear or smoked, are cleaned in the same way as wall mirrors. Use glass cleaner on a paper towel or piece of newspaper to quickly remove spots and spatters. Do not use soap on mirror tile; it will streak and leave a film.

much elbow grease your paper can take, first work on a scrap.

■ Lift grease stains from washable wallpaper with a paste made of cornstarch and water. Alternately, rub dry borax over stains.

■ To remove crayon marks on wallpaper, rub carefully with a dry, soap-filled, fine-grade steel-wool pad; or use a wad of white paper towel moistened with dry-cleaning solvent and delicately sponge the surface. Carefully blot to prevent the solvent from spreading and discoloring the paper.

■ Smudges, finger marks, and pencil marks can be removed from the surface of papered walls by very gently rubbing the spots with an art gum eraser.

■ To clean a grease spot, blot it with a paper towel and sprinkle cornstarch on the stain. After the cornstarch absorbs the grease, rub it off gently and vacuum.

■ To remove a grease spot from nonwashable wallpaper, place a blotter over the spot and press it with a moderately hot iron. The blotter will soak up the grease.

■ Clean nonwashable wallpaper with rye bread. Make a fist-size wad of bread, and rub it across discolorations and dirt.

WOOD PANELING

Wood paneling can have a natural, stain, oil, or wax finish. Routine care requires occasional vacuuming with a brush attachment. Never use water to clean wood paneling. Many commercial oil and wax finishes are available. For best results follow the manufacturer's instructions.

WOODWORK

Woodwork is either painted, stained, or left natural with an oil or varnish finish. Like walls, it benefits from a regular cleaning routine.

■ Vacuum or dust woodwork regularly.

■ Keep a small container of matching paint or stain handy to touch up nicks and scratches.

■ Wash door and window frames from the bottom up.

■ Clean woodwork with a wood cleaner or polish. Do not use water-base cleaners on stained or natural woodwork except for light touch-ups that you buff quickly. Spray the cleaner on a cloth instead of directly on the wood.

■ Many commercial oil and wax finishes are available. Follow the manufacturer's instructions.

THE KITCHEN

Cooking is a messy task, but it is easily controlled with quick daily cleanups. Smoke and grease are the major culprits behind the grime that accumulates in the kitchen. An exhaust fan vented to the outside minimizes the buildup of grime. But while keeping the kitchen fairly clean beats having to spend long stretches of time cleaning it, plenty of unavoidable kitchen chores will eventually have to be done. Refer to the following when you want to get these jobs done fast.

CERAMIC COOKTOPS

The ceramic cooktop is a glass cook-top with electric heating elements under the glass. While smooth tops may appear to be easy to clean, special care must be taken to avoid damaging or discoloring the ceramic surface. The best way to clean a ceramic cooktop is to sprinkle a nonabrasive cleanser or baking soda over the surface and rub with a synthetic scouring pad or sponge.

Rinse well with clear water, and buff with a soft cloth for a clean finish.

■ Wait until the top cools to wipe up spills. Never use a wet sponge or cloth on a hot panel.

■ Don't set soiled pots or pans on the surface; they can mar it permanently.

■ Abrasive cleaning products will scratch the surface, discoloring it and making it difficult to keep clean.

GAS AND ELECTRIC STOVETOPS AND RANGE EXTERIORS

The exteriors of most gas and electric ranges are baked-on porcelain enamel; the trim is usually chrome; and the control knobs are plastic. The easiest way to keep these clean is to wipe the surface around the heating elements after each use. Avoid using harsh abrasives or steel wool, which will damage the stove's enamel finish.

■ Wash reflector bowls, or drip pans, and grids in warm soapsuds whenever food or grease is spilled on them.

■ Gas burners should be washed occasionally. Clear the holes with a fine wire. Do not use a tooth-pick; it could break off and clog the hole.

■ Electric heating elements are self-cleaning and should never be submerged in water.

■ Remove all the control knobs when you clean the exterior of the range to make the job easier. Soak the knobs in warm sudsy water, and dry them with a soft towel before putting them back in place.

COOKWARE AND SERVING WARE

Basic care for all cookware and serving ware starts with reading the manufacturer's care instructions. Wash all pots and pans thoroughly inside and out soon after use. Clean seasoned omelet pans with a paper towel. If baked-on food requires washing the pan in soapsuds, dry it thoroughly after washing over a warm burner and rub vegetable oil into the pan with a paper towel.

Prevent heat stains on the outside of pans by keeping gas flames low so that they cannot lick up the side of the pot. Do not subject cookware to sudden temperature

ALUMINUM COOKWARE CURE

To remove interior discoloration, fill the pan with water, add 1 tablespoon cream of tartar or 1 tablespoon lemon juice per quart of water, and simmer until the discoloration is gone. Complete the process by scouring the pan with a steel-wool soap pad. Caution: Wear rubber gloves.

changes; allow all cookware to cool before washing or soaking.

ALUMINUM

To protect aluminum cookware from discoloration, never wash it in a dishwasher or let it soak in soapy water for long periods of time. Use a steel-wool soap pad to remove burned-on food on cast-aluminum cookware. Liquid nonabrasive bathroom cleanser or a paste of baking soda and water used with a synthetic scouring pad will polish both cast and sheet aluminum.

CAST IRON

Cast-iron cookware has a tendency to rust if it is not kept properly seasoned. Some cast-iron cooking utensils come from the factory already sealed, but most will have to be seasoned before their first use. Season cast-iron cookware in the traditional way: Scour cast-iron pots with a steel-wool soap pad, rinse, then wipe the inside of the pot with vegetable oil, place it in a warm oven for two hours, and wipe off the excess oil. Repeat this procedure periodically and whenever rust spots appear.

Wash cast-iron cookware in hot sudsy water, then dry it thoroughly, and store in a dry cupboard without its lid in place. Never wash cast-iron cookware in the dishwasher; it will remove the seasoning and cause rust.

CLAY

Soak new clay cookware in water for about ½ hour before using it for the first time. Be sure to soak both the top and the bottom, then scrub them well with a stiff brush to remove any clay dust. Line the cooker with parchment paper to prevent the  porous surface from absorbing food stains and strong flavors. If your clay pot becomes stained or takes on pungent odors, fill the cooker with water, add 1 to 4 tablespoons baking soda, and let it stand.

■ Never put hot clay cookware on a cold surface—it might crack.

■ Never wash clay cookware in the dishwasher or scrub it with a steel-wool soap pad.

■ Carefully dry the cooker before storing it to prevent mold. Store clay cookware with its lid off.

■ If mold spots appear on a clay cooker, brush the surface with a paste made of equal parts baking soda and water. Let stand 30 minutes, preferably in strong sunlight; brush the paste away, rinse well in clear water, and dry.

COPPER

Copper darkens with use and exposure to air. If you prefer shiny copper, you can clean and polish it easily with commercial copper cleaner. Copper cookware is lined with some other metal, usually tin or steel, to prevent harmful chemical reactions with food. Use only wood, nylon, or nonstick-coated spoons for stirring to prevent scratches.

■ Some copper cookware comes with a protective lacquer coating that must be removed before the utensil is heated. Follow the manufacturer's instructions or place in a solution of 1 cup baking soda and 2 gallons boiling water. Let it stand until the water is cool, peel off the coating, wash, rinse, and dry.

■ Protect copper pans from scorching by making sure there is always liquid or fat in the pan before it is placed on the heat.

■ When melting butter, swirl it around in the bottom of the pan and up the sides. Lower the heat as

COPPER POLISH

To clean a discolored copper pot, use a paste of 1 tablespoon salt, 1 tablespoon white vinegar, and 1 tablespoon flour. Caution: Wear rubber gloves. Because the vinegar is acid, wash the pot in hot soapy water and rinse it before vigorously buffing for shiny results. You'll have the same success with a paste made of 2 tablespoons lemon juice and 1 tablespoon salt.

soon as the contents of the pot reach the boiling point.

DINNERWARE

To make short work of dinnerware, remove food residue as quickly as possible. Scrape dishes with a rubber scraper or plastic brush to prevent scratches. Never scrape plates with knives or other sharp objects.

■ Rinse out cups before residues have a chance to stain them.

■ Acidic foods, such as tomatoes, vinegar, and wine, allowed to remain on glazed dinnerware can pit the surface.

■ To protect glass and china from breaking while you are washing it, use a plastic dish pan or rubber sink mat. You can also pad the bottom of the sink with a towel.

■ Do not wash delicate, hand-painted, gold- or silver-trimmed, or antique dinnerware in the dishwasher. Metal-trimmed dinnerware should also not be soaked in soapy water for long periods of time; this will damage the trim.

ENAMEL

Always let enamel cookware cool before washing. Rapid changes in temperature can crack the enamel coating. If necessary, soak a dirty pot to loosen cooked-on foods. Use a synthetic scouring pad—never abrasive cleansers or steel wool—to scrub stubborn soil. Enamelware can be washed safely in the dishwasher.

FLATWARE AND CUTLERY

Most people wash knives, forks, and spoons along with other dishes. If washing by hand, wash flatware after the glasses and before the plates.

Cutlery (knives and other cutting instruments) can be cleaned in the same way as flatware, but observe the manufacturer's instructions to be sure that the cutlery is dishwasher-safe.

■ Always wash gold-plate flatware by hand and buff to bring up the shine and prevent water spots.

■ Sterling-silver and silver-plate flatware may be washed in the dishwasher, but will need to be polished less often if it is washed by hand.

■ Rinse salt and acidic food off flatware as soon as possible to avoid stains.

■ Clean streaks on your everyday flatware by rubbing with a soft cloth sprinkled with a little olive oil. Use a second cloth to buff.

■ Make a paste of cornstarch and water and apply to tarnished silverware. Let dry; wipe clean with a dry cloth.

■ Mix a solution of 5 ounces dry milk powder, 12 ounces water, and 1 tablespoon white vinegar. Pour into a 9×13-inch cake pan. Drop in tarnished silverware, and let it sit overnight. Rinse and dry all pieces thoroughly.

■ Store silverware in rolls, bags, or cases made with special tarnish-resistant cloth.

■ Place 1 or 2 pieces of white chalk in your silverware chest to prevent tarnishing.

■ Do not allow stainless-steel flatware to touch anything made of silver in the dishwasher. It will set up an electrolytic action that pits the stainless steel and leaves black spots on the silver.

GLASSWARE

Most glassware can be safely washed in the dishwasher, but gilt- and silver-trim glass, delicate crystal, milk glass, and ornamental glass must be washed by hand. If you have soft water, wash all glassware by hand—the combination of soft water and detergent will etch and permanently dull glassware.

■ Before you wash glassware, cushion the bottom of the sink with a towel or rubber mat.

■ Add vinegar to the wash water or rinse water for more sparkle; ammonia in the wash water will cut grease on glassware.

■ Slowly slide stemware into the water, holding the glass by the base; if you push a glass into the water bottom first, it is likely to crack.

■ Remove dirt from crevices with a soft brush; remove stains by rubbing with a cut lemon or washing in a vinegar solution.

■ Allow glassware to drip-dry upside down, or polish with a soft cloth.

■ Clean stained decanters by filling them with water and adding 1 cup ammonia or vinegar. Soak overnight.

GLASS AND CERAMIC-GLASS

Most heat-resistant glass and ceramic-glass cookware is designed for oven use only, but some can be used on stovetops. Read the manufacturer's instructions carefully to make sure that you use your cookware appropriately. All glass and ceramic-glass cookware is dishwasher-safe.

■ Glass cookware that is allowed to boil dry is likely to shatter. If a pot boils dry, turn off the heat and leave the pot where it is until it has cooled.

■ Remove mineral deposits from glass coffeepots and teapots by boiling full-strength cider vinegar in the container for 15 minutes.

NONSTICK FINISHES

Nonstick finishes or coatings are relatively thin and easily damaged. Use wood, nylon, or specially coated spoons and spatulas to prevent surface damage. Most nonstick cookware can be safely washed in the dishwasher. Wash new pans before using them, and lightly coat the inside with vegetable oil. Apply vegetable oil again after each washing in the dishwasher and after treating for stains. Do not soak pans in soapy water; the coating can retain a soap flavor.

NONSTICK COOKWARE CLEANER

When you want to remove stains from nonstick cookware, mix 2 tablespoons baking soda with 1 cup water and ½ cup liquid bleach. Boil the solution in the pan for several minutes until the stains disappear, then wash as usual.

PLASTIC AND RUBBER

Plastic and rubber utensils and containers should never be exposed to high heat, because some plastics will melt and warp, and heat and sunlight can cause rubber products to crack. Check the manufacturer's instructions to see if an item is dishwasher-safe. Do not use solvents, harsh abrasives, or scouring pads to remove stains from plastic or rubber.

■ A paste made of baking soda and water is very effective for removing stubborn soils and stains from plastic and rubber utensils. Apply the paste to plastic with a sponge or soft cloth; a synthetic scouring pad can be used on rubber.

■ Remove odor from a plastic container by crumpling a piece of newspaper into the container. Secure the lid tightly, and leave it overnight. The paper will absorb the odor.

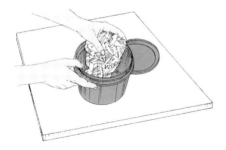

STAINLESS STEEL

Stainless steel requires little special care. It is dishwasher-safe, but if you wash it by hand, dry it promptly to prevent water spots. Letting a pot

STAINLESS-STEEL POLISH

Sprinkle baking soda on the wet surface of a pan, and scrub the metal with a synthetic scouring pad. Caution: Wear rubber gloves. After rinsing and drying, the pan will be bright as new.

CLEANING WOODENWARE

Baking soda cleans and deodorizes wood. Mix ½ cup baking soda with 1 quart warm water, and rub it on the wood surface. Caution: Wear rubber gloves. Use a synthetic scouring pad to clean a cutting board. Scour the gummy residue on the edges of the board. Rinse with clear water; blot the moisture with a towel, and air-dry. Bring back the natural finish by giving woodenware a coat of boiled linseed oil or vegetable oil, rubbed in with a synthetic scouring pad. Apply two thin coats 24 hours apart, wiping off the excess ½ hour after each application.

boil over high heat for a long period of time will discolor stainless steel. Storing the cookware stacked with other pots and pans may cause surface scratches.

WOOD

Wood bowls, trays, rolling pins, spoons, salad utensils, and cutting boards need special care to prevent warping and cracking. Because wood is porous, it absorbs moisture. When it dries out, the wood may be rough because the water may have raised the grain. Periodically clean and oil cutting boards to restore their smooth surfaces and to protect them from moisture. Some salad bowls are finished with a waterproof varnish, but many people prefer to keep their bowls untreated to absorb seasonings and enhance the flavor of salad.

■ Wipe immediately after use with a sponge or paper towel moistened in cold water.

■ If the item needs to be washed, don't let it soak in water and never put it in the dishwasher.

■ Remove stains with a solution of ¼ cup chlorine bleach and 1 quart warm water. Rinse and dry, then coat with vegetable oil.

■ Eliminate odors by rubbing the surface with a slice of lemon.

COUNTERTOPS

Kitchen countertops have to be able to handle anything, from a paring knife that goes off course to a slosh of grape juice. Acrylic, ceramic tile, cultured marble, marble, and plastic laminate countertops can take the abuse of cooking if we make it up to them with regular cleaning and care. These surfaces are all easy to clean.

ACRYLIC

You have to go out of your way to harm an acrylic countertop. A very hot pan will leave a permanent burn mark on the surface, but scouring powder or steel wool will remove stains and scratches. For routine cleaning, use a mild abrasive cleanser applied directly to the wet surface. Rinse well and buff with a soft cloth.

CERAMIC TILE

Glazed and unglazed ceramic tile are used for kitchen countertops. Unlike most other kitchen surfaces, ceramic-tile counters can take the heat from hot pots and pans. Ceramic tile is extremely durable, but the grout between the tiles is soft, porous, and prone to cracks.

■ Use a toothbrush or nailbrush to scrub grout clean. To remove mildew, dip the brush in laundry bleach.

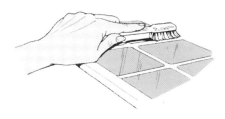

■ When you clean grout, don't use harsh abrasive cleaners, which might scratch the glaze on ceramic tile.

■ Many foam and spray tile-and-grout cleaners are available. Follow the manufacturer's instructions, and rinse with clear water to finish

GROUT CLEANER

To make this heavy-duty cleaner, put 3 cups baking soda in a medium-size bowl and add 1 cup warm water. Caution: Wear rubber gloves. Mix to form a smooth paste; scrub into the grout with a sponge or toothbrush and thoroughly rinse after cleaning. Mix a fresh batch for each cleaning.

the job. Caution: Wear rubber gloves, and do not breathe the mist from spray cleaners.

CULTURED MARBLE

Cultured marble is an acrylic material that resembles real marble, but is easier to care for because it is less porous and does not have to be sealed. Avoid abrasive cleaners and steel-wool soap pads; they will scratch the surface. Mild abrasive cleansers should be applied directly to the wet surface. Rinse well and buff with a soft cloth. Note that hot pots will leave permanent burn marks on cultured marble.

MARBLE

Marble countertops are porous and susceptible to stains, but they are not affected by heat. Seal marble with a special stone sealer to reduce its porosity, and wipe up wine, fruit juice, and other acidic food spills immediately to prevent permanent surface etching. Abrasive and caustic cleaners will mar the surface of marble, and oil polish and soft waxes may discolor it. While many appropriate commercial cleaners are available, borax rubbed into the surface with a moistened cloth will also clean marble. Rinse with warm water, and buff with a soft cloth.

PLASTIC LAMINATE

Most kitchens have plastic laminate countertops. They're practically seamless, giving cooks a smooth, waterproof work surface that is easy

PRESERVING A WOOD COUNTERTOP

Always use a cutting board on a wood countertop. Wipe up stains, and keep your wood countertops as dry as you possibly can. Periodically, rub oil into wood countertops to protect them from moisture. Use boiled linseed oil or salad oil.

■ Remove stains with a solution of ¼ cup chlorine bleach in 1 quart warm water. Rinse, dry, and coat with oil.

■ To get rid of odors that are absorbed by wood countertops, rub the surface with a slice of lemon.

■ To clean wood countertops, mix ½ cup baking soda in 1 quart warm water. Rub the paste into the wood using a synthetic scouring pad. Rinse well, and blot up excess moisture. When dry, restore the finish by using boiled linseed oil or salad oil rubbed in with a fine steel-wool pad. Treat the countertop with two coats of oil, applied 24 hours apart, blotting up the excess after each application.

HOMEMADE COUNTERTOP CLEANER

Use this cleaner on acrylic, ceramic tile, cultured marble, and plastic laminate countertops.

Mix ½ cup vinegar, 1 cup ammonia, and ¼ cup baking soda in 1 gallon hot water. Caution: Wear rubber gloves, and work in a well-ventilated area when using this powerful solution. Apply it to the acrylic countertop with a sponge, rinse with clear water, and buff. Dirt and soap film are quickly and inexpensively removed with this mixture.

to clean. Unfortunately, plastic laminate burns, scratches, and stains fairly easily, so you'll have to be considerate of your countertops to keep them looking good.

■ Regular applications of appliance wax or light furniture wax will help laminate surfaces resist stains and scratching.

■ Never use abrasive cleansers or steel wool on laminate countertops.

■ For general cleaning, a two-sided scrubbing pad with fiber on one side and a sponge on the other works particularly well. Moistened slightly with water, the fiber side is just abrasive enough to loosen greasy smears and other soil.

LARGE APPLIANCES

Large appliances range from enamel-coated metal boxes that clean up with the swipe of a wet cloth to ranges that have at least four depressions to trap and hold spilled food. If you keep up appearances by regularly wiping sticky fingerprints off the refrigerator door and drips off the front of the dishwasher, you can put off cleaning the messes that lurk within your large appliances until you have time to deal with them thoroughly.

DISHWASHERS

■ Baking soda comes in handy when the dishwasher needs cleaning. Dip a cloth into the soda, and use it to clean smudges from the exterior; the same method will also remove stains from the liner. Use a synthetic scouring pad to clean stubborn soil.

■ Clean out hard-water stains, deodorize, and sparkle the inside of the dishwasher by running a wash load using powdered lemonade mix. The ascorbic acid in the powder helps the cleaning action.

■ If the interior of your dishwasher retains odors, sprinkle 3 tablespoons of baking soda in the bottom of the machine and allow it to sit overnight. The odors will be washed away with the baking soda during the next wash cycle.

MICROWAVES

Use a mild dishwashing detergent, baking soda, or glass cleaner to clean the inside of the microwave, and wash the glass tray in the sink or the dishwasher when it is soiled. Never use a commercial oven cleaner in a microwave oven.

■ If your microwave is splattered with old sauces and greasy buildup, place a glass measuring cup with 1 cup water and ¼ cup vinegar inside microwave. Boil for 3 minutes, then remove measuring

GREASE CUTTER CLEANUP

Use this homemade solution to cut grease buildup on stoves, backsplashes, or glossy enamel surfaces:

¼ cup baking soda

½ cup white vinegar

1 cup ammonia

1 gallon hot water

Wear rubber gloves and use in a well-ventilated area.

cup and wipe inside of oven with a damp sponge. You'll be surprised how easily it will wipe away.

■ Deodorize your microwave by keeping a dish of vinegar inside overnight. If smells continue, change vinegar and repeat procedure nightly until the odor is gone.

RANGE HOODS

Many ranges have separate or built-in range hoods above their cooking surfaces. Range hoods are usually vented to the outside and remove grease, steam, and cooking odors from the kitchen. Some hoods do not have outside vents and rely on replaceable charcoal filters to clean smoke and odors from the air. Both vented and nonvented hoods have fans to draw air and smoke from the cooking area, and both need to be cleaned to keep them free from buildup and working effectively.

■ Wipe the exterior and interior of the range hood regularly. When you need to give it a thorough scrub, use a solution of hot water, dishwashing detergent, and ammonia to cut the grease; wear rubber gloves.

■ Remove the filter cover, and wash it in soapy hot water. Allow it to dry completely before replacing. Wipe the blades of the fan with an ammonia solution.

■ Clean metal mesh filters when they are dirty, and replace the filters on nonvented range hoods every six to nine months or as often as the manufacturer recommends.

■ Avoid washing charcoal filters; washing will reduce their effectiveness.

OVENS

There are many strong cleaning products designed to clean standard ovens. Caution: Many oven cleaners are dangerous when they come in contact with your skin or eyes. Wear rubber gloves, and protect your eyes while cleaning. Don't breathe the spray mist or the fumes. Avoid dripping the cleaner on any surfaces other than those it is intended to clean. Carefully read and follow the manufacturer's instructions when you use a commercial oven cleaner.

HOMEMADE OVEN CLEANER

Pour 1 cup ammonia in a glass or ceramic bowl, place it in a cold oven, and allow it to sit in the closed oven overnight. The next morning, pour the ammonia into a pail of warm water and use this solution and a sponge to wipe away the loosened soil. Caution: Wear rubber gloves whenever you work with an ammonia solution. The fumes are strong at first, but they soon dissipate.

When you clean a traditional oven, protect the heating elements, oven wiring, and thermostat from commercial oven cleaners with strips of aluminum foil.

Many stoves are equipped with self-cleaning or continuous-cleaning ovens. A self-cleaning oven uses a pyrolytic, or high heat, system to incinerate oven grime, creating a powdery ash. A continuous-cleaning, or catalytic, system eliminates small spatters through the porcelain-enamel finish on the oven liner, which absorbs and spreads soil to promote cleaning at normal temperature settings. Large spills must be wiped up; they will burn and may permanently stain the oven surface. Dust continuous-cleaning ovens weekly and self-cleaning ovens after the cleaning cycle, using the dusting attachment of your vacuum to remove dried food particles or ash.

Follow the manufacturer's instructions when using the cleaning cycle of a self-cleaning oven, and follow the manufacturer's recommendations to care for a continuous-cleaning oven. Neither kind of oven should be cleaned with commercial oven cleaners. Continuous-cleaning ovens should never be scrubbed with abrasives or powdered cleansers; these products will damage the surface.

■ Oven racks that have stubborn baked-on blackened areas can be cleaned by "steaming" off the soot with ammonia vapors. Just lay the racks on old towels in your bath-tub. Fill the tub with warm water and ½ cup ammonia, and let it sit ½ hour. Be sure the bathroom is well ventilated. Rinse.

■ If a pie or similar sugary item boils over in your oven, sprinkle the sticky spill with salt. Let it sit until the spilled area becomes crisp, then lift off with a spatula when the oven cools.

■ When cleaning your oven, finish by wiping the entire surface with a sponge using a mixture of equal parts white vinegar and water. This will help prevent grease buildup.

REFRIGERATORS

A frost-free refrigerator should be cleaned when dirty or about every four to six months. Clean a manual-defrost refrigerator when you defrost the freezer compartment.

■ Wash the drip pan whenever you defrost or clean your refrigerator.

■ Defrost the freezer section of your refrigerator when the frost gets to be ½-inch thick. Turn off the freezer, and remove all food. Remove shelves, bins, racks, and trays, and wash them in a mild soap solution. Dry thoroughly.

■ Do not put food back into the freezer until you have wiped off any condensation that develops and the freezer has been running for at least ½ hour. Wipe the interior of the refrigerator to prevent puddles from remaining in the bottom when you replace the bins.

■ Vacuum the dust behind the bottom grille of your refrigerator at least once every six months.

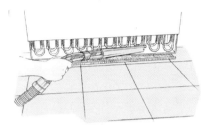

■ Control refrigerator odors with a box of baking soda placed at the back of a shelf. Replace the box every other month. Also, place a box in the freezer if odors are a problem there.

■ Wipe the inside of your refrigerator with a sponge soaked in vanilla extract to deodorize it.

■ Commercial kitchen cleaners will remove smudges and dirt and leave a protective wax coating on the exterior of the refrigerator, but baking soda will also clean and shine your refrigerator. Rub the exterior with a cloth dipped in baking soda, rinse well, and dry with a soft cloth.

SMALL APPLIANCES

The little machines that line up along our kitchen countertops or park themselves in appliance corrals save us time and effort when we cook. Most small appliances are designed to be easy to clean, but they still require some work.

BLENDERS AND FOOD PROCESSORS

Most plastic work bowls and blender jars can be washed in your dishwasher; some cannot. Some blades are dulled by repeated exposure to the dishwasher detergents; some are not. Always read and follow the manufacturer's cleaning instructions. If you wipe the bases of food preparation appliances after each use, you will rarely have to scrub them.

■ To clean the blender jar, fill it with a warm detergent solution and run the blender at high speed for about 15 seconds. Rinse well and dry.

■ To retain the sharpness of the blades, do not wash the blender's assembly in the dishwasher.

■ Wash the food processor's work bowl, cover, pusher, blade, and discs in warm soapy water or in the dishwasher. Because the blade is sharp, carefully wash it by hand.

■ Glass cleaner is excellent for cleaning stainless-steel blender bases and trim. Simply spray it on and buff with a soft cloth.

■ An all-purpose cleaner or a solution of baking soda and water cleans plastic blender and food-processor bases.

COFFEEMAKERS

Drip coffeemakers are easy to clean— all you have to do is change the filter; wash the pot, lid, and basket in a detergent solution; and quickly wipe the base with a cloth. Percolators need a thorough, occasional cleaning to get rid of oil buildup that can affect the taste of the coffee.

- Remove coffee and mineral stains from the glass pot of an automatic drip coffeemaker by adding 1 cup crushed ice, 1 tablespoon water, and 4 teaspoons salt to carafe when it is at room temperature. Gently swirl mixture, rinse, and then wash as usual.

- Allow a heated percolator to cool before cleaning.

- Clean the spout and tubes of a percolator with a special percolator brush and sudsy warm water.

- Use a synthetic scouring pad— never harsh abrasives or steel wool—to remove stubborn soil from percolator parts. If the surface becomes scratched, oil and other coffee residues will accumulate in the scratches.

ELECTRIC CAN OPENERS

Your can opener needs light but regular care. Always remember to unplug a can opener before cleaning it; do not immerse the case in water. Wipe the can opener after each use to remove food spills or drips. Use a sponge dampened in a warm soapy solution made from liquid dishwashing detergent. Periodically remove the cutting wheel and lid holder and soak them in hot sudsy water. Scrub caked-on food with a toothbrush; rinse, dry, and replace the parts.

GARBAGE DISPOSERS

Garbage disposers are self-cleaning, but they can get smelly, especially if you let food sit in them for any length of time. To keep your disposer odorless and running smoothly, operate it with a full stream of running cold water. Flush the disposer for a few seconds after turning it off to ensure that all debris is washed away. Keep the following materials out of the disposer: metal, wood, glass, paper, or plastic objects; fibrous organic waste, such as artichoke leaves and corn husks; and caustic drain cleaners. If an unpleasant odor begins to come from your disposer, eliminate it by tearing up the peels of citrus fruit and putting them into the disposer. Grind them with a stream of cold running water, and enjoy the fresh smell. Or sprinkle baking soda over ice cubes and grind them in the disposer.

TOASTER OVENS AND BROILERS

Cleaning your toaster oven or broiler after you use it prevents a squalid buildup of food spatters and crumbs.

- Wipe the exterior of the oven and the crumb tray regularly; wipe the interior of the oven with a warm dishwashing solution after cooking greasy foods. A synthetic scouring pad will remove stubborn soil from the tray and racks. The plastic parts are best cleaned with a warm detergent solution.

■ Clean a toaster oven only when it is cool and has been disconnected.

■ Never immerse the oven in water, and don't use harsh abrasives, steel wool, or a commercial oven cleaner to clean a toaster oven.

TOASTERS

Toasters are crumb catchers and smudge collectors; they need regular attention to keep them clean, shiny, and crumb-free.

■ Remember to unplug the toaster and let it cool before cleaning it. Never immerse the toaster in water.

■ Wipe the exterior of the toaster regularly. Remove the crumb tray at the base of the toaster and shake out accumulated crumbs; wash the tray in warm soapy water.

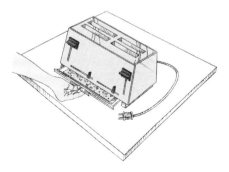

■ If your toaster does not have a crumb tray, turn the toaster upside down and shake it over the sink or a large garbage can.

■ Use a thin soft brush to remove crumbs from the interior.

■ Metal utensils should not be used to clean the inside of the toaster.

WAFFLE IRONS

Waffle irons need little care. The grids are made from seasoned cast iron or a nonstick surface and generally do not require washing after ordinary use.

■ Never clean a waffle iron until it is cool and has been unplugged. Do not immerse a waffle iron in water.

■ Wipe the exterior of your waffle iron and clean up batter spills after each use.

■ Wipe the grids with a paper towel that has been dampened with vegetable oil.

■ If waffles stick to the grids and burn, remove the grids and wash them in warm soapy water.

WINDOWS AND WINDOW COVERINGS

Windows look best if they are cleaned on a regular basis, at least twice a year on the inside and outside. Home recipes work just as well as commercial products for washing windows, and you'll save money. But remember that window cleaners pose a threat to woodwork. Don't let them drip on the windowsill where they can harm the paint or varnish.

HOMEMADE GLASS CLEANER

2 tablespoons ammonia
½ cup rubbing alcohol
¼ teaspoon dishwashing detergent
Add all ingredients to a small spray bottle, then fill the bottle with water and shake well. You can substitute 3 tablespoons vinegar or lemon juice for the ammonia. Use as you would any commercial window cleaner.

WINDOW COVERINGS

BLINDS

Blinds are made from narrow slats of wood, metal, or plastic held in place by tapes, cords, or colored yarns and ribbons. Blinds can be adjusted up and down or side to side; venetian blinds can also have the angle of their slats adjusted for light control.

- Vacuum blinds regularly with the brush attachment of your vacuum. Close adjustable slats when vacuuming so you can reach more of their surface.

- Remove finger marks with a sponge.

- When blinds require a thorough cleaning, immerse plastic, metal, and painted blinds in water.

- Natural wood blinds with decorative yarn tapes should not be immersed in water.

- Touch up dingy white tapes on venetian blinds with white shoe polish.

CURTAINS

Carefully read all the care labels attached to new curtains, and follow the manufacturer's instructions for cleaning.

- Using the upholstery attachment on your vacuum, regularly go over curtain panels for quick cleaning.

TECHNIQUES FOR CLEANING WINDOWS

■ Wash one side of a window with horizontal strokes and the other side with vertical strokes so you can pinpoint which side of the window has a streak.

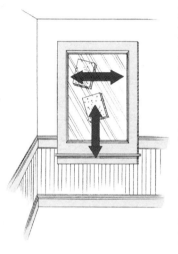

■ Use a squeegee on a long handle or a sponge/squeegee combination to prevent streaks on large windows.

■ Eliminate tiny scratches on glass by polishing the affected areas with toothpaste.

■ Wash windows on a cloudy day, because direct sunlight dries cleaning solutions before you can polish the glass properly.

■ Use a soft toothbrush or cotton swab to clean corners.

■ To give an extra shine to window glass, polish it with well-washed cotton T-shirts or old cloth diapers. Or rub a clean blackboard eraser over a freshly washed and dried window to give it a diamond-bright shine.

■ Polish windows to a sparkling shine with crumpled news-paper. The paper also leaves a film that's resistant to dirt.

■ Wash windows from the top down to prevent drips.

■ Vacuum curtains to remove excess dust before washing. Remove curtain rings and clips unless they are permanently attached.

■ Fiberglass curtains should always be hand-washed and never dry-cleaned, but you must wear rubber gloves when washing them to protect your hands from glass filaments. Do not wash fiberglass in a washing machine.

■ Handle cotton curtains gently if they have been hanging in a sunny window; sunlight may have weakened the fabric.

■ Machine-wash sheers, open weave, and other delicate fabrics in a mesh bag, or hand-wash so that the fabric does not stretch or tear.

■ Use curtain stretchers for drying lace or net curtains; if they need to be pressed, iron curtains before they are completely dry.

DRAPERIES

Draperies are often lined and are usually made of fabrics that are much heavier than those used for curtains. It is usually best to dry-clean draperies. Some drapery fabric is washable; check the care label for this information. Dust draperies with the upholstery attachment on your vacuum. Don't forget to dust the tops of the drapes, valances, and drapery hardware.

■ Remove all hooks and pins—unless they are permanently attached—before washing or dry-cleaning.

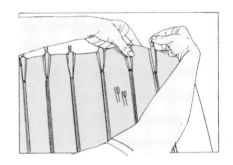

■ If you plan to wash your draperies, test a corner of the fabric in a bowl of warm water and detergent to see if it bleeds. Use only the gentle cycle to wash draperies.

SHADES

Light-diffusing or opaque shades are usually made of fabric that is wash-able, and some shades have a protective vinyl coating that makes them easy to clean. Other shades are not washable and must be dry-cleaned.

■ Vacuum shades regularly using the brush attachment. Lower the shades completely before vacuuming to

CLEANING WASHABLE WINDOW SHADES

Make a mild soapy solution using a liquid dishwashing detergent, and apply it to a rolled-out shade with a sponge. Rinse with a clean sponge dipped in clear water, and allow it to dry before rerolling.

CLEANING NONWASHABLE WINDOW SHADES

Thoroughly rub the surface with a rough, absorbent cloth dipped in cornmeal. The secret of this treatment is that the abrasiveness and absorption of the cloth and cornmeal pick up the soil and grease. Terry cloth is good for this job, but an old sweatshirt turned inside out is even better. Kitchen flour can be substituted for cornmeal.

clean the full length; don't forget the tops and valances.

- Remove finger marks with a sponge or a quick spray of an all-purpose spray cleaner.

- To thoroughly clean the shades, remove them from the window and spread them out on a flat surface. Test a corner of the shade with a detergent to see if the color bleeds.

SHUTTERS

Painted or stained shutters are the most common, but some people choose only to seal or varnish their wood shutters. For painted shutters, the best care is probably the least since some polishes and waxes can damage the color or decoration.

- Vacuum all shutters regularly with a brush attachment, and wipe occasionally with a sponge to remove smudges and finger marks.

- Use warm soapy water and a cloth to wash painted shutters; wash each louver separately on both sides. If you feel you must wax, use a hard paste wax only once a year.

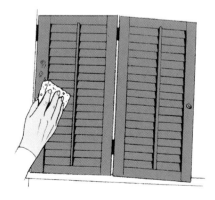

Clothes Care

Although automatic washing machines and dryers have removed much of the misery of doing laundry, someone still has to sort it, load the clothes in the washer, select detergent and water temperature, move the clothes to the dryer, fold the dried clothes, and press some garments. In other words, it's still a chore. And the multitude of fabrics and special care instructions can complicate the job. With guidelines and tips on how to care for your favorite clothes, you can speed through piles of laundry and save some time for more enjoyable activities.

KNOWING YOUR MATERIALS

The first step in doing your laundry quickly and efficiently is to know what an item is made of and the best way to care for it. Most garments manufactured and sold in the United States have permanently attached care labels. These labels can be of enormous help in determining exactly how you should remove stains and clean an item.

Certain information is not included on care labels. Neither the manufacturer nor the retailer is required to inform a consumer that a

certain fabric will shrink. The label assumes that the purchaser knows that an item labeled "Hand-wash Only" should be washed in lukewarm water and that all nonwhite articles should not be treated with chlorine bleach. Check the accompanying chart—"Understanding Fabric Care Labels" on pages 74 and 75—if you don't understand the meaning of a label or if you want clarification on caring for a particular garment.

Another important piece of information contained on fabric care labels is the fiber content of the material. This is especially important with blends. These fabrics are combinations of fibers, such as cotton and wool, cotton and polyester, or wool and acrylic. Blends should be cared for in the same way as the fiber with the highest percentage in the fabric. For example, a blend of 60 percent cotton and 40 percent polyester should be cleaned as though it were 100 percent cotton. However, when you remove spots and stains, you should follow procedures recommended for the most delicate fiber in the blend. For example, to remove stains from a blend of cotton and

silk, use the procedure for silk. If the stain is still apparent after treatment, follow the procedure for cotton, the most durable fiber in this blend.

NATURAL FABRICS

COTTON

Cotton fabric is strong, long-wearing, and absorbent. It will shrink and wrinkle unless it is given special treatment. Cotton is often blended with other fibers or treated with a finish to make it wrinkle-resistant. It is available in a wide variety of weights and textures.

■ Machine-wash and tumble-dry cotton fabrics, using a water temperature ranging from cold to hot, depending on the manufacturer's care instructions, and an all-purpose detergent.

■ If needed, chlorine bleach can be used on white or colorfast cotton unless a fabric finish has been applied. Do not use more than the recommended amount of bleach; this can damage the fibers.

■ Use a fabric softener to improve softness and to reduce wrinkling, but be aware that fabric softener makes cotton less absorbent and should not be used on towels, washcloths, or diapers.

■ Iron cotton with a hot iron for best results. Use spray starch or spray sizing to restore a crisp appearance.

LINEN

Pure linen fabric wrinkles easily, so many manufacturers make linen blends or add wrinkle-resistant finishes to overcome this problem. Linen is absorbent and comfortable to wear, but it can crack or show wear at the seams, along the creases, or on the finished edges of the garment.

- Machine-wash and tumble-dry linen. An all-purpose detergent is the best cleaning agent.

- Chlorine bleach can be used on white linen, following the manufacturer's recommended amount.

- Press with a hot iron while the fabric is still slightly damp for the best results.

SILK

Silk is a delight to wear, but it requires special care. Most silk garments are marked "Dry-clean Only," but some can be washed by hand. Always test a corner of the fabric for colorfastness before washing a whole article made of silk. Some dyed silk will bleed.

- Use a hair shampoo containing protein and warm or cool water for hand-washing. The protein in the shampoo feeds the protein in the silk. Handle washable silk gently during washing; never twist or wring it. Hang silk out of direct sunlight to dry.

- Press silk while it is still damp with a warm iron (below 275°), or use a steam iron.

WOOL

Wool fabric is highly resilient, absorbent, and sheds wrinkles well, but it will shrink and mat if exposed to heat and rubbing. It is popular in both knit and woven fabrics. Wool fabric textures range from fine wool crepe and jersey to felt and mohair.

- Woolens (except felt) should always be dry-cleaned unless it is specifically marked "Washable."

- If the garment is washable, allow it to soak for a few minutes before starting the washing process. Use only cold water and a gentle cycle.

- Handle woolens carefully when they are wet to avoid stretching. To remove excess moisture, roll a wool article in a towel, then block it into shape and dry it on a flat surface.

- Clean felt by wiping it with a dry sponge; for a more thorough treatment, hold the material over the steam from a teakettle, brushing lightly with a dry sponge or lint-free cloth to smooth the surface.

■ Machine-dry woolens only if the manufacturer's instructions recommend it.

■ Press wool with a hot iron, using lots of steam. Cover the article with a damp cloth.

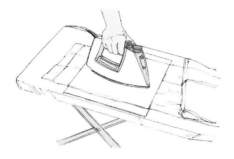

■ Allow any wool garment to dry thoroughly before storing it.

SYNTHETIC FABRICS

ACETATE

Acetate is made from cellulose and has a silklike appearance. It is closely related to rayon and has good body and drapes well. Taffeta, satin, crepe, brocade, and double knits often contain acetate. It is not very absorbent or colorfast and loses its strength when it is wet.

■ If the care label specifies that the article is washable, hand-wash it carefully in warm water, using a light-duty detergent.

■ Do not soak colored items or wash them with white articles.

■ Line-dry acetate away from heat or direct sunlight.

■ Press acetate at the coolest setting, on the wrong side, while the article is damp.

■ Nail polish remover and perfumes will permanently damage acetate.

ACRYLIC

Many acrylic weaves resemble wool's softness, bulk, and fluffiness. Acrylics are wrinkle-resistant and usually machine-washable. Often acrylic fibers are blended with wool or polyester fibers. Acrylic's biggest drawback is its tendency to pill. Blends will do this less than pure acrylic.

■ Dry-clean acrylic garments, or wash them by hand or in the machine.

■ Turn garments inside out before laundering to reduce pilling.

■ Wash delicate items by hand in warm water, gently squeezing out the excess. Machine-wash sturdy articles with an all-purpose detergent, and tumble-dry at low temperatures.

FIBERGLASS

Fiberglass fabrics are wrinkle- and soil-resistant, but they have poor resistance to abrasion. They are not absorbent, but stand up well to sun and weather, which makes fiberglass fabrics ideal for curtains and draperies. Fiberglass is never made into wearing apparel because it sheds small glass fibers.

■ Dust fiberglass periodically with the upholstery attachment of your vacuum cleaner.

■ For best results, hand-wash fiberglass using an all-purpose detergent. Wear rubber gloves to protect your hands from fibers.

■ Drip-dry fiberglass articles; do not iron them.

MODACRYLIC

Modacrylic is a fiber often used in fake furs, fleece robes, blankets, stuffed toys, and wigs. It is resilient, soft, and warm, and it resists mildew, sunlight damage, and wrinkling.

■ Hand-wash delicate modacrylic items, such as wigs, and machine-wash sturdy items in warm water with a gentle cycle and a light-duty detergent. Use fabric softener to reduce static electricity.

■ Use a low-heat setting in the dryer, removing modacrylic articles as soon as the tumbling stops.

■ If pressing is needed, use a cool iron.

NYLON

Nylon fabrics are extremely strong, lightweight, smooth, and lustrous. They are also nonabsorbent and have excellent wrinkle resistance. Often combined with spandex, nylon knits are very stretchy but recover their original shape. Nylon is used to make many items, including lingerie, carpets, rainwear, and tents.

■ Machine-wash sturdy articles in warm water with an all-purpose detergent.

■ Hand-wash lingerie and hosiery, using warm water and a light-duty detergent, or machine-wash in a mesh bag to prevent stretching or tearing.

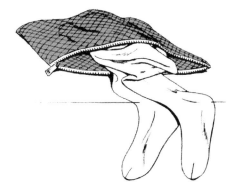

■ Use fabric softener to significantly reduce static electricity.

■ Tumble-dry nylon at a low temperature setting. Press at a cool temperature setting.

POLYESTER

Polyester fabrics are strong, resilient, wrinkle-resistant, colorfast, crisp, and hold pleats and creases well. But they are also nonabsorbent, attract and hold oil stains, may pill when rubbed, and may yellow with age. Polyester is used for clothing and filling garments and coats; some bed linens and towels are also made from polyester blends. Polyester can be safely dry-cleaned or machine-washed.

■ Turn polyester-knit garments inside out before washing to prevent snags.

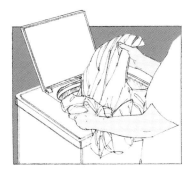

■ Machine-wash polyester in warm water, using an all-purpose detergent. Use a chlorine bleach if necessary. Fabric softener will reduce static electricity.

■ White polyester fabric will look even whiter if you soak it overnight in a mixture of ½ cup automatic dishwashing detergent and 1 gallon warm water. Launder as usual, but add ½ cup vinegar to the final rinse.

■ Tumble-dry at a low temperature setting. Do not overly dry polyester; this will cause gradual shrinkage.

■ Press polyester fabrics at a moderate temperature setting, or use steam.

RAYON

Rayon is a strong, absorbent fabric, but it tends to lose strength when it is wet. It is used for drapery and upholstery fabrics as well as for clothing.

■ Dry-clean rayon, or wash it by hand unless it is labeled "Machine-washable." For hand-wash, use lukewarm water with a light-duty detergent. Machine-wash rayon in warm water on a gentle cycle with a light-duty detergent.

■ Chlorine bleach can be used on rayon unless it has been treated with a resin finish.

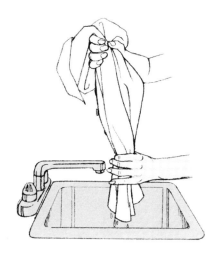

■ Drip-dry and press rayon on the wrong side with an iron at a medium temperature setting while the fabric is damp.

SPANDEX

Spandex is a lightweight fiber that resembles rubber in durability. It has good stretch and recovery, and it is resistant to damage from sunlight, abrasion, and oils. Always blended with other fibers, spandex provides the stretch in waistbands, foundation garments, swimwear, and exercise garments.

- Hand- or machine-wash spandex-blend garments in warm water using an all-purpose detergent.

- Use only oxygen bleach. Rinse thoroughly.

- Line-dry or tumble-dry garments made with spandex at a low temperature setting.

TRIACETATE

Triacetate resembles acetate, but it is less sensitive to heat; this allows it to be creased and crisply pleated. Triacetate is often used in jersey, textured knits, and taffeta.

- Pleated garments can be hand- or machine-washed in cold water. Set the gentle cycle to agitate for three minutes. Drip-dry permanently pleated garments.

- Most triacetate articles can be machine-washed with an all-purpose detergent in hot or warm water.

- Tumble- or line-dry triacetate. Press using a hot temperature setting.

THE BASICS OF LAUNDRY

Doing the laundry properly will extend the life of your clothes. Once you know the basics—how to sort clothes, pretreat stains, select laundry products, and use the washer and dryer—getting the laundry done is quite simple.

SORTING THE WASH

Sorting the laundry is the first step to a clean wash and helps to keep clothes, linens, and other household items looking their best through repeated washings. First sort the laundry by color. Put all the white articles in one pile, the light colors and pastels in another pile, and the bright and dark colors into a third. Then separate the dark pile into two piles: one for colorfast items and one for noncolorfast items. Further separate each pile into three smaller piles based on how dirty they are: lightly soiled, moderately soiled, and heavily soiled. You may have up to 12 piles of laundry. Sort them until you come up with a reasonable number of compatible, washer-size loads. The following hints will help you with the final sorting:

- Combine white and light-color items that have similar degrees of soil into the same pile.

continued on page 76

UNDERSTANDING FABRIC CARE LABELS

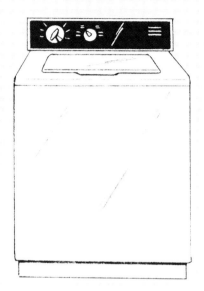

Machine Washable

When label reads	It means
Machine-wash	Wash, bleach, dry, and press by any customary method, including commercial laundering and dry-cleaning.
Home Launder Only	Same as above, but do not use commercial laundering.
No Chlorine Bleach	Do not use chlorine bleach. Oxygen bleach may be used.
No Bleach	Do not use any type of bleach.
Cold Wash/ Cold Rinse	Use cold water or cold washing machine setting.

When label reads	It means
Warm Wash/ Warm Rinse	Use warm water or warm washing machine setting.
Hot Wash	Use hot water or hot washing machine setting.
No Spin	Remove wash load before final machine spin cycle.
Delicate Cycle/ Gentle Cycle	Use appropriate machine setting; otherwise, wash by hand.
Durable Press/ Permanent Press Cycle	Use appropriate machine setting; otherwise, use warm wash, cold rinse, and short spin cycle.
Wash Separately	Wash alone or with like colors.

Nonmachine Washable

When label reads	It means
Hand-wash	Launder only by hand in lukewarm water; may be bleached; may be dry-cleaned.
Hand-wash Only	Same as above, but do not dry-clean.
Hand-wash Separately	Hand-wash alone or with like colors.
No Bleach	Do not use bleach.

When label reads	It means
Damp-wipe	Surface-clean with damp cloth or sponge.

Home Drying

When label reads	It means
Tumble-dry	Dry in tumble dryer at specified setting— high, medium, low, or no heat.
Tumble-dry/Remove Promptly	Same as above, but in absence of cool-down cycle, remove at once when tumbling stops.
Drip-dry	Hang wet, and allow to dry with hand-shaping only.
Line-dry	Hang damp, and allow to dry.
No Wring	Hang-dry, drip-dry, or dry flat only.
No Twist	Handle gently to prevent wrinkles.
Dry Flat	Lay garment on flat surface.

Ironing and Pressing

When label reads	It means
Cool Iron	Set iron at lowest setting.
Warm Iron	Set iron at medium setting.
Hot Iron	Set iron at hot setting.
Do Not Iron	Do not iron or press with heat.

When label reads	It means
Steam-iron	Iron or press with steam.
Iron Damp	Dampen garment before ironing.

Miscellaneous

When label reads	It means
Dry-clean Only	Garment should be dry-cleaned only, including self-service.
Professionally Dry-clean Only	Do not use self-service dry-cleaning.
No Dry-clean	Use recommended care instructions only. No dry-cleaning materials.

continued from page 73

■ Create a separate pile for delicate items that must be hand-washed.

■ Separate white synthetic articles, and wash them only with other white fabrics.

■ Separate synthetics, blends, and permanent-press fabrics from natural fabrics.

PREPARING THE WASH

Follow these hints to minimize damage to the articles you are washing and to help clean them thoroughly:

■ Pretreat spots, stains, and heavily soiled items with either a prewash spot-and-stain remover, a liquid detergent, a paste made from granular soap or detergent, a bar of soap, or a presoak.

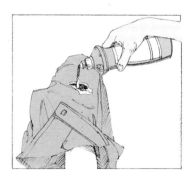

■ Know the fiber content and finishes of fabrics so you can select the proper water temperature and cleaning products.

■ Save care information so you can follow the recommended cleaning procedures.

■ Close all zippers, hook all hooks, and button all buttons.

■ Turn pockets inside out to get rid of debris.

■ Remove any nonwashable trim, decorations, pins, or buckles that might make holes or snag other articles in the wash.

■ Mend seams, tears, holes, or loose hems to prevent further damage during the wash cycle.

PREWASH SPOT-AND-STAIN REMOVERS

While soaps and detergents can be worked directly into spots and heavily soiled areas before you put the laundry into the washer, a special product designed just for removing spots and stains is more convenient to use. These are called prewash spot-and-stain removers and typically come in aerosols or pump sprays. They are excellent for treating stubborn stains, especially grease marks on synthetic fabrics.

■ Treat the stain while it is still fresh. Saturate the soiled area completely, then lightly rub the fabric together to work in the prewash product.

■ Some prewash products can damage the exterior finish of the washer and dryer, so be careful where you spray them.

■ Do not soak dark- and light-color fabrics together for long periods of time; this can cause colors to run.

■ Wash the laundry as usual after using a presoak.

SELECTING LAUNDRY PRODUCTS

Most commercial laundry preparations are designed to be used in washing machines, but some can be used for both hand- and machine-washing. Read the label carefully before purchasing any product to make sure it is the right one for the job you want it to do. When you use a laundry product, follow the directions precisely and measure accurately.

DETERGENTS AND SOAPS

Soap, a mixture of alkalies and fats, is a good cleaner in soft water, breaks down well in city sewer systems, and does not harm the environment. Soap is less effective in hard water, however, because it reacts with the high mineral content to form a curd that leaves a gray scum on clothing.

Detergents are synthetic washing products derived from petroleum and other nonfatty materials. They are less affected by hard water than soap and have excellent cleaning power. Detergents contain a wetting agent that lifts off dirt and agents that help to make hard-water minerals inactive, which is why they do not create scum.

BLEACH

Bleach works with detergent or soap to remove stains and soil, whiten white items, and brighten the colors of some fabrics. It also acts as a mild disinfectant. The two basic types of laundry bleach are chlorine and oxygen. Common liquid chlorine bleach is the most effective and least expensive, but it cannot be used on all fabrics. Oxygen bleach is safer for all washable fabrics, resin-finish fibers, and most washable colors.

■ Give fabrics a colorfastness test before using any bleach by mixing 1 tablespoon chlorine bleach with ¼ cup water or 1 tablespoon oxygen bleach with 2 quarts hot water. Apply this solution to an inconspicuous place; wait a few minutes, and check for a color change.

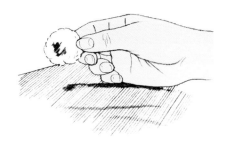

■ Bleach should be poured into the wash water or otherwise diluted before clothes are added. Bleach should never be poured directly onto fabrics.

■ Always bleach the whole item and not just a single stain.

■ Use the hottest water possible when using bleach; this improves its performance.

■ Bleach clothes only in the wash cycle so the bleach can be completely removed during the rinse cycle.

■ When washing fabrics that contain spandex, use only oxygen bleach.

FABRIC SOFTENERS

Fabric softeners add softness and fluffiness, reduce static electricity, and help decrease lint. They are available in liquid or sheet form. Liquid fabric softeners are added to the wash or rinse cycle; sheets are used in the dryer.

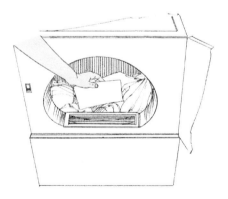

■ Dilute liquid fabric softeners with water before adding them to the dispenser or to the rinse water. Fabric softener can stain fabric if it is poured directly onto clothes.

■ Sheet fabric softeners may stain polyester articles if they are used in the dryer when these fabrics are drying. If you stain an item with fabric softener, rub the area with liquid detergent or a prewash spot-and-stain remover and rewash.

■ When laundering baby clothes, it's best to use fabric softener sparingly because some babies are sensitive to softener buildup.

■ If a laundered garment feels greasy or slick, you may have used too much fabric softener. Leave the softener out of the next few washes to see if the condition improves.

USING AN AUTOMATIC WASHER

For the best results from your washing machine, you must know how to combine multiple load capacities, water levels, temperature settings, and cycles properly.

LOADING THE MACHINE

Read the manufacturer's instruction booklet thoroughly, keep it for reference, and follow the recommended laundry procedures.

■ Do not overload the machine; garments should not exceed the manufacturer's recommendation.

■ Loading the washer to full capacity each time you wash will save time and energy, but don't be tempted to mix dark and light clothes in one load just to fill it.

■ Mix small and large items in each load for the best circulation, and distribute the load evenly around the wash basket.

SELECTING WATER TEMPERATURE

The correct water temperature setting for a load of wash varies according to the kinds of fabric being washed and the amount of soil. Use the chart on page 74 to help you select the proper wash and rinse settings.

SELECTING WATER LEVEL

Use enough water to provide good circulation, but do not use so much that you waste water and energy. Most machines have a water-level control, and you should adjust this control to match each load you wash. Refer to the manufacturer's instructions for this information.

SELECTING MACHINE CYCLE

Select the type of cycle and the length of washing time according to the kind of load and the degree of soil. Use a longer cycle for heavily soiled laundry.

■ Sturdy white and colorfast items: Use normal cycle, with a 10- to 12-minute wash time.

■ Sturdy noncolorfast items: Use normal cycle, with a 6- to 8-minute wash time.

USING WATER CONDITIONERS

The amount and type of chemicals and minerals dissolved in water determine whether the water is hard or soft. The condition of the water affects the cleaning potential of laundry products: the softer the water, the more effective it is for cleaning. Determine the hardness of your water so you will know if you need to condition it for effective cleaning.

Hard water leaves a residue, known as washing film, on laundered articles. You can soften hard water with a mechanical water softener that attaches to your water tank or by adding a water-conditioning product to the wash and rinse water during laundering.

■ Follow the directions on product labels precisely.

■ Use a nonprecipitating water conditioner to remove previously formed washing film or buildup. You can also remove light hard-water washing film from fabrics by soaking them in a solution of 1 cup white vinegar and 1 gallon water in a plastic container.

■ Use a nonprecipitating conditioner if you use soap in hard water or if you use a phosphate-free detergent.

HAND-WASHING

Most washable fabrics can be put into the machine, but some items are marked "Hand-wash Only." Never disregard this label—even when you're in a hurry.

Sort hand-wash items the same way you sort machine-wash clothes. Separate into piles by color, putting white and light colors together, dark and noncolorfast items into separate piles. Pretreat stains and heavily soiled areas.

Use a light-duty detergent, and dissolve it in the warm or cool wash water before adding the clothes. Let them soak for 3 to 5 minutes. Gently squeeze the suds through the fabric, being careful not to rub, twist, or wring excessively. Rinse articles thoroughly in cool water until the water runs clear.

Hang blouses, dresses, scarfs, and lingerie to dry. Use towels to blot excess moisture from sweaters, stockings, panties, and bras. Hang these items to dry only if the weight of the water will not stretch them out of shape; otherwise, dry them on a towel on a flat surface.

- Sturdy permanent press and wash and wear: Use permanent-press cycle, with a 6- to 8-minute wash time.

- Delicate fabrics and knits: Use gentle or delicate cycle, with a 4- to 6-minute wash time.

DRYING CLOTHES

Most clothes dried in an automatic dryer come out soft and almost wrinkle-free. If you have time and a backyard, you may prefer to dry the laundry on the clothesline on sunny days, reserving the dryer for bad weather and for permanent-press fabrics.

MACHINE DRYING

Read the manufacturer's instruction book to familiarize yourself with the dryer's operating procedures and recommended cycles.

- Do not overload the dryer; this will cause uneven drying and excessive wrinkling.

- Remove items from the dryer as soon as it stops, and hang or fold them to keep them from getting wrinkled.

- Clean the lint filter after each use of the dryer.

LINE DRYING

- Attach items to the clothesline by their most sturdy edges. Dry white and light items in the sun and bright items in the shade.

- Make sure that clothespins and clotheslines are clean.

- Use plastic rope or plastic-coated wire for your clothesline, and wipe it with a damp cloth before using it.

IRONING TIME-SAVERS

- Do your ironing in the bedroom. You'll be able to use the bed to sort your laundry, and you'll have hangers close at hand in the closet.

- Cut your ironing time by putting a piece of aluminum foil under the ironing board cover. The foil will reflect heat so you're actually ironing from both sides at once.

- Progress from articles or garments needing the lowest temperature to those requiring the highest.

- For a perfect fit, place your ironing board cover on the board while it's still damp, and let it dry in place.

- To prevent wrinkles, keep moving freshly ironed surfaces away from you.

- To prevent collars, cuffs, and hems from puckering, iron them on the wrong side first.

- Iron double-thickness fabric on the inside first, then on the outside.

- Acrylic knits can stretch out of shape if moved when wet and warm. Press each section dry, and let it cool completely before moving it on the ironing board.

- When pressing badly wrinkled corduroy, hold the iron just above the garment and steam the fabric thoroughly. While the corduroy is still damp, quickly smooth it along the ribs with your palm.

- Revive the nap of velvet or corduroy by pressing it right side down on a piece of the same fabric.

- If you don't have a sleeve board, insert a rolled-up towel in sleeves so they can be pressed without leaving creases. Or make your own sleeve board from a cardboard tube covered with soft fabric.

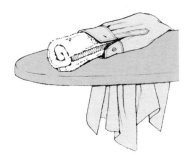

- Quick spray starch can be made at home by slowly adding 1 tablespoon cornstarch to 2 cups water. Stir until the starch is dissolved, and pour the blend into a clean spray bottle. Spray fabrics lightly when ironing.

- Restore a shiny look to chintz by ironing the fabric right side down on waxed paper.

- To keep from giving your wash-and-wear garments a sheen when you do touch-up ironing, turn the clothing inside out and iron the wrong side.

■ To remove wrinkles from a tie, insert a piece of cardboard cut to fit its inside. Cover the tie with cheesecloth, and press lightly with a steam iron.

■ To avoid flattening embroidery or eyelets when ironing, iron them facedown on a thick towel.

■ Hold pleats in place with paper clips when ironing. Be careful that the clips don't snag the fabric— particularly if it has a loose weave.

ELECTRIC IRONS

The obvious problem with a clogged steam iron is that it doesn't deliver enough steam. An even worse problem is the tendency of clogged irons to become suddenly unclogged and spew white mineral globs all over your best black suit. A clean iron speeds your pressing and protects your clothes.

■ Follow the manufacturer's instructions to keep the steam

vents from becoming clogged. Some irons use tap water; others require distilled water.

■ When you clean the soleplate of your iron, remove residue from the vents with a cotton swab or pipe cleaner. A sharp knife or other tool may scratch the soleplate.

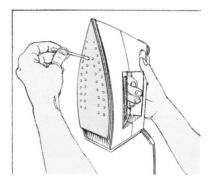

■ Use a cloth dipped in baking soda to clean the soleplate of a slightly warm iron. Scrub starch buildup or other soil. Rinse well, taking care to clear the vents.

■ If your iron is sticky from pressing starched clothes, clean it by running it across a piece of aluminum foil, fine sandpaper, or paper sprinkled with salt. If your iron is plastic-coated, though, avoid salt or other abrasives.

CLEANING WATER RESERVOIRS

Remove mineral deposits from the water reservoir when the steam action begins to decrease. Pour a solution of ⅓ cup white vinegar and ⅓ cup water into the water reservoir. Heat the iron, and let it steam for

SOLVING LAUNDRY PROBLEMS

Here are some common laundry problems and simple, quick ways to solve them.

Brown Stains

Cause: Detergent reacting with iron or manganese in the water.

Solution: Install an iron filter on your water system. Use a water conditioner in both the wash and rinse water.

Tears, Holes, or Snags

Cause: Excessive wear leads to damaged garments.

Solution: Make all repairs before washing an item, and hook all hooks, close zippers, and remove pins before putting articles in the washer.

Gray and Dingy Fabric

Cause: Incorrect sorting, insufficient detergent, or water temperature too low.

Solution: Follow suggestions for sorting and proper washing techniques.

Cause: Hard water.

Solution: Use a water conditioner, or install a water softener.

Greasy Spots

Cause: Undiluted liquid fabric softener coming into contact with fabric.

Solution: Dilute liquid fabric softener.

Harsh-feeling Fabrics

Cause: Hard water.

Solution: Install a water softener, or use a water conditioning product.

Linting

Cause: Not enough detergent.

Solution: Increase the amount of detergent.

Cause: Overloaded washer.

Solution: Reduce load size so the wash can circulate freely.

Scorching During Ironing

Cause: Iron temperature setting too high.

Solution: Reduce the heat setting on the iron.

Cause: Heat of iron reacting with a buildup of laundry products.

Solution: Run clothes through one or two complete washing cycles with 1 cup precipitating water conditioner.

Yellowing

Cause: Incomplete removal of soil, especially body oils.

Solution: Pretreat heavily soiled areas, increase the amount of detergent, and use hotter water and bleach.

Cause: Iron in the water.

Solution: Install an iron filter; use extra detergent and a nonprecipitating water conditioner.

about three minutes. Unplug the iron, and position it, soleplate down, on a small glass dish that has been placed in a larger shallow pan. Allow the water to drain from the vents for about an hour. Drain away any remaining solution, and flush the reservoir with clear water before using the iron.

DEFEATING STAINS

If all we had to worry about was ring around the collar, laundering would be a much easier job. Unfortunately, stains are easy to come by in the normal course of living. With the right treatment, however, most stains can be eliminated.

A RINGING SOLUTION

Remove ring around the collar with one of these methods:

■ Rub chalk into the collar, then wash as usual.

■ Pour shampoo along the collar, and allow it to soak into the ring. Let it sit—the longer the better— then wash.

■ The grease-cutting agents in liquid dishwashing detergent can help remove ring around the collar. Paint on, let sit, then launder.

BASIC RULES FOR STAIN REMOVAL

Successful stain removal relies on the correct technique and the appropriate removal agent for the particular stain and the material that is stained. If you ignore the basic rules for stain removal, you may be stymied in your attempt to get rid of a spot.

■ The best time to treat a stain is the moment after it occurs. The longer it sets, the more likely it is that a stain will become permanent.

■ Identify both the staining agent and the stained surface. Both will affect the way you treat the stain.

■ Remove as much of the staining agent as you possibly can before you begin the stain-removal process.

■ Rubbing, folding, wringing, and squeezing cause stains to penetrate more deeply and may damage delicate fibers.

■ Avoid using hot water, high-heat clothes dryers and irons on stains; heat makes some stains impossible to remove.

■ Pretest stain removers. Even water can damage some fabrics, so test every cleaner you plan to use in an inconspicuous spot.

■ Read manufacturers' care labels and product directions before you start to clean a stain.

■ Work from the edges toward the center to avoid spreading the stain.

DIFFERENTIATING STAINS

There are many different types of stains. In general, they break down into three major categories: greasy, nongreasy, and combination stains.

GREASY STAINS

Greasy stains come in all flavors—from butter or margarine to the oil from your car. You can sometimes remove grease spots from washable fabrics by laundering. Pretreating by rubbing a little detergent directly into the spot often helps. If you are treating an old stain or one that has been ironed, a yellow stain may remain after treatment with a solvent. Bleach is often effective at eliminating this yellow residue.

To remove grease spots from nonwashable fabrics, sponge the stain with a dry-cleaning solution. Total elimination of the stain may

require several applications, and you must allow the spot to dry completely between each sponging. Greasy stains may also be removed from nonwashable fabrics by using an absorbent substance, such as cornstarch, cornmeal, or fuller's earth (a natural mineral clay). Dust it on the greasy spots. When the absorbent material begins to look caked, shake or brush it off.

■ Pour cola or club soda directly on a greasy spot. Let it sit for a few minutes to loosen the stain, then wash as usual.

■ To cut grease on really dirty clothes, pour a can of cola into the wash along with your usual detergent.

■ Loosen grease spots on clothes by rubbing them with chalk before washing.

■ Greasy spots on suede can be removed by blotting the area with a cloth dipped in vinegar. Dry the fabric, then brush to bring back the nap.

NONGREASY STAINS

Fruit juice, black coffee, tea, food coloring, ink—nongreasy stains are easy to acquire but not impossible to remove. If you are treating a non-greasy stain on a washable fabric, sponge the stain with cool water as soon as possible. If this doesn't remove the stain, try soaking the fabric in cool water. If some of the stain remains after this treatment, try gently rubbing liquid detergent into it, then rinse with cool water. The very last resort is to use bleach, but always read the fabric-care label before you bleach. If the stain is old or has already been ironed, it may be impossible to remove completely.

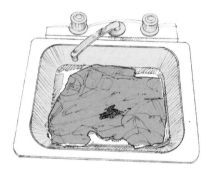

A nongreasy stain on fabric that cannot be washed can be sponged with cool water. Place an absorbent pad under the stained area, and slowly drip water through the fabric with an eye dropper or plastic spray bottle. If water fails to remove the stain, work liquid detergent into the stain and rinse it by sponging or flushing with cool water. Sponge the spot with rubbing alcohol after you've rinsed it to remove any detergent residue and to speed drying. (Caution: If you're treating acetate, acrylic, modacrylic, rayon, triacetate, or vinyl, be sure to dilute the alcohol with water: 1 part alcohol to 2 parts water.)

■ To remove ink stains, spray hair spray on the spot, and blot with a paper towel.

■ If blood leaves a stain, try cleaning with 3 percent hydrogen peroxide. Test a hidden area first to be sure the fabric is colorfast. Dab on the peroxide, then blot, repeating as necessary.

■ Perspiration stains can sometimes be removed by soaking the clothes in salt water. Dissolve ¼ cup salt in a tub of water, soak overnight, then wash.

■ For older perspiration stains, soak area in undiluted vinegar. Let it soak 15 to 20 minutes, then launder as usual.

COMBINATION STAINS

Some stains are double trouble. Coffee with cream, salad dressing, and lipstick leave a trail of combination stains behind them; they're both greasy and nongreasy. Getting rid of such stains is a two-part operation. First you need to eliminate the nongreasy stain, and then attack the greasy residue. On most fabrics, you'll need to sponge the stain with cool water, then work liquid detergent into the stain and rinse thoroughly. After the fabric has dried, apply a dry-cleaning solution to the greasy part of the stain. Allow the fabric to dry, and repeat as necessary.

TIPS FOR SPECIAL CARE ITEMS

■ Place delicate items in a mesh bag in the washing machine; they will be less likely to get tangled or damaged.

■ If you give your panty hose an occasional bath in a mixture of ½ cup salt to 1 quart of water, they'll last longer.

■ Turn a turtleneck sweater wrong side out before you put it in the laundry hamper. When it's washed, any makeup or skin oils that have come off on the neck area will be exposed to the suds and will come clean faster.

■ To prevent fraying, wash a foam rubber pillow in its case, then air-dry the pillow. Do not put it in the dryer.

■ Glycerin will keep plastic items such as shower curtains soft and pliable; add to the rinse water.

■ Plastic or rubber rainwear should be air-dried, not put in a clothes dryer.

■ Hand-wash leather gloves in saddle soap while they're on your hands, but don't rub them. Rinse them well, and remove them. If they're hard to remove after washing, run a stream of water into them.

■ Before drying leather gloves you've just hand-washed, blow into them to help reshape the fingers. When the gloves are almost dry, put them on once more, flexing the fingers to soften the leather. Then take off the gloves and dry them flat.

YOUR STAIN-REMOVAL KIT

To beat stains, you have to be prepared. A well-stocked stain-removal kit, like a first-aid kit, should be ready to help you handle cleaning emergencies whenever they occur. Here are the tools you'll need:

■ Clean white cotton cloths

■ Disposable diapers for absorbing flushed cleaning solutions

■ White blotting paper

■ White paper towels

■ A spoon, blunt knife, or spatula for scraping

■ An eyedropper or spray bottle

■ A small brush

Your kit will also need to include a variety of stain-removal agents. What you need depends on what you are likely to have to clean. You will be able to purchase most of them at your local hardware store, grocery store, or pharmacy.

ABSORBENTS

■ Absorbents "soak up" grease stains. Cornmeal is the best absorbent for light colors, and fuller's earth is best for dark colors. Spread the absorbent material on the stained areas, and allow it to work. As the grease is soaked up, the absorbent material will cake or become gummy. It should then be shaken or brushed off. Repeat the process until the stain has been removed.

BLEACHES

■ Chlorine is commonly used to bleach white cotton, linen, and synthetic fabrics. It is a powerful stain remover and can weaken fibers if allowed to stay on fabric for too long. Never use chlorine bleach on silk, wool, or fabrics that are exposed to sunlight, such as curtains. Always pretest chlorine bleach. Caution: Chlorine bleach is poisonous. If it comes in contact with the skin or eyes, it will cause burns and irritation.

■ Color remover contains hydro-sulfite chemicals, which lighten the color of fabrics before they are redyed a lighter color. They also remove some stains from colorfast fibers. Always pretest color remover. If the product causes a distinct color change instead of fading the fabric, you may be able to restore the original color by rinsing immediately with cool water. Color remover should not be used in a metal container.

Caution: Color removers are poisonous. Avoid prolonged contact with skin. Observe all precautions on the label.

■ Hydrogen peroxide is sold in a 3 percent solution and is a mild antiseptic. It is a safe bleach for most fibers. Buy peroxide in small quantities, and store it in a cool, dark place; it loses strength quickly after it is opened.

■ Oxygen bleach can be purchased in crystal form under trade names or generically. It is safe for all fabrics and surfaces. This type of bleach is slower-acting than hydrogen peroxide. When you use this bleach, be sure to rinse the treated articles.

CHEMICALS

■ Acetic acid can be bought in a 10 percent solution at pharmacies and photo-supply stores. It is a clear fluid that can be used to remove stains on silk and wool. It must be diluted with 2 parts water for use on cotton and linen (test for colorfastness). Never use this chemical on acetate. If acetic acid causes a color change, try sponging the affected areas with ammonia; this may restore the color.

■ Acetone is the base for nail polish remover. (Never substitute nail-polish remover for pure acetone because it contains ingredients that can worsen stains.) You can purchase acetone at pharmacies

SAFETY PRECAUTIONS

To treat stains and spots as soon as they occur, you have to be prepared. Many products in your stain-removal kit are flammable or toxic, and certain safety tips should be kept in mind when storing and using these products.

■ Store products out of the reach of children. The storage area should be cool, dry, and away from food-storage areas. Keep bottles tightly capped and boxes closed.

■ Do not transfer cleaning products to new containers.

■ Follow the directions on the product label, and heed all warnings.

■ Glass and unchipped porcelain containers are preferable to metal or plastic when working with stain-removal agents. Never use plastic with solvents. Never use any container that is rusty.

■ Protect your hands with rubber gloves. Don't touch your eyes or skin while

handling chemicals. If you do accidentally touch your eyes or spill chemicals on your skin, flush immediately with clear water.

■ Remember that the fumes of solvents are toxic; work in a well-ventilated area.

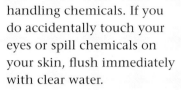

■ Do not use chemicals near an open flame or electrical outlet. Do not smoke while using chemicals.

■ When using a solvent on a washable fabric, be sure to rinse all traces of the solvent out of the fabric.

■ Do not experiment with mixtures of stain-removal agents. Never combine products unless specifically directed to do so in the home recipes for cleaning solutions.

and paint stores. The colorless liquid smells like peppermint, and it can be used on stains caused by substances such as nail polish or household cement. Acetone should not be used on fabrics containing acetate.

■ Isopropyl alcohol in a 70 percent solution is sufficient for most stain-removal jobs that call for alcohol. Stronger denatured alcohol (90 percent solution) can also be used. Be sure you do not buy alcohol with added color or fragrance. Since alcohol will fade some dyes, test it on the fabric you will be cleaning. Alcohol will damage acetate, triacetate, modacrylic, and acrylic fibers.

■ Ammonia, the plain household variety without added color or fragrance, can be used for stain removal. Because ammonia affects some dyes, test it on the stained article. To restore color changed by ammonia, rinse the affected area in water and apply a few drops of white vinegar, then rinse with clear water. Ammonia damages silk and wool; if you must use it on these fibers, dilute it with an equal amount of water and use sparingly.

■ Amyl acetate, or banana oil, is available in drugstores; it's safe for use on fibers that could be damaged by acetone, but it should not be allowed to come in contact with plastics or furniture finishes.

■ Coconut oil can be bought in drug and health-food stores. It is used in the preparation of dry spotters that are used to remove many kinds of stains. If you cannot obtain coconut oil, substitute mineral oil, which is almost as effective. To make a dry spotter, combine 1 part coconut oil and 8 parts liquid dry-cleaning solvent. Store in a tightly capped container to prevent evaporation.

■ Glycerin is used in the preparation of wet spotters that are used to remove many kinds of stains. To make a wet spotter, mix 1 part glycerin, 1 part white dishwashing detergent, and 8 parts water. Store in a plastic squeeze bottle, and shake well before each use.

■ Oxalic acid, sold in many pharmacies, is effective in treating ink and rust stains. The crystals must be dissolved in water (1 tablespoon crystals to 1 cup warm water). Test the solution on a hidden corner of the spotted item before using it on the stain. Moisten the stained area with the solution. Allow it to dry, then reapply. Be sure all traces of the solution are rinsed out.

■ Sodium thiosulfate, also known as photographic "hypo" or "fixer," is available in crystal form at photo-supply houses. Although considered safe for all fibers and harmless to dyes, this chemical should be tested on an inconspicuous area before use to ensure colorfastness and prevent damage.

■ Vinegar for stain removal refers to white (clear) vinegar. It is a 5 percent acetic acid solution and should be diluted if you use it on cotton or linen. Vinegar is safe for all other colorfast fibers, but it can change the color of some dyes. If an article changes color, rinse the affected area with water to which you've added a few drops of ammonia. Rinse thoroughly with clear water.

WASHING AGENTS

■ When instructions call for a mild detergent, use only a white dishwashing liquid detergent; the dyes in nonwhite detergents may worsen the stain. When instructions call for a pretreating paste made of detergent and water, use a powdered detergent that does not contain bleach.

■ Enzyme presoaks are most effective on protein stains, such as meat juices, eggs, and blood; they may harm silk and wool. Make sure you have exhausted every alternative before you use enzyme presoaks on these two fabrics.

■ Pretreaters start the cleaning process before the stained item is put in the washer. Pretreaters must be used in conjunction with the rest of the laundering process; do not try to use a pretreater alone, as

though it were a spot remover. Check the manufacturer's instructions to find out how long to let the pretreater soak before washing.

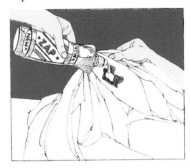

■ Soaps with added moisturizers, fragrance, dyes, or deodorant, such as bath soaps, should not be used to treat spots.

EIGHT WAYS TO BEAT STAINS

It would be nice to be able to squirt a little dab of the right solution on a stain, stand back, and watch the spot fade away forever. Unfortunately, stain removal is not that simple. There are eight basic techniques for stain removal: brushing, flushing, freezing, presoaking, pretreating, scraping, sponging, and tamping. The right technique for a particular spot or stain depends on what was spilled and where it fell.

BRUSHING

Some spots, such as dried mud, can be removed completely by brushing. For other kinds of stains, brushing is only a step in the cleaning process. A small brush, such as a toothbrush, is best for this technique. When you're working on fabric, stretch the piece on a firm, clean surface. Hold a sheet of paper next to the stain, and brush the staining material onto the paper. Gentle brushing pulls the stain off the surface and onto the paper.

hard. Hold an ice cube against the stain to freeze it. If the stained item is not washable, place the ice in a plastic bag. After the stain has solidified, it can usually be gently lifted or scraped from the surface.

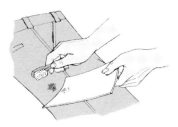

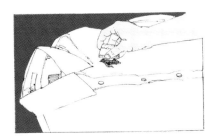

FLUSHING

Use flushing to remove loosened staining materials and the residue from stain-removal agents. If cleaning products are left in the material, they may cause additional staining or damage the treated article. An eyedropper or a plastic spray bottle that can be adjusted to a fine stream lets you control the amount of water flushed through the fabric. Before you begin this treatment, place a clean absorbent pad, such as a disposable diaper, under the spot. Work slowly, replacing the absorbent pad often to prevent the deposited material from restaining the fabric. If you're treating a stain on a washable fabric, rinse the article in warm water after you have flushed the stain.

FREEZING

Candle wax, chewing gum, and other gooey messes are easier to remove when they are cold and

PRESOAKING

When your wash is grayed, yellowed, or heavily soiled, washing alone will not get it clean and bright—you will have to presoak. Sort the soiled items before presoaking; items that are not colorfast should be presoaked separately from colorfast items because their colors may bleed. You may add bleach, laundry detergent, or an enzyme presoak to the soaking water. You can leave colorfast, stained articles in a presoak for as long as it takes to get them clean, but items that aren't colorfast should be soaked only briefly. Rinse thoroughly before washing to ensure that no residue of the presoak is left on the items.

PRETREATING

Pretreat oily, greasy stains with liquid laundry detergent, a pretreating spray, bar soap, or a pretreating paste made from powdered detergent and water. Rub the pretreater into the stain gently, and wash the item as usual.

SCRAPING

Scrape away excess staining material with a dull knife, spoon, or spatula before you apply stain remover. Don't press too hard; move the edge of your scraping tool back and forth across the stain in short strokes.

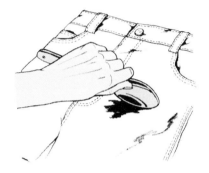

SPONGING

Put an absorbent pad under the stain before you sponge it. Sponge the stain gently using light strokes. Change the pad or sponge as soon as any of the stain is deposited on it. Some fabrics, such as acetate, triacetate, and rayon, are likely to develop rings when they are sponged. When you work on stains on these fabrics, barely wet the sponge with stain remover and touch the fabric lightly so that the stain remover is absorbed as slowly as possible. Blot the treated area between absorbent pads. Allow it to air-dry. Ironing or drying with heat may cause the stain remover itself to stain the fabric.

TAMPING

The best way to get some stains out of durable, tightly woven fabrics is to tamp them with a toothbrush or other small brush. Place the stained article on a hard work surface, not on a pad, and lightly rap the stain with the tips of the bristles. Repeat until the stain is removed. Use this technique sparingly since tamping will harm most fabrics.

MENDING AND REPAIR

Every stitch you sew saves you the expense of a tailor's bill and extends the life of your clothes. Although most mending jobs can be done by hand without a sewing machine, make sure you have the essentials of the basic sewing kit so that you can follow the step-by-step instructions of basic mending techniques.

THE BASIC SEWING KIT

■ A selection of buttons

■ A selection of needles

■ A selection of threads

- Sewing scissors
- Pins and pin cushion
- Thimble
- Tape measure
- Fasteners, such as snaps and hooks and eyes
- Self-fastening tape
- Patches

If you don't have these items already, keep the following tips in mind when shopping for them:

- Light trimming scissors or shears in a 6- or 7-inch length are best. Use these scissors only for sewing.

- Pins with large glass or plastic heads are the easiest to use. Buy the longest ones you can find—up to 1½ inches.

- A package of assorted sharps— medium-length needles with round eyes—are suitable for all fabric weights.

- Thimbles come in various sizes; find one that fits the middle finger of your sewing hand.

- Hooks and eyes in assorted sizes (1, 2, and 3) and snaps in sizes 3/0, 2/0, and 0 solve most replacement problems.

- A 6-inch metal sewing gauge is more useful for sewing than a tape measure, particularly in hemming where it can be used for keeping a desired measurement.

- Other items that make sewing a lot easier include a seam ripper—the sharp, curved edge is used to cut seams open, while the fine point is used to pick out threads; a needle threader, which saves lots of time and frustration; and pinking shears, which have zigzag edges, allowing you to trim fabric without fraying.

BASIC TECHNIQUES

- Fix it when you find it. The old adage that the longer you take to fix something, the worse it gets holds true in mending.

- Make it like the original. Study the garment before you repair it to see how to match the buttons, thread, and stitch patterns.

- Press as you go. Pressing prepares fabric for smooth stitching, helps keep folds flat and in place, and makes it easy to achieve professional-looking results. When you press, lift the iron up and down with a light touch, rather than sliding it back and forth.

- Follow the manufacturer's directions. This is especially important for patches, gripper snaps, and zippers.

THREADING THE NEEDLE

Hold the needle upright with one hand, and rotate it in your fingers until you can see the eye. Hold the cut thread about ¾ inch from the end with the fingers of the other hand, and push the thread through the eye of the needle until about ½ inch extends beyond the eye. Pull about ⅓ of the thread length through for a single thread; match the ends if a double thread is needed for the mending job. If you have trouble threading the needle, the following tricks may help:

■ Position the needle in front of a white surface so the eye is more visible.

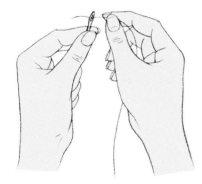

■ Stiffen the thread end by moistening it or running it through some beeswax.

■ Dip the end of the thread into a bottle of red nail polish, and allow to dry. Colored polish will make the thread easier to see and will provide a slick end for threading.

■ Spray your fingertips with hair spray and then stiffen the tip of the thread by rolling it back and forth in your fingers.

■ Try a needle with a larger eye, or use a needle threader.

KNOTTING THE THREAD

Place the end of the thread along the ball of the index finger of your left hand (right hand if you're left-handed). Hold the thread with your left thumb, and position the point of the needle over the thread about ½ inch from the end of the thread. Hold the end of the thread and the needle in place with your left thumb. With your right hand, wrap the thread snugly around the tip of the needle, twice for a small knot or four times for a large knot.

Pinch the wrapped thread between the thumb and index finger of your left hand. Push the needle up between those fingers as far as you can with the second finger of your right hand. Then grasp the point of the needle with the thumb and index finger of your right hand, and slide the wrapped thread slowly and smoothly down the needle, over the eye, and down the length of the thread into a snug knot. Trim away the excess thread below the knot.

REPLACING A BUTTON

Most buttons can be sewn with general-purpose thread. Buttons should be sewn on loosely to allow for the overlapping garment layer containing the buttonholes. Buttons sewn too tightly will make the button difficult to close. Sew-through buttons usually have two or four holes through which the button is sewn to the garment. Shank buttons

  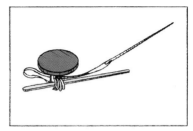

(Left) Replacing some sew-through buttons requires shank builders. (Middle) When removing a shank builder, wind the thread under the button bottom. (Right) A shank button has a small loop on its underside.

have a loop on the back through which they are sewn to the garment.

To replace a sew-through button, you will need a shank builder—either a toothpick or a thick matchstick. Insert the needle into the fabric on the side of the garment where the button will be, and bring the point up ⅛ inch away. Pull through to the knot. Make two small stitches to mark the spot for the button and to give your work a firm base—the button will cover the knot and stitches. Now insert the needle through one of the holes of the button from the wrong side. Let the button fall down the needle and the thread to the garment. Place your shank builder across the top of the button. Hold it in place with your finger, and stitch over the shank builder as you sew on the button. Match your stitches to the stitch design of the other buttons. Take three to six stitches through each pair of the button's holes, depending on how much stress the button will receive. Then bring the needle up through the fabric but not through

the button. Remove the shank builder, hold the button tightly away from the garment, and wind the thread snugly two or three times around the threads under the button. Insert the needle through to the wrong side of the garment, and push the needle under the button stitches. Pull the thread partially through, forming a loop. Insert the needle through the loop, and pull the thread snugly to form a knot. Cut the threads close to the knot.

To replace a shank button, begin by inserting the needle on the side of the garment where the button will be located. Bring the needle up ⅛ inch away, and pull the thread through to the knot. Make two small stitches to mark the spot for the button and to give a firm base for your work. The button will cover the knot and stitches. Position the button at the marking with the shank parallel to the buttonhole. Insert the needle through the shank and then down through the fabric. Stitch through the shank four to eight times. Be careful to keep the stitches on the underside of the garment small and neat. Finally, make a knot. Insert the needle under the button stitches on the wrong side of the garment. Pull the thread partially through, forming a loop. Insert the needle through the loop, and pull the thread snugly to form a knot. Trim the threads close to the knot.

BASIC STITCHES

Four basic stitches can get you through almost any type of hand-sewing repair. If you haven't sewn before, you may want to practice a bit to develop the ability to stitch evenly in a straight line.

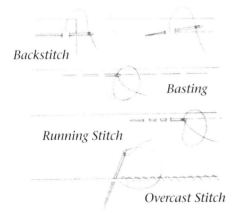

Backstitch

Basting

Running Stitch

Overcast Stitch

■ Backstitch—Viewed from the top, backstitching appears as a continuous line of even stitches; viewed underneath, the stitches are twice as long as those on top and they overlap at the ends. Use a single knotted thread, and work from right to left. Insert the needle from the underside of the fabric layers ⅛ inch to the left of where your stitching will begin. Pull the thread through to the knot. Insert the needle ⅛ inch behind where the thread emerges (that is, where your stitching will begin). Bring the needle up ¼ inch beyond this insertion, and pull the thread snugly. Bring the needle up ¼ inch beyond the insertion, and pull the thread through. Continue in this manner, forming evenly spaced stitches about ⅛ inch long.

■ Basting—Basting is used to hold two or more layers of fabric together temporarily during fitting or construction. You may want to baste a hem or cuff to make sure you like the length before completing the hem with a more permanent stitch. Use an unknotted single thread, so it will be easy to pull out, and work from right to left. Insert the needle from the right side, and weave the point of the needle in and out two or three times. Basting stitches may be as long as 1 inch. Pull the thread partially through, securing the unknotted end between your thumb and forefinger so that you don't pull it through entirely. Reinsert the needle, and repeat the process. Leave the thread loose at the end so that it can be easily removed.

■ Running stitch—The running stitch, used for delicate repairs, topstitching, and gathering, is worked in much the same way as basting, but the stitches are shorter and even. Secure the thread at both ends with a knot. Use a single knotted thread, and work from right to left. Insert the needle from the wrong side, then weave the point evenly in and out of the fabric two or three times. Pull the thread through firmly, but avoid puckering the fabric.

■ Overcast stitch—This stitch is used to keep a fabric edge from fraying. Use a single knotted thread, and work from right to left. Insert the needle from the underside of your work. Pull the thread through to the knot, and insert the needle from the wrong side again, ⅛ to ¼ inch to the left of the knot. Pull the thread through, but not too tightly or the fabric will curl. The more your fabric frays, the closer the stitches should be. Keep the depth of the stitches uniform, and make them as shallow as possible without pulling the fabric apart.

ORGANIZING YOUR SUPPLIES

■ Keep a small magnet in your sewing basket. When needles and pins drop on the carpet while you're sewing, retrieve them quickly with the magnet.

■ Sewing needles can get rusty and dull. Rub off any rust with an abrasive soap pad or steel wool.

■ Leave a length of thread in a needle before storing it in a pincushion. You'll be able to see it

more easily, and the needle will be less likely to slip inside the pincushion.

■ A bar of soap makes a perfect pincushion. In addition to storing pins and needles, it lubricates the tips so that they slide easily through stiff fabrics.

■ To keep scissors from damaging other items in your sewing basket, cover the points with the rubber protectors sold for knitting needles.

■ Before throwing out clothing you no longer wear, stock up on notions by saving any usable zippers, buttons, or decorative trim. These can come in handy when you're trying to replace a fastener.

■ Thread looks darker on the spool than it will on fabric. Choose a thread a shade darker than the material you'll be using it on.

HEMMING TECHNIQUES

■ Before hemming a skirt, dress, or pants, let the garment hang for a day on a hanger to allow the fabric to settle.

■ You can often steam out small puckers at the top edge of a hem. Don't redo a slightly puckered hem until you've tried to press it.

■ Clip-type clothespins can be more convenient than pins for holding a hem in place while you sew it.

CARING FOR YOUR CLOTHES

Along with good laundering and mending techniques, your clothes will benefit from proper care and storage. Clothes that will be stored for a season or longer need to be free of moths, moisture, and sunlight.

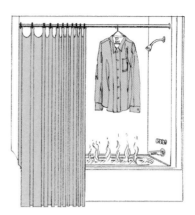

GENERAL CLOTHING CARE

- When you buy a new garment, dab the center of each button with clear nail polish to seal the threads.

- Wrap tape around your finger with the sticky side out to remove lint from a small area quickly.

- For a do-it-yourself lint remover, roll up a magazine and wrap wide adhesive tape around it with the sticky side out.

- When brushing clothes to remove dust and lint, you'll get better results if you brush with the nap rather than against it.

- Rub zipper teeth occasionally with wax to keep the zipper working smoothly. The stub of a candle works well for this procedure.

- You can de-wrinkle clothing in a hurry by running hot water into the bathtub and hanging the garment on the shower rod. The steam will remove the wrinkles.

SEASONAL STORAGE

If your wool sweaters need to be protected from moths or your heirloom items require special care, you'll find that the time spent on storing your clothes properly will reward you the next time you get them out of storage. There will be no moth holes, no mildew, and no need for replacements.

REPELLING MOTHS

- New garbage cans make good storage containers for clothing. If they are airtight, and you are storing freshly cleaned clothes, you won't need to add mothballs.

- If your cedar closet is old and no longer smells of cedar—which deters moths—lightly sand its surfaces. The sanding will open the wood's pores and release a fresh cedar odor.

- The cedar odor only repels moths; it doesn't kill them. Clean all clothes before storage to remove any moth eggs.

■ Mothproofing products should be placed as high as possible in the closet because the fumes filter downward.

DETERRING MOISTURE

■ To prevent mildew from forming in a leather purse during storage, fill the purse with crumpled newspaper and leave it unfastened.

■ In humid climates, corrugated boxes can be used for clothes storage if you coat the box with shellac to keep out moisture.

CARING FOR SHOES

■ Neaten up the frayed ends of shoelaces (and make it easier to lace them) by dipping them in clear nail polish.

■ Remove scuff marks on shoes by rubbing with a baking-soda paste.

■ Use petroleum jelly to shine leather shoes. Apply with a soft cloth, wipe off the excess, and buff with a clean cloth.

■ Spray furniture polish on shoes, then buff with a clean, dry cloth.

■ Use a light coating of spray starch on new fabric tennis shoes before wearing them—dirt can't become

embedded in the canvas, and the shoes will always be easy to clean.

■ Clean the rubber on athletic shoes with baking soda sprinkled on a sponge or washcloth.

■ Use lemon juice to clean and shine black or tan leathers. Apply with a soft cloth.

■ To keep shoes shiny after you've polished them, spray them with hair spray.

■ Hand lotion can be used to shine shoes. Just put a dab on each shoe, rub in with your fingers, and buff.

■ Clean the salt residue common on winter boots with a cloth dipped in a solution of 1 cup water and 1 tablespoon vinegar. This will work on leather and vinyl.

■ Use a soft cloth dipped in vinegar to shine a pair of patent-leather shoes or any patent-leather item.

■ Shoes that are starting to smell can be helped by sprinkling with a little salt. Let sit overnight. The salt will help control moisture, which contributes to odors.

■ Keep smelly feet at bay by sprinkling baking soda into shoes to control odor and moisture.

STAIN REMOVAL CHART

ALCOHOLIC BEVERAGES

ACETATE BURLAP FELT FIBERGLASS RAYON SILK TRIACETATE WOOL	Blot any excess liquid. Spray on fabric spot cleaner, or flush area with cool water. Apply a wet spotter and a few drops of white vinegar. Cover with an absorbent pad dampened with the wet spotter, and let stand as long as any stain is being removed. Keep the stain and pad moist, changing the pad as it picks up the stain. Flush with cool water, blotting excess liquid with a clean absorbent pad. Dry thoroughly.
ACRYLIC FABRIC COTTON LINEN NYLON POLYESTER SPANDEX	Apply fabric spot cleaner, or sponge stain promptly with cool water. If possible, presoak the stain in cool water for at least 30 minutes or overnight. Work undiluted dishwashing or liquid laundry detergent into stain. Rinse well. Launder as soon as possible. Old or ironed-in stains may be impossible to remove.

BABY FOOD/FORMULA

ACETATE BURLAP CARPET, SYNTHETIC CARPET, WOOL FIBERGLASS RAYON SILK TRIACETATE WOOL	Blot up excess liquid, or scrape excess solids from fabric. Sponge with a dry-cleaning solvent, or apply a dry spotter to the stain and cover with an absorbent pad dampened with the dry spotter. Let it stand as long as any stain is being removed. Keep pad and stain moist, changing the pad as it picks up the stain. Flush with one of the recommended liquid solvents. Allow to dry completely.
ACRYLIC FABRIC COTTON LINEN NYLON POLYESTER SPANDEX	Blot up or scrape excess material, and rinse stain in cool water. Soak for 30 minutes in an enzyme presoak. Launder immediately, if possible. If not, flush with cool water and allow to dry thoroughly. If stain has dried, repeated laundering may be necessary.

BERRIES (BLUEBERRY, CRANBERRY, RASPBERRY, STRAWBERRY)

ACETATE CARPET, SYNTHETIC CARPET, WOOL FIBERGLASS RAYON TRIACETATE	Spray on fabric spot cleaner. If stain remains, sponge with cool water. Then sponge the area with lemon juice. Flush with water. Blot as much excess liquid as possible, and allow to dry. If stain persists, apply a wet spotter. Cover with an absorbent pad moistened with wet spotter. Let stand as long as any stain is being removed. Change the pad as it picks up the stain. Flush with water. If any trace of stain still appears, moisten the area with a solution of 1 cup warm water and 1 teaspoon enzyme presoak product. Cover with a clean absorbent pad. Let it stand for 30 minutes. Flush with water, and allow to air-dry.
ACETATE BURLAP FIBERGLASS RAYON SILK TRIACETATE WOOL	Spray on fabric spot cleaner. If stain remains, sponge with cool water immediately. Then sponge with lemon juice. Flush with water. Blot as much excess liquid as possible, and allow to dry. If any trace of stain still exists, soak in a solution of 1 quart warm water, ½ teaspoon liquid dishwashing or laundry detergent, and 1 tablespoon white vinegar for 15 minutes. Rinse with water, and launder as soon as possible.

BLOOD

ACETATE BURLAP FIBERGLASS RAYON SILK TRIACETATE WOOL	Sponge the stain with cold water. If any stain remains, apply a wet spotter and a few drops of ammonia (do not use ammonia on silk and wool). Cover with an absorbent pad dampened with the wet spotter and ammonia. Let it stand as long as any stain is being removed, changing the pad as it picks up the stain. Flush thoroughly with cool water. If stain persists, moisten it with a solution of ½ teaspoon enzyme presoak—except on silk or wool—and ½ cup warm water. Cover the stain with an absorbent pad. Let it stand for 30 minutes.
ACRYLIC FABRIC COTTON LINEN NYLON POLYESTER SPANDEX	Blood can usually be removed by a thorough laundering in cold water. If any stain remains, soak it in a solution of 1 quart warm water, ½ teaspoon dishwashing or liquid laundry detergent, and 1 tablespoon ammonia for 15 minutes. Tamp or scrape, blotting occasionally with an absorbent pad. Rinse well with water, making sure to remove all traces of the ammonia, then dry or launder as usual.

BUTTER/MARGARINE

ACETATE
CARPET, SYNTHETIC
CARPET, WOOL
FIBERGLASS
RAYON
SILK
TRIACETATE

Scrape as much of the solid butter as you can without driving any of it further into the fibers. Apply an absorbent (cornmeal for light colors, fuller's earth for darks), but do not press it in. Give the absorbent plenty of time to work. Remove the absorbent and, if needed, repeat the application. If any residue remains, sponge the spot with cleaning fluid or spot remover.

ACRYLIC FABRIC
COTTON
LINEN
MODACRYLIC
NYLON
POLYESTER
SPANDEX

Scrape up any excess. Pretreat with stain remover, blot the stained area, and launder as usual. If the stain remains, or if immediate laundering is impossible, place the fabric stain side down on an absorbent pad. Flush with cleaning fluid through the back of the stain, and blot with a clean absorbent pad. Pretreat again, and rinse well or launder.

CHOCOLATE/COCOA

ACETATE
FIBERGLASS
RAYON
SILK
TRIACETATE
WOOL

Blot up any excess, or scrape any matter from the surface. Flush the stain with club soda to prevent setting. Sponge the stain with a dry-cleaning solvent. Then apply a dry spotter to the stain, and cover with an absorbent pad dampened with the dry spotter. Keep the stain and pad moist with the dry spotter. Change the pad as it picks up the stain. Flush with dry-cleaning solvent. If a stain remains, moisten it with a solution of 1 cup warm water and 1 teaspoon enzyme pre-soak product—but do not use on silk or wool. Cover with a clean pad that has been dipped in the solution and wrung almost dry. Let it stand at least 30 minutes. When the stain is lifted, flush thoroughly with water and allow to dry.

ACRYLIC FABRIC
COTTON
LINEN
MODACRYLIC
NYLON
POLYESTER
SPANDEX

Wipe up as much excess as possible. Flush the stain with club soda. Sponge the area with a dry-cleaning solvent. Apply a dry spotter to the stain, and cover with an absorbent pad dampened with the dry spotter. Keep the stain moist with dry spotter. Change the pad as it picks up the stain. Flush with dry-cleaning solvent. If any stain remains, apply a few drops of dishwashing detergent and a few drops of ammonia, then tamp or scrape. Flush well with water to remove all traces of ammonia.

COFFEE

ACETATE
FIBERGLASS
RAYON
TRIACETATE

Blot with a clean cloth. Sponge the stain with water. Apply fabric spot cleaner or a wet spotter and a few drops of white vinegar. Cover with an absorbent pad dampened with the wet spotter. Keep the stain and pad moist with the wet spotter and vinegar. Change the pad as it picks up the stain. Flush with water. If a stain remains, moisten it with a solution of 1 teaspoon enzyme presoak and 1 cup warm water. Cover with a pad that has been dipped in the solution and wrung almost dry. Let it stand for at least 30 minutes. When the stain is removed or no more is being lifted, flush thoroughly with water and allow to dry.

ACRYLIC FABRIC
MODACRYLIC
NYLON
POLYESTER
SPANDEX

Blot with a clean cloth. Presoak the stain in a solution of 1 quart warm water, ½ teaspoon dishwashing detergent, and 1 tablespoon white vinegar for 15 minutes. Rinse with water. Sponge the remaining stain with rubbing alcohol and launder, if possible. If not, soak it in a solution of 1 quart warm water and 1 tablespoon enzyme presoak product for 30 minutes. Rinse well with water.

CRAYON

ACETATE
FIBERGLASS
RAYON
SILK
TRIACETATE
WOOL,
NONWASHABLE

Gently scrape to remove excess matter. Place an absorbent pad under the stain, and flush with a dry-cleaning solvent. Allow to dry. Repeat if necessary.

ACRYLIC FABRIC
COTTON
LINEN
MODACRYLIC
NYLON
POLYESTER
SPANDEX
WOOL, WASHABLE

Scrape to remove the excess matter. Place the stain between two pieces of white blotting paper, and press with a warm iron. Change the papers as the stain is absorbed. This stain can easily spread, so use care while pressing. On colorfast white cotton or linen, try pouring boiling water through the stain. After using either method, allow fabric to dry. If any trace remains, flush it with a dry-cleaning solvent. Rinse well with water, and allow to dry.

CREAM

ACETATE CARPET, SYNTHETIC CARPET, WOOL FIBERGLASS RAYON SILK TRIACETATE WOOL, NONWASHABLE	Remove any excess matter immediately. Sponge with dry-cleaning solvent. Then apply dry spotter to the stain and cover with an absorbent pad dampened with dry spotter. Change the pad as it picks up the stain. Flush with a dry-cleaning solvent. If any stain remains, moisten the area with a solution of 1 cup warm water and 1 teaspoon enzyme presoak—do not use on silk or wool. Cover with a clean pad that has been dipped in the solution and wrung almost dry. Let it stand for 30 minutes. When no more stain is being lifted, flush the area thoroughly with water and allow to dry.
ACRYLIC FABRIC COTTON LINEN MODACRYLIC NYLON POLYESTER SPANDEX WOOL, WASHABLE	Immediately remove any excess matter. Sponge the stain with a dry-cleaning solvent. Apply a dry spotter, and cover with an absorbent pad dampened with dry spotter. Let it stand as long as any stain is being removed. Change pad as it picks up the stain. Keep stain and pad moist with dry spotter. Flush with dry-cleaning solvent. If any stain remains, apply a few drops of dishwashing detergent and a few drops of ammonia to the area, then tamp or scrape. Flush with water to remove all ammonia, and allow to dry completely.

DEODORANT

ACETATE CARPET, SYNTHETIC CARPET, WOOL COTTON FIBERGLASS LINEN RAYON SILK TRIACETATE WOOL	Apply rubbing alcohol to the stain, and cover with an absorbent pad dampened with alcohol (dilute alcohol with 2 parts water for acetate, rayon, and triacetate; test silk for colorfastness before using alcohol). Keep moist. Allow to stand as long as any stain is being removed. If the stain remains, flush with a solution of warm sudsy water with a little ammonia added (use special care on silk and wool). Rinse with water. Apply a solution of warm water with a little white vinegar added, taking special care with this solution on cotton and linen. Rinse again. Dry thoroughly. Caution: Never iron material with a deodorant stain. The chemical and heat interaction will ruin most fabrics.
ACRYLIC FABRIC MODACRYLIC NYLON POLYESTER SPANDEX	Most deodorant stains can be removed by pretreating with a liquid detergent or prespotter and laundering as usual. If the stain doesn't seem to be loosening with the pretreatment, rinse and flush with white vinegar. Rinse in clear water. If the stain remains, flush the area with denatured alcohol. Rinse with clear water, and dry or launder as usual.

GLUE

ACETATE FIBERGLASS RAYON SILK TRIACETATE WOOL	Immediately sponge the area with water. Spray on fabric spot remover. Then apply a wet spotter and a few drops of white vinegar. Cover with an absorbent pad dampened with wet spotter. Change the pad as it removes the stain. Flush with water and repeat until no more stain is removed. For a lingering stain, moisten the area with a solution of 1 cup warm water and 1 teaspoon enzyme presoak product—do not use on silk or wool. Cover with a clean pad that has been dipped in the solution and wrung dry. Let it stand 30 minutes. Flush thoroughly with water, and allow to dry.
ACRYLIC FABRIC COTTON LINEN MODACRYLIC POLYESTER SPANDEX	Soak in a solution of 1 quart warm water, ½ teaspoon liquid dishwashing or laundry detergent, and 1 tablespoon white vinegar. (Omit vinegar when treating cotton and linen.) Let soak for 15 minutes, and rinse well with water. Soak in a solution of 1 quart warm water and 1 tablespoon enzyme presoak product for 30 minutes. Rinse well, and launder as soon as possible.

GRASS

ACETATE CARPET, SYNTHETIC CARPET, WOOL RAYON SILK TRIACETATE WOOL	Sponge the area with a dry-cleaning solvent. Apply a dry spotter to the stain, and cover with an absorbent pad dampened with the dry spotter. Change the pad as it picks up the stain. Flush with dry-cleaning solvent, and allow to dry thoroughly. When working on carpets, be sure to blot up the excess liquid during the procedure and before drying.
ACRYLIC FABRIC COTTON LINEN MODACRYLIC NYLON POLYESTER SPANDEX	Work liquid dishwashing or laundry detergent into the stain, and rinse well. If any stain remains, soak in enzyme presoak product. Rinse thoroughly, and launder as soon as possible. If stain persists, test for colorfastness in an inconspicuous place, then use a mild sodium perborate bleach or 3 percent hydrogen peroxide. Thoroughly rinse, then launder as usual.

GREASE: AUTOMOTIVE OR COOKING

ACETATE **CARPET, SYNTHETIC** **CARPET, WOOL** **RAYON** **SILK** **TRIACETATE** **WOOL**	Blot up as much excess as possible, and apply an absorbent. After letting the absorbent work, brush it out of the fabric. If stain remains, sponge with a dry-cleaning solvent. Then apply a dry spotter to the area. Cover the stain with an absorbent pad dampened with dry spotter. Change the pad as it picks up the stain. Allow to dry.
ACRYLIC FABRIC **COTTON** **LINEN** **MODACRYLIC** **POLYESTER** **SPANDEX**	Blot up excess as soon as possible. Apply an absorbent, and let it soak up the spill. After brushing out the absorbent, sponge the area with a dry-cleaning solvent. Then apply a dry spotter to any remaining stain. Cover the stain with an absorbent pad, and let it remain in place until no more stain is lifted. Change the pad as it picks up the stain. Occasionally tamp the area, blotting up any loosened material. Flush with dry-cleaning solvent. Flush the area with water, and repeat until no more stain is removed. Allow to dry.

MUD/DIRT

ACETATE **FIBERGLASS** **RAYON** **SILK** **TRIACETATE** **WOOL**	Let mud dry, then brush off excess. If any stain remains, sponge the area with water and apply a few drops of wet spotter and a few drops of white vinegar. Cover with an absorbent pad dampened with wet spotter. Change the pad as it picks up the stain. Flush with water. If stain remains, apply rubbing alcohol to the area and cover with an absorbent pad dampened with alcohol. (Do not use alcohol on acetate, rayon, or triacetate.) Let the pad stand as long as any stain is being removed. When no more stain is being removed, flush thoroughly with water and allow to dry.
ACRYLIC FABRIC **COTTON** **LINEN** **MODACRYLIC** **NYLON** **POLYESTER** **SPANDEX**	Let mud dry, then brush off excess. Laundering should remove any remaining stain. If more treatment is needed, sponge the stain with rubbing alcohol. (Do not use alcohol on acrylic fabric or modacrylic.) Flush with water. If stain persists, sponge it with a dry-cleaning solvent. Allow to dry, then launder.

OIL: AUTOMOTIVE, HAIR, LUBRICATING, MINERAL, OR VEGETABLE

ACETATE CARPET, SYNTHETIC CARPET, WOOL RAYON SILK TRIACETATE WOOL	Blot up excess, and apply an absorbent, such as cornmeal. After letting the absorbent work, brush the powder off the fabric. If a stain remains, sponge with a dry-cleaning solvent. Apply a dry spotter. Cover with an absorbent pad that has been dampened with dry spotter. Change the pad as it picks up the stain. Flush the area with the dry-cleaning solvent. If a stain persists, sponge the area with water and apply a wet spotter with a few drops of white vinegar. Cover the stain with an absorbent pad moistened with wet spotter. Change the pad as it picks up the stain. Flush with water, and repeat the procedure until no more stain is removed. Allow to dry.
ACRYLIC FABRIC COTTON LINEN MODACRYLIC NYLON POLYESTER SPANDEX	Blot excess. Apply an absorbent, and allow it to work. After brushing out the powder, sponge the area with a dry-cleaning solvent. Apply a dry spotter, and cover with an absorbent pad moistened with dry spotter. Change the pad as it picks up the stain. Occasionally tamp the area, blotting any loosened material. Flush with a dry-cleaning solvent. If stain remains, sponge with water and apply a wet spotter and a few drops of ammonia. Tamp the stain again, blotting with an absorbent pad. Flush the area with water, and repeat until no more stain is removed. Allow to dry.

SOFT DRINKS

ACETATE FIBERGLASS RAYON SILK TRIACETATE WOOL	Blot with a clean cloth. Sponge the remaining stain with water. It is imperative that all the sugar be removed. Usually water will completely remove the stain, but if any remains, spray on spot cleaner or apply a wet spotter and a few drops of white vinegar. Cover with an absorbent pad. Change the pad as it picks up the stain. Flush well with water. Repeat until the stain is lifted. If any sugar remains and turns yellow, it cannot be removed.
ACRYLIC FABRIC COTTON LINEN MODACRYLIC NYLON POLYESTER SPANDEX	Blot up excess, flush with water, and launder immediately. If that is not possible, soak the stain in a solution of 1 quart warm water, ½ teaspoon liquid detergent, and 1 tablespoon white vinegar for 15 minutes. Rinse well with water to remove enzyme and sugar residues. Allow to dry, but launder as soon as possible.

URINE

ACETATE CARPET, SYNTHETIC CARPET, WOOL FIBERGLASS RAYON SILK TRIACETATE WOOL	Sponge the area with water or club soda immediately. Apply a wet spotter and a few drops of ammonia. (Do not use ammonia on silk or wool.) Cover with an absorbent pad moistened with wet spotter. Change the pad as it picks up the stain. Flush with water, then apply wet spotter with a few drops of white vinegar. Flush well, and repeat if necessary. Allow to dry.
ACRYLIC FABRIC COTTON LINEN MODACRYLIC NYLON POLYESTER SPANDEX	Flush immediately with water or club soda. Soak the stain in a solution of 1 quart warm water, ½ teaspoon liquid detergent, and 1 tablespoon ammonia for 30 minutes. Rinse well with water. If stain persists, soak in a solution of 1 quart warm water and 1 tablespoon white vinegar for 1 hour. (Use white vinegar with care on cotton and linen.) Rinse well, and allow to dry. If stain is set, try applying rubbing alcohol to the area and tamping (do not apply full-strength rubbing alcohol to acrylic fabric or modacrylic—dilute with 2 parts water). Rinse well, and allow to dry.

VOMIT

ACETATE CARPET, SYNTHETIC CARPET, WOOL FIBERGLASS RAYON SILK TRIACETATE WOOL	Gently scrape up solids. Sponge the area with water, and apply a wet spotter and a few drops of ammonia. (Do not use ammonia on silk and wool.) Cover with an absorbent pad moistened with wet spotter and ammonia. Change the pad as it picks up the stain. Flush thoroughly with cool water, making sure to remove all traces of ammonia. If stain persists, moisten it with a solution of ½ teaspoon enzyme presoak and ½ cup warm water—do not use on silk or wool. Cover with an absorbent pad dampened with the solution, and let it stand for 30 minutes. Flush with water, and dry thoroughly.
ACRYLIC FABRIC COTTON LINEN MODACRYLIC NYLON POLYESTER SPANDEX	Quickly scrape to remove solids. Soak the stain in a solution of 1 quart warm water, ½ teaspoon liquid detergent, and 1 tablespoon ammonia. Tamp or scrape to help loosen the stain. Blot occasionally with an absorbent pad. Rinse well with water, making sure to remove all ammonia traces. If stain persists, soak in a solution of 1 quart warm water and 1 tablespoon enzyme presoak for 30 minutes. Rinse well, and launder as soon as possible.

Food

Buying, preparing, and storing food are activities that take quite a bit of planning and effort. As a result, most cooks are quite receptive to tips that help make these chores quicker and easier. The following pages have information for all kinds of kitchen questions. Whether you are a cooking novice who wants to learn food basics in order to prepare simple meals or an old pro who wants a refresher course, you'll find details to help you fine-tune your individual cooking style.

STORAGE TIPS

■ Purchase food-storage containers that do several jobs, such as freezer-to-oven casserole dishes.

■ Store heavy pots, pans, and casseroles at lower levels to avoid having to reach up for them.

■ Save screw-top glass containers for storing dry goods in the pantry.

■ A small plastic or glass saltshaker with no metal parts makes an excellent sprinkler for lemon juice.

■ The shaker bottles and containers that some spices come in can be filled with flour for no-mess flouring of cutlets and other foods. If you add seasonings to the flour, you've got an instant seasoned coating mix.

■ A large pair of tweezers or needle-nose pliers can help you get olives and pickles out of narrow jars; they are also useful for removing bones from fish fillets.

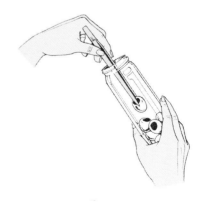

- If you store sharp knives in drawers, keep them in a holder to prevent the blades from getting dull.

- Mesh bags and wire baskets make good storage containers for potatoes and onions because they allow necessary air circulation.

GLOSSARY OF FOODS

DAIRY PRODUCTS

All dairy products are made from milk, whether it be from cows, goats, or sheep. With the exception of nonfat dried milk, store dairy products in the refrigerator or freezer.

BUTTER AND MARGARINE

Butter is made from cream and must have a milk fat content of 80 percent. It is sold both unsalted (sweet) and salted. Margarine is made from milk, milk emulsions, and vegetable oil. Fat content can be up to 80 percent.

- If you're short on butter, stretch it by adding evaporated milk. Two cups of evaporated milk added to 1 pound of butter makes almost 2 pounds of butter. Add the milk a little at a time to butter that has been brought to room temperature and beaten until creamy. Chill. (Don't use this mixture in cakes such as pound cake.)

- Store butter in the butter keeper or on the bottom shelf of the refrigerator; otherwise it will absorb flavors from other foods.

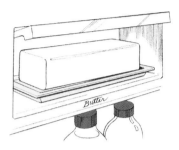

- If you're going to store unsalted butter in your freezer for a long time, wrap it carefully and seal it airtight. Salted butter that you're freezing for a short time can be stored in its original container.

- Use unsalted butter for cooking and baking. It's generally fresher than salted butter.

CREAM

Creams, made from the fatty part of milk, differ according to the percentage of fat. Half-and-half, the lightest, has about 12 percent fat. Light cream and sour cream have about 20 percent fat, although nonfat sour creams are available. Whipping cream is about 40 percent fat.

- Half-and-half or undiluted evaporated milk can be substituted in a recipe that calls for light cream.

- When beating heavy or whipping cream, chill the cream, bowl, and beaters first—the cold keeps the fat in the cream solid, thus increasing the volume.

■ For optimum volume, beat whipped cream in a deep, narrow bowl. Generally 1 cup of cream will yield 2 cups of whipped cream.

■ Do not overbeat, or whipped cream will clump together and form butter.

■ Add flavorings, such as powdered sugar and vanilla extract, to the cream after it has begun to thicken.

■ Sour cream will curdle if it becomes too hot, and there are no culinary tricks to restore it. Always add sour cream at the end of the cooking time, and heat it only until it is warm, not hot, and never to a boil.

CHEESE

Cheeses, all made from animal milk, range from fresh, unripened cheeses to aged, hard cheeses. Fat content varies as well.

■ Unripened cheeses include cottage cheese, farmer's cheese, cream cheese, and ricotta.

■ Soft cheeses, which have been ripened for a short time, include feta, Brie, Camembert, and chèvre.

■ Hard cheeses, ripened for various lengths of time, range from semihard to hard and can be cut or grated. They include cheddar, Edam, Emmenthaler, fontina, Gouda, Gruyère, Havarti, Muenster, Parmesan, provolone, and Romano.

■ Blue cheeses, which are ripened by green molds, include Gorgonzola, Roquefort, and Stilton.

CHEESE TIPS

■ Refrigerate all cheeses with the exception of Parmesan. While some grated Parmesan cheese products can be kept out of the refrigerator after opening, others cannot. Check the label.

■ Cheese should not be exposed to air, which will dry it out.

■ Always check the labels on cheese, particularly if you are looking for low-fat or low-cholesterol varieties. Fat content should be listed in grams of fat per ounce. Given that cheese can be very fatty, a low-fat

WHAT TO DO IF THE FREEZER FAILS

- If your freezer goes out but you expect the stoppage to be temporary, avoid opening the freezer if possible.

- If you expect your freezer to be out of action for more than a day or two, call around to find a school, church, or store with a freezer in which you can store your frozen goods temporarily.

- Dry ice will keep your food frozen in a freezer that's temporarily out of commission, but it must be handled carefully. Caution: Never touch dry ice with your bare hands—it freezes everything, including skin. Also, work in a well-ventilated area.

- If you use dry ice to preserve the contents of a nonfunctioning freezer, avoid letting it touch the packages. Place the ice on empty shelves, or cover the frozen goods with a layer of cardboard and place the dry ice on top.

- To determine how much dry ice you need to keep your frozen foods in good condition, use the following calculation: For a 10-cubic-foot freezer that is full, you'll need 25 pounds of dry ice to keep the contents below freezing for three to four days. If the freezer is only half full, the same amount of ice will only keep the contents frozen for two to three days.

- After a thaw, check if meat or poultry still contains ice crystals. If it does, you can refreeze it safely. Otherwise it should be cooked.

cheese doesn't necessarily mean it's low in fat.

- To soften cream cheese quickly, remove it from the wrapper and place it in a microwave-safe bowl. Microwave on medium 1½ to 2 minutes or until slightly softened, turning the bowl after 1 minute.

- When using ricotta cheese in recipes, first dry it thoroughly. Place the cheese in a clean cotton or linen towel and, holding it over a large bowl or sink, squeeze it into a tight ball and wring. Keep moving the ricotta to dry parts of the towel, and wring it until all excess moisture is gone.

- Cheese will have added freshness and flavor if it's wrapped in a cloth soaked in wine and vinegar and then stored in the refrigerator.

- Mold won't form on cheese if you store it with a few sugar cubes in a tightly covered container.

- When cheese gets too hard, you can soften it by soaking it in buttermilk.

- It's easier to grate cheddar or any soft cheese if you chill it in the freezer for a few minutes before grating.

- If you like to use cheese strips in salads and as garnish, try cutting strips with a potato peeler.

- A good way to clean the grater after grating cheese is to rub a slice of bread over it. As a bonus, you've made cheese-flavored bread crumbs for topping a casserole.

EGGS

Rich in protein, calcium, iron, and vitamins, chicken eggs are a nearly perfect food—unless you're watching your cholesterol intake. Eggs are classified by size, jumbo being the largest. For most recipes, medium or large eggs suffice. The color of the shell—brown or white—has nothing to do with the nutrient value.

- Always use clean, uncracked, grade A eggs, and cook them until the yolks are thickened and set.

- Always use fresh eggs. To check if an egg is fresh, place it in a bowl of cold water. A fresh egg will sink; a stale egg will float.

- Store fresh eggs in the refrigerator for 3 to 5 weeks; hard-cooked eggs can be refrigerated for up to 1 week. Egg whites will keep in the freezer for up to 1 year; after you defrost

them remember that 2 tablespoons of egg white that's been frozen equal 1 tablespoon of fresh egg white. Egg yolks do not freeze well.

- Eggs absorb odors through their shells and should be kept away from foods with strong aromas.

- When slicing hard-boiled eggs, the yolk will not crumble if you first dip your knife in cold water.

MILK

Whether it's homogenized, whole, nonfat dried, evaporated, or condensed, milk provides many nutrients. Milk also contains various amounts of fat. The percentages on milk labels refer to the amount of fat in the milk. No fat is removed from whole milk; fat is removed from 2 percent, 1 percent milk, and skim milk. Nonfat milk contains no fat.

Buttermilk used to be the part of the milk that was left behind after butter was churned. Today, buttermilk is made from pasteurized skim milk to which a bacterial culture is added to produce the tart flavor.

Fresh milk can be soured and used as a substitute for buttermilk. If a recipe calls for 1 cup buttermilk, place 1 tablespoon lemon juice or distilled white vinegar in a measuring cup and add enough milk to measure 1 cup. Stir, and let the mixture stand at room temperature for 5 minutes.

■ It's safe to store milk in the freezer. Be sure to defrost it in the refrigerator, not at room temperature.

■ Keep nonfat dried milk in the cupboard, and reliquefy it for use in place of whole or skim milk.

■ Nondairy soy milk (made from soybeans) can be used in most recipes that call for cow's milk. The tastes are similar in cooked dishes.

YOGURT

Yogurt is a popular dairy product for snacks, desserts, and in cooking. Yogurt is made from milk and a culture. Most of the fat is removed in low-fat yogurt, and nonfat yogurt contains no fat. There's even a nondairy soy yogurt for people who do not eat dairy products.

■ Store yogurt in the refrigerator, and watch the labels. Throw out any yogurt with mold.

■ Plain (nonflavored) yogurt can be substituted in many recipes for sour cream and mayonnaise. Take care when adding yogurt to hot foods. Too much heat or vigorous stirring can cause yogurt to separate or become stringy.

FROZEN DAIRY PRODUCTS

Ice milk, frozen yogurt, and other frozen dairy products should all be stored in the freezer, where they will keep for varying lengths of time. These products will take on a cardboard taste if frozen too long. Melted ice cream shouldn't be refrozen.

FRUIT

Along with providing fiber and vitamins to the diet, fruits have a very low fat content and are low in sodium. Since most fruits can be eaten raw, the only real trick to serving delicious fruit is to make sure they're ripe, when their taste and texture are at their peak. Fruits also need to be carefully watched for perishability. Along with the following tips, be sure to check the explanations under individual categories for more information.

■ Whenever possible, avoid buying prepackaged fruits; the packaging may disguise rotten spots.

■ Use stainless-steel knives to cut fruit—carbon steel knives react with fruit and cause discoloration.

■ To easily peel thick-skinned fruit, put the fruit in a bowl, pour boiling water over it, and wait 1 minute. Remove the fruit, and peel the skin with a paring knife.

■ To prevent freshly cut fruit from browning, keep the fruit submerged in water to which you've added juice from half a lemon.

APPLES

For adaptability, availability, nutritional content, and taste, you simply can't beat apples. Refrigerate apples to slow down the ripening process. If you don't have room in the refrigerator, keep your apples stored in a cool place, with a wet towel placed over the top of the container to keep the apples moist but not wet. Don't let apples freeze—they will spoil.

■ To tell if an unpicked apple is ripe, twist it clockwise on the stem. A ripe apple should come away from the tree easily.

■ If you have an apple tree in your garden, you can test apples for ripeness by cutting one open and looking at the seeds. A mature apple will have dark brown seeds. An immature apple will have seeds that are tan or white in color.

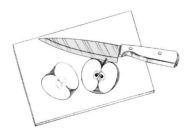

SORTING OUT APPLES

If you've ever made an apple pie that wasn't a winner, it's probably because you used the wrong apples. Some apples are great for eating; some are great for cooking; and a few varieties are great whether they're eaten raw, cooked, or baked in a pie.

All-Purpose: Baldwin, Granny Smith, Jonathan, McIntosh, Winesap

Eating: Gala, Golden Delicious, Red Delicious

Cooking: Rhode Island, Greening, Rome Beauty, York Imperial

■ Store apples in clear plastic or mesh rather than in a paper bag. You'll be able to spot any that are spoiling and remove them before they contaminate other fruit.

■ To maintain the crispness of apple slices and to prevent them from browning, immerse them in salted water for ten minutes before you use them.

■ To prevent apples from shrinking when you bake them, remove a horizontal belt of peel from around the middle of each one. To prevent wrinkling during baking, cut random slits in each one before placing them in the oven.

BERRIES

While the many varieties of berries differ in taste, they're very similar when it comes to choosing and handling. Nearly all berries are fragile and perishable. Select berries that are firm but not hard. If they're covered with plastic, look at the container bottoms. If they are wet or stained, much of the fruit is probably moldy or mushy. If you discover one or two bruised and spoiled berries when you get home, discard them; molds quickly spread from berry to berry. To keep berries in prime condition, don't wash them until you're ready to eat them. They can be stored for a few days in the refrigerator in a colander, which helps the air circulate around them to keep them fresh.

■ **Blackberries** grow on thorny shrubs and are extremely fragile. Their peak months are June, July, and August. In addition to making a wonderful pie, blackberries combine beautifully with other berries for a fruit salad. Pureed, strained, and combined with a little sugar, they make a splendid sauce for ice cream.

■ **Blueberries** are either wild or commercial. Wild blueberries, which are much smaller and more flavorful than commercial berries, are available only in certain parts of the country because they are very perishable. Look for plump, fresh berries of good blue color with a waxy bloom. If you're lucky enough to pick wild blueberries, use them immediately or pack clean, dry blueberries in freezer containers and freeze for later use in baking. Rinse gently before using, and remove any stems.

■ **Cranberries**—small, sour, red berries—are native to North America. They are usually cooked with sweetener to make them edible. Cooking cranberries requires less sugar if you add ¼ teaspoon of baking soda to the pot. When cooking cranberries, add a teaspoon of butter to each pound of berries to prevent overboiling and foaming. Cranberries are done cooking when they look as though they're ready to burst. If you cook them until they actually pop, they'll taste bitter.

■ **Raspberries** are extremely perishable. Look for berries that are plump and fresh looking, and use them as soon as possible after purchase. Wash gently just before using. For recipes that require the juice to be separated from frozen raspberries, thaw the raspberries in a strainer that is set over a bowl.

■ **Strawberries** come in a wide assortment. Although some are huge, bright red, and well shaped, the flavor of these berries does not always measure up to their beauty. Often, smaller berries have a sweeter, more distinct strawberry flavor. Choose fruit that is fresh, clean, and bright red, with green caps attached. Strawberries should be stored in the refrigerator, caps attached, until ready to use. Rinse gently just before preparing, and use as soon as possible. Always be sure to hull strawberries after they are washed, never before, or they will absorb some of the water, causing the fruit to soften. For coarsely crushed strawberries, use a potato masher.

CITRUS FRUITS

■ **Grapefruit** are low in calories, natural diuretics, and perfect palate cleansers. Although grapefruit look the same on the outside, they can be either white or pink inside. The pink or red grapefruit is sweeter. To select the juiciest grapefruit, look for firm, heavy fruit with the thinnest skins. Grapefruit do not ripen once picked, so they can be refrigerated immediately, where they will keep for up to 6 weeks.

■ **Oranges** come in a variety of shapes, sizes, colors, and degrees of sweetness. Eating oranges, such as navels, temples, and Jaffas, have a sweet-tart flavor and thick peels that are easy to remove. Valencia and Parson Brown are two varieties of juicing oranges. They are sweet and may have a thin, difficult-to-remove peel and lots of seeds. When selecting oranges, don't be misled by the intensity of their color—most oranges are dyed to make them look more appetizing. Instead, look for brown spots—surprisingly enough, they indicate top quality. Oranges store well for up to two weeks at room temperature.

■ **Tangerines** are best when they're juicy. When selecting tangerines, choose heavy fruit, which indicates good juice content. They may feel slightly puffy, which is normal, since the skin zips off easily. Fresh tangerines are very perishable—handle them with care. Keep them cold and humid, and use as soon as possible.

GRAPES AND RAISINS

■ **Grapes** are grown all over the world in warm climates, but nearly all the grapes sold in the United States are grown in California. The same grapes that are eaten fresh are used for making wine and raisins. Select grapes with deep color and firm fruit, and refrigerate immediately. Rinse them with water only before eating or they will get soft.

■ **Raisins** are most often made from Thompson seedless grapes. They are loaded with sugar and packed with vitamins and iron. When incorporating raisins into a batter or dough, dust them lightly with flour first. This will prevent them from sticking together and from sinking to the bottom of the pan. Store leftover raisins in a tightly covered glass jar or in an airtight plastic bag.

GETTING THE MOST FROM LEMONS AND LIMES

Lemons and limes are rarely eaten on their own, but they are used for everything from flavoring beverages and pies to adding zest to vegetables, fish, and poultry. Lemons can even prevent some fruits (such as apples) from turning brown when sliced. Fresh lemons and limes are found in supermarkets year-round, and bottled juice is also widely available.

■ A medium-size lemon will yield about 3 to 4 tablespoons of juice and 1 to 2 teaspoons of grated rind.

■ To get the juiciest, most flavorful lemons and limes, pick those with smooth skins and small points at each end. As soon as you bring them home from the store, put them in the refrigerator in a tightly sealed container of water. Doing so encourages them to yield more juice.

■ To get the most juice from your lemons and limes, warm the fruit to room temperature. Roll them on the countertop with the palm of your hand before squeezing.

■ If only a small amount of juice is needed, make a hole in the lemon or lime with a toothpick. Squeeze out the amount you need, then seal the hole by inserting the toothpick in it; store it in the refrigerator.

■ To remove peel in strips, use a vegetable peeler or a lemon zester. Remove only the colored part of the peel. Scrape off any white left on a peel before adding it to the recipe.

■ When using both the juice and peel of a lime or lemon, grate the peel first, then squeeze the juice.

■ Limes should be kept out of the sunlight to prevent them from turning yellow.

MELONS

Melons are great to eat on their own or in a fruit salad. Select melons that are heavy. If you hold a melon to your ear, shake it, and hear the juice and seeds sloshing around, it's over-ripe. Ripen melons for a few days before refrigerating. For maximum enjoyment, let melons develop at room temperature.

■ **Cantaloupes** should be well shaped with a smoothly rounded, depressed area at the stem end. A fragrant aroma is also a sign of good quality. Allow cantaloupes to mellow at room temperature for a few days after purchase.

■ **Crenshaw melons** have a golden rind tinged with green when ripe. They can be smooth or slightly ribbed. Look for those that are round at the base and taper to a point at the stem end.

■ **Honeydew melons** have a smooth surface and a creamy white or yellow rind. Avoid honeydews with a stark white rind tinged with green, as these are likely to be unripe. Keep honey-dews at room temperature for a few days before serving or using in recipes.

■ **Persian melons** resemble cantaloupe, but the rind is dark green and covered with a pale yellow netting. The rind turns lighter green as the melon ripens. The flesh of the Persian melon is thick and orange-pink in color. Keep this melon at room temperature for a few days before enjoying its delicate flavor.

■ If you want to take a **watermelon** on a picnic, wrap it in newspaper or burlap as soon as you remove it from the refrigerator. It will stay refreshingly cool until you're ready to eat it.

STONE FRUITS

■ **Apricots** are usually dried because they are very fragile when they are ripe for picking and they do not ripen once picked. If you're lucky enough to find fresh apricots in a grocery store, look for ones that are both soft and juicy.

■ **Cherries** should be plump, firm, and fresh. They should be brightly colored, ranging from yellow, red, deep red, reddish brown, mahogany to black. Avoid buying immature fruit, which is hard, smaller, light in color, or overly soft and shriveled. Fresh cherries can be frozen for later enjoyment. Simply wash the fruit, remove stems and pits, drain well, and place in a plastic bag. They'll keep in the freezer up to a year.

■ **Dates** are usually sold dried, but fresh dates have an excellent flavor. If you have never tasted them, try to find them at a specialty food store. They are a good source of vitamins and are very sweet.

■ **Nectarines** are the result of a cross between a plum and a peach. Choose fruit that is smooth, plump, highly colored, and free from blemishes. Yellow skin should be brightly blushed with red. Avoid hard, dull-looking nectarines. Nectarines should mellow and soften at room temperature. They can be easily substituted for peaches in recipes.

■ **Olives,** the fruit of the olive tree, must be cured in brine to be fit to eat. The size of an olive is no indication of its flavor. Some tiny varieties are bitter, while others are quite mild, and the same is true for large olives. Green olives are harvested before they are fully ripe; black olives have ripened on the tree.

■ **Peaches** are widely available canned, but fresh peaches are usually only available from June to September. Select plump, well-shaped peaches with a creamy or golden undercolor. The red blush differs with varieties and is not a

sign of ripeness. Avoid peaches tinged with green because they will not ripen properly. Most peaches are sold before they are ripe. To ripen them, store at room temperature in a loosely closed paper bag until they yield to gentle palm pressure. Once ripe, use immediately or refrigerate for a few days. To easily peel peaches for pies or other desserts, put them in boiling water for 10 to 20 seconds, then run them under very cold or ice water and peel.

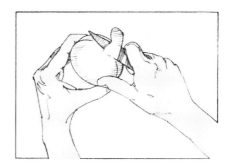

■ **Plums** come in a rainbow of colors—purple, blue, scarlet, green, and yellow—and shapes. Tastes range from tart to sweet. When selecting plums, choose those with good color. They should be fairly firm and should yield to slight pressure under your thumb. At home, allow plums to soften at room temperature for a few days to bring out their full flavor; then refrigerate and use as soon as possible. Prunes are made from dried plums.

TROPICAL FRUITS

■ **Bananas** contain nearly 5 teaspoons of sugar—almost twice as much as many popular candy bars—but an average-size banana only has 80 to 90 calories because they're low in fat. Choose bananas that are plump and not bruised or split. Select bananas that have not yet become fully yellow so that they will be firm and free of bruises when you get them home (where they will ripen easily at room temperature). To hasten the ripening of green bananas, place them so that they touch overripe ones, or wrap them in a damp cloth and put them in a bag.

■ **Coconut,** easily available in packages, is best when it's fresh. When choosing a coconut, check that the three soft eyes on the shell are intact, dry, and free of mold. Shake it to make sure that it is full of milk. To release the milk, pierce the eyes on the shell and drain the liquid.

Coconut milk can be refrigerated for 24 hours or frozen for future use. To remove the shell from a coconut, heat the coconut in the oven for 15 minutes at 350°F. Tap it all over with a hammer, remove the cracked shell, and peel away the brown skin. The full flavor of shredded coconut is released when it is toasted. Spread the shredded coconut in an even layer on a baking sheet, and place it in a preheated 350°F oven for 8 to 10 minutes. Store leftover coconut in an airtight container for up to one week in the refrigerator or up to six months in the freezer.

■ **Kiwi** has fuzzy brown skin covering emerald flesh that is often described as a combination of melon, pineapple, and strawberry. Dotted with edible black seeds, slices of kiwi are a festive addition to any recipe. Kiwi needs to be ripened for full tangy sweet flavor. To ripen the fruit at home, place it in a plastic bag with an apple, and leave it at room temperature until it yields to gentle palm pressure. When storing ripe kiwi in the refrigerator, place it in the fruit bin away from other fruits so that the flavors don't get mixed. Kiwis contain an enzyme that prevents gelatin from setting, so don't include them in a gelatin salad mold.

■ **Mangoes** vary in size, shape, and color. The yellow-orange flesh of the mango has a rich flavor and a spicy aroma. They must be fully ripe before eating or using in recipes. The skin of most mangoes becomes tinged with more red or yellow as the fruit ripens. Mangoes are ready to eat when they yield to gentle pressure. Allow them to ripen at room temperature until soft, then use or refrigerate for a few days.

▪ **Papayas** are a tropical fruit native to the Americas. When ripe, the skin is usually deep yellow and the flesh is light orange to pink in color and has a soft texture. Ripe papayas will be soft when gently squeezed. Allow fruit to ripen at room temperature until the skin has turned at least half yellow. Once ripe, it can be refrigerated. It can be served either raw or cooked. The center of the papaya contains lots of edible black seeds that have a peppery taste and can be used as a garnish or added to salad dressings. The flesh contains an enzyme called papain, which is an ingredient in commercial meat tenderizers. If you make a gelatin mold with papaya, cook the fruit first or the papain will prevent it from gelling.

▪ **Pineapples** do not ripen after they are picked. If they have been harvested too early, the fruit will not be very sweet. Select fruit that is firm, plump, and heavy for its size. Serve it as soon as possible, or cut it up in rings or wedges and refrigerate, where it will keep for one week. If a fresh pineapple isn't quite ripe, you can make it taste ripe this way: Prepare it as usual, and then put the pieces in a pot, cover them with water, add sugar,

and boil for a few minutes. Then drain off the water, let the fruit cool, and chill it in the refrigerator. If a recipe calls for gelatin and pineapple, use either canned fruit or fresh pineapple that has been boiled for five minutes. There is an enzyme in fresh pineapple that will prevent gelatin from setting.

▪ **Starfruit,** or carambola, is a tropical fruit that ranges in taste from tart to sweet. The flavor of a sweet carambola is likened to a combination of orange and pineapple; tart varieties are similar to lemon. Carambolas are golden yellow when ripe. Ripe carambolas may also be tinged with brown.

OTHER FRUITS

▪ **Currants** are actually the names for two very different fruits. One, made from the tiny, dark Zante grape, is most often dried and used in baking. The second variety is a tiny berry related to the gooseberry. It comes in black, red, and white varieties and is used in preserves and jellies, liqueurs, and pie fillings.

▪ **Pears** are available throughout the year. Pears do not ripen on the tree, which is why they are hard when harvested. Choose firm fruit of good color for the variety of pear. Surface blemishes and russeting are natural for some varieties and do not affect fruit quality. Ripen pears at room temperature until they yield to gentle pressure at the stem end. When ripe, refrigerate pears immediately. For cooking or baking, use firm, slightly underripe pears.

■ **Rhubarb** is also known as "pieplant" because it is frequently teamed with strawberries and used as a filling for pies. The long pink or red stalks of the rhubarb are very tart and must be sweetened with a generous dose of honey or sugar. When cooking rhubarb into a sauce, take care not to overcook it, and add only a small amount of water to the pan. Always discard the rhubarb leaves; they contain oxalic acid and are toxic.

GRAINS

Grains are the seeds of grasses that are either used whole or ground into flour. The type of grass—barley, corn, oats, rice, wheat—determines the nutrient value and taste of the grain. Grains are purchased dried and keep well for about six months if stored in an airtight container in a cool, dark place. Some grains, such as cornmeal and oats, are more susceptible to insect larvae and should be used quickly.

■ **Barley** needs to be rinsed well before cooking if the whole grain is used. The outer husk is removed to produce pearl barley, often used in soups and casseroles.

■ **Buckwheat** is ground from the seeds of a plant in the rhubarb family. It is a Japanese staple and is used to make flour and soba noodles. Because it is gluten free, it is a good choice for people sensitive to wheat.

■ **Corn** is ground into both coarse cornmeal (polenta) and fine cornmeal, hominy, or grits.

■ **Couscous** is a tiny grain made from semolina, or the hard part of durum wheat. A staple in Middle Eastern cooking, couscous combines well with vegetables and spices.

■ **Oats** are typically used for oatmeal by removing the hulls from whole oats. The resulting oat groats are then steamed and rolled to flatten them into flakes.

■ **Rye,** when ground, is added to white and whole wheat flours to make dark breads.

■ **Quinoa** is a South American grain loaded with nutrients. It can be substituted for rice in many dishes.

■ **Wheat** is typically ground into flour and is available as cracked wheat, wheat flakes, and wheat germ. Wholewheat flour is more nutritious than white flour, but it does not store as well.

MEAT

Meat typically refers to the four types of red meat—beef (from cattle); pork (from pigs); lamb (from young sheep); and veal (from calves or young cattle). All meat in the United States is inspected for wholesomeness, and most meat is graded. In most supermarkets beef, pork, and veal cuts are graded choice. Only a prime grade is superior. These cuts are usually only available at specialty markets. Avoid buying meat that is graded select.

Most people differentiate meat by the cut, such as a chop, roast, or steak. The cut is determined by where the piece of meat comes from on the animal's body.

Usually cuts that require more cooking time will be less expensive, but they are often more flavorful. The most tender cuts, which come from little-used muscle, can be cooked most quickly. Pork chops, for example, come from the mid, upper side of the pig and can be easily broiled or grilled very quickly at high heat. A flank steak, which comes from the well-used lower, rear side of a steer, needs to be marinated or pounded before broiling or grilling. Always make sure you're buying the cut of meat called for in a recipe. If you're unsure, ask your butcher. The most well-known and common cuts of meat are described in the following sections, along with buying tips. Some tips that apply to meats in general:

■ To french a bone means to scrape it clean of fat and meat so that a 2-inch length of clean bone is exposed. This is usually done to beef and pork rib bones. In lamb, the most common cut that is frenched is the rack. In addition to enhancing the appearance of the meat (frenched bones are often decorated with paper frills), exposing the bones makes it easier to carve between them.

■ Thaw meat in the refrigerator or microwave, not at room temperature. Allow about 5 hours for each pound of meat to thaw in the refrigerator. Follow your microwave's instructions for thawing meat. Never refreeze meat that has been thawed and not cooked.

■ Marinating less tender cuts of meat in a bath of oil, vinegar, and herbs infuses the meat with a wonderful flavor and also penetrates the meat fibers to help tenderize them.

BEEF

For years, beef has been considered the mainstay of American families. Americans continue to consume beef in much higher proportions than other countries, due to its availability and ease of preparation.

■ To meet USDA standards, all ground beef must be at least 70 percent lean. Ground sirloin and ground round are the leanest; ground chuck contains more fat. Ground beef, which can be broiled, fried, or grilled, is typically used for burgers, meatballs, and meatloaf. Use or freeze ground beef within 24 hours after purchase.

■ With the exception of a standing rib roast, roasts need time and added moisture to release their flavors. Rump roasts, rolled roasts, and chuck roasts can be browned and then roasted until well done or cooked on top of the stove in a pot with added vegetables and stock. The larger the roast, the longer it can keep in the refrigerator, but freeze any roast if you do not plan to use it within three to four days.

■ Steaks come in various types. Steaks from the short loin portion include club, T-bone, and porterhouse. Tournedos are small beef steaks cut from the tenderloin. Rib steaks come from the rib portion. All of these can be broiled or grilled. Flank and round steaks, from the lower part of the animal, need to be marinated before grilling or cooked slowly at lower heat. Freeze steaks if you do not plan to use them within two to three days.

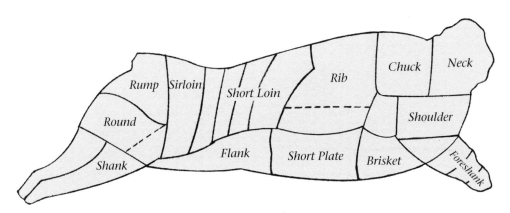

Cuts of Beef

LAMB

From six weeks to a year old, a lamb produces lightly flavored, relatively lean meat. Mutton, the meat from sheep older than a year, is common in England and Australia. Ground lamb, often used in Middle Eastern recipes, can be substituted for ground beef, but it has a distinctive flavor and more fat. Lamb riblets or spareribs come from the breast portion of the lamb, not the rib portion. The lamb breast is cut between the ribs to make riblets. They are best braised or marinated and grilled. Cook ground lamb within 24 hours, roasts within three to four days.

PORK

Pork is available cured or uncured in a wide variety of cuts. Curing refers to a variety of processes by which the meat is prepared before sale, but it does not mean that the meat is precooked. Bacon, for example, is cured but requires further cooking. All pork must be thoroughly cooked because of the possible presence of the trichina parasite.

■ Bacon is highly perishable. It will keep in the refrigerator about ten days or can be frozen for up to three months. Canadian bacon is a lean smoked meat and a popular breakfast food. Because it is purchased fully cooked, it heats quickly in a skillet over medium-high heat.

■ Pork chops and roasts refer to center-cut, loin, and rib chops and sirloin roasts cut from the loin. They can be broiled, grilled, roasted, and even baked. The tenderloin, the most tender meat cut from the loin, is a strip of meat that lies along each side of the backbone. Freeze pork chops and roasts if you don't plan to cook them within two to three days.

■ Ham comes from the hind leg of a pig. It is usually thought of as a cured meat, although it can be purchased uncured and is then referred to as fresh ham or pork

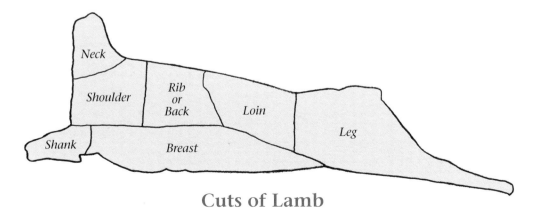

Cuts of Lamb

leg. The distinctive flavors of hams are produced by the pigs' diets—peanuts, acorns, apples, corn, or peaches—and the type of wood over which they are smoked—apple, hickory, or oak. Fully cooked hams and even canned hams should be refrigerated. Check the label for storage information. Packaged ham slices or whole hams should be stored in the coldest part of the refrigerator. Use ham slices within three or four days; whole hams within a week. Ham does not freeze well.

■ When a recipe calls for ribs, you must choose between spareribs, baby ribs, country-style ribs, and back ribs. They all come from the midsection of the pig, and most of the weight is in the bones. Spareribs have the least amount of meat; baby or baby-back ribs, which are cut from the loin, have more meat; and country-style ribs have much more meat per pound. All of them can be grilled, broiled, or baked. Cook ribs within one to two days of purchase.

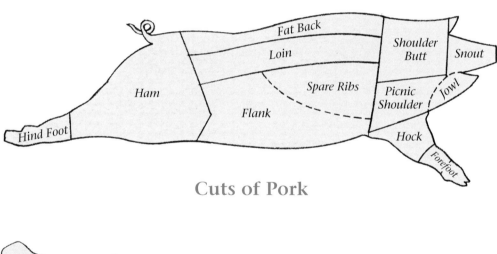

Cuts of Pork

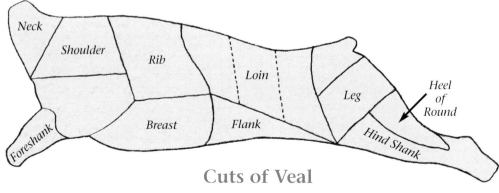

Cuts of Veal

VEAL

Veal refers to the meat from young calves fed a special diet to produce lean, light-colored meat. It is typically the most expensive meat per pound. Because of the delicacy, nearly all cuts of veal benefit from low-temperature roasting, sautéing, or braising. The most well-known cuts are chops, which are cut from the shoulder and can be braised or fried; roasts, cut from the shoulder or loin; and breast, which can be cooked slowly. Veal should be used within one to two days of purchase.

NUTS

Whether they're whole, chopped, or ground, nuts add nutrition and flavor to meals and dishes. Their high oil content, however, negates some of the benefits of their high protein content. Varieties include almond, brazil, cashew, chestnut, coconut, hazelnut (or filbert), macadamia, peanut, pecan, pine (or pignoli), pistachio, and walnut, both black and English. Most varieties can be bought whole, chopped, or ground; salted or unsalted; roasted or spiced. Generally, whole, unshelled nuts are the least expensive.

Most unshelled nuts will keep at room temperature for up to six months, but shelled nuts should be stored in airtight containers in the refrigerator or freezer to keep them from becoming rancid. Throw out any that have mold.

■ To remove thin skins, place the nuts on a baking sheet and bake them in a preheated 350°F oven until the skins begin to flake off. This will vary with the variety. Nuts can easily burn, so watch them closely. Remove them from the oven, wrap them in a heavy towel, and rub them against the towel to remove as much of the skins as possible.

■ To grind nuts, use a nut grater or grinder and grind only a few nuts at a time to prevent them from becoming oily.

■ To toast nuts, place them in a single layer on a baking sheet and toast in a preheated 350°F oven until very lightly browned. Watch them closely. Depending on the variety, this should take from 3 to 10 minutes. Use them immediately or store them in a covered container in the refrigerator.

POULTRY

Poultry refers to domesticated birds, including chicken, capon, Rock Cornish hens, duck, goose, and turkey. Game birds include wild ducks, geese, and pheasants.

POULTRY PACKAGING

Most poultry sold today is packaged according to size:

- Broilers or fryers are young chickens weighing 2½ to 4 pounds. They are available whole or in packages with various parts.

- Roasters, weighing between 4 and 8 pounds, are sold whole. Smaller roasters can be cut up for baking or frying.

- Stewing hens, weighing between 3 and 7 pounds, are older birds with tougher meat. They are best for making stocks and stews.

- Capons, young cocks that were castrated, are tender and fat and command a premium price.

- Rock Cornish hens, the result of two breeds of chicken, are small, young birds weighing between 1 and 2 pounds.

- Turkeys, sold by weight, include small (4 to 10 pounds), medium (10 to 20 pounds), and large (more than 20 pounds).

- Ducks usually weigh between 5 and 6 pounds, while a goose usually weighs between 8 and 15 pounds.

BUYING AND STORING POULTRY

- Although it's difficult to see through the packaging, avoid poultry that has bruised or dry-looking skin.

- Uncooked chicken can be refrigerated for up to two days.

- To properly freeze poultry, remove it from its original packaging. Rinse it under cold water, pat dry with paper towels, and trim away excess fat. For a whole chicken, remove the giblets from the body cavity. Wrap the chicken in freezer paper, label it with the date, and freeze. Wrap, label, and freeze the giblets separately. Use this same procedure to freeze chicken pieces, but be sure to separate the pieces into several packages.

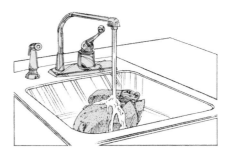

- Freeze whole chickens for up to eight months, chicken pieces for up to six months, and giblets for up to three months.

- Frozen turkeys should be put in the freezer in their original wrappings as soon as possible after purchase.

- To defrost chicken, thaw it in its wrapping in the refrigerator. Allow about three to four hours per pound. Caution: Never defrost chicken at room temperature.

SAVORY STUFFING

Whether you call it dressing or stuffing, what goes inside the bird can be delicious, but it takes a few tips to get it just right:

■ Stuff a chicken or turkey just before roasting. If you need to make the stuffing ahead of time, store it in an airtight container in the refrigerator separately from the bird. Make sure the stuffing is cool before you stuff the bird.

■ Always stuff a chicken or turkey loosely—don't cram dressing into the cavity. If the bird is stuffed loosely, heat will penetrate more easily to cook the stuffing all the way through.

■ When stuffing a chicken, allow about ¾ cup of stuffing for each pound of chicken.

■ Immerse the thermometer in warm water before sliding it into the turkey. When you insert it, keep it away from fat and bones, both of which render inaccurate readings.

■ To hold in stuffing, truss a turkey with unwaxed dental floss—it's extra strong and doesn't burn.

■ When preparing a stuffed chicken or turkey, check the stuffing as well as the bird for doneness. Place the thermometer in the stuffing, and leave it for 5 minutes before taking a reading. For complete cooking, the stuffing should register 165°F and the bird 185°F.

■ You'll be able to remove the dressing from a turkey easily if it is held in a cheesecloth bag that you've pushed into the cavity. When you're ready to serve, pull out the bag and turn the dressing into a bowl.

■ To prepare fresh chestnuts for a stuffing, use a small, sharp knife to slit the flat side of each chestnut. Put the nuts in a saucepan, cover them with cold water, and bring to a boil. Cook for several minutes, then remove the pan from the heat. Working quickly with only a few nuts at a time, peel the outer and inner shells. Cook the peeled nuts covered with water or stock in a saucepan. Simmer until tender (about 30 minutes).

■ When storing leftovers, always remove the stuffing from the cavity and store separately.

■ Defrost turkey in its original wrapper in the refrigerator. Be sure to allow enough time for complete thawing—about two days for a 12-pound turkey, three to four days for larger birds.

SEASONINGS

Herbs are the leaves of various plants. They are available fresh, dried, or ground. Spices are the seeds, buds, fruits, flowers, bark, and roots of plants. Spices are much more pungent than herbs. In some cases, a plant produces both a spice and an herb. Other seasonings are made from a mix of spices, such as chili powder, or a mix of herbs, such as bouquet garni.

Herbs and spices should be stored in airtight containers in a cool cupboard. Most ground spices store well for about a year, twice as long as ground or dried herbs, which only have a shelf life of about six months.

HERBS

Basil: Fresh or dried, the sweet taste of basil is essential in Italian dishes.
Bay leaf: The dried whole leaves of this herb add tang to stews and meat dishes, but make certain that you remove the bay leaf before serving.
Chives: Chives have a delicate flavor and are generally used as a fresh garnish.
Dill: A member of the parsley family, dill weed is the dried, soft, feathery leaves of the dill plant. Its distinctive flavor can easily dominate any dish, so use it sparingly.
Marjoram: With a taste close to oregano, marjoram is typically used in fish, meat, and poultry dishes and in tomato sauces.
Mint: Available both fresh and dried, mint is used in vegetable and fruit dishes, as well as teas.
Oregano: The strong flavor of oregano can easily overpower delicate dishes, but it is perfect in most Italian dishes.
Parsley: When purchasing fresh parsley, look for bright green bunches with a fresh aroma. To store, wash parsley well, shaking off excess water. Wrap parsley in paper towels before placing it in a plastic bag. Refrigerate until ready to use. Parsley is usually used as a garnish.
Rosemary: Although it does not combine well with other herbs, the distinctive flavor of rosemary makes it a good choice for meats and poultry or on any grilled food.
Sage: Fresh sage is much stronger than dried sage, but either combines well with game, poultry, and stuffing.
Tarragon: Tarragon is widely used on chicken, fish, and vegetables, as well as in many sauces. Dried tar-

ragon loses much of the pungency of the fresh leaf.

Thyme: Thyme is widely used to add flavor to vegetables, meat, poultry, fish, soups, and cream sauces. English thyme is one of the most popular varieties.

SPICES

Allspice: This spice gets its name because it resembles the combined flavors of cinnamon, nutmeg, and cloves.

Capers: These are the pea-size buds of a flower from the caper bush. Found mostly in Central America and the Mediterranean, capers add pungency to sauces, dips, and relishes.

Cayenne: This hot red pepper needs to be used sparingly to avoid overpowering a dish, but it is essential in many Latin American and Southwestern dishes.

Chili powder: Like curry powder, chili powder is a blend of fairly hot spices and ground chilies.

Cinnamon: While the ground bark is used mainly in desserts, whole bark sticks can be used to flavor cider and other hot drinks.

Clove: This sweet spice is available whole and ground and is used in both baked meat dishes and desserts.

Cumin: Ground cumin is used in many Latin American and Southwestern dishes for its smokey and hot flavor. Use it sparingly.

Curry powder: Curry powder is formed by blending together a number of spices, including turmeric, cardamom, cumin, pepper, cloves, cinnamon, nutmeg, and sometimes ginger. Chilies give it heat, and ground dried garlic provides a depth of taste. Curry blends vary depending on their use.

Ginger: A gnarled tan root, ginger adds a distinctive aroma and flavor to foods and is used extensively in Asian dishes.

Nutmeg: This spice has a pungent fragrance and a warm, slightly sweet taste that is used to flavor baked goods, candy, puddings, meats, sauces, vegetables, and eggnog.

Paprika: Ground paprika adds zip without much heat to dishes such as potato salad and seafood.

Saffron: This fragrant spice is used most often in soups and rice dishes.

Turmeric: Related to ginger, turmeric is an essential component of curry powder and was once known as Indian saffron. Use it sparingly—a little goes a long way.

SEAFOOD

Low in cholesterol, fat, and sodium, seafood makes a nutritious entrée. Freshwater fish live in lakes and rivers, while saltwater fish come from the ocean or bays. Shellfish refers to fish that live in hard shells.

FRESHWATER FISH

Brook Trout
Buffalo Fish
Carp
Catfish
Crappie

Lake Trout
Mullet
Pickerel
Salmon (some varieties)
Whitefish
Yellow Perch
Yellow Pike

OCEAN FISH

Atlantic Herring
Bluefish
Flounder
Grouper
Haddock
Halibut
Pollack
Pompano
Red Snapper
Salmon (some varieties)
Sea Bass
Scrod
Sole
Swordfish
Tuna
Turbot
Whiting

SHELLFISH

Abalone
Clams
Crab
Crawfish
Lobster
Mussels
Oysters
Prawns
Shrimp
Snails
Squid

BUYING SEAFOOD

The best way to tell if a fish is fresh is to look it in the eye, examine its gills, and smell it. If the eyes are clear and bulge a little, the gills are pink, and the smell is fresh, the fish is fresh. There are only a few exceptions to this rule. If fish are already cut into fillets or steaks, the test is more difficult. You then have to rely on firm and shiny flesh. There should be no darkening around the edges or discolorations.

■ Avoid prepackaged fish because it's hard to tell how old it is.

■ When buying shellfish in the shells, be sure shells are tightly closed. If the shell is slightly open, tap it lightly. It should snap shut. If it doesn't, the creature is dead and should be discarded.

■ Make sure live lobsters are really alive. Their legs should move, and their tails should not be limp.

■ Most shrimp are previously frozen and thawed for sale. If they are mushy, discard them immediately.

■ Don't buy crabs with slimy or greasy shells.

STORING SEAFOOD

■ Before refrigerating, take off any wrappings, rinse the fish under cold water, and pat them dry with a paper towel. Then refrigerate fish immediately at between 32° and 37°F. Use within 24 hours.

■ To freeze fish, remove wrappings, rinse under cold water, and pat dry with paper towels. Wrap in plastic and then in aluminum foil before placing it in the freezer. Use it within a month for best quality.

■ Never refreeze fish that has been previously frozen and thawed.

■ Always thaw frozen fish in the refrigerator, not at room temperature.

■ Store live shellfish in the refrigerator for no more than 24 hours. Keep them moist with a damp cloth or paper towel, but make sure they can breathe.

VEGETABLES

Vegetables are the bulbs, leaves, roots, shoots, or even seeds of various plants. While they vary in nutritional content, storage needs, and ways to be cooked, there are a few tips to keep in mind about all vegetables:

■ Vegetables stored in the refrigerator will keep better if the crisper is at least ⅔ full. When storing only a few vegetables, put them in airtight plastic bags or containers, then into the crisper.

■ To freshen blemished or wilted produce, snip off all brown edges, sprinkle the vegetables with cold water, wrap them in towels, and place them in your refrigerator for an hour or more.

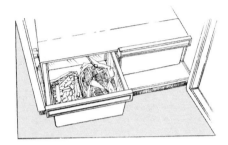

■ If you're simmering vegetables and you need to add more water, use hot water, not cold. Adding cold water may toughen the fibers.

■ To make frozen vegetables taste as much as possible like fresh ones, pour boiling water on them before cooking. This flushes away all traces of frozen water.

■ If you've purchased fresh vegetables and find live insects in them, drive them out by soaking the food for 30 minutes in cold water to which you've added a few tablespoons of salt or vinegar.

BRASSICAS

Bok choy	Cabbage
Broccoli	Cauliflower
Brussels sprouts	Kale

Choose brassicas that have bright leaves and show no signs of wilting. Store them in the refrigerator and use as soon as possible. To prepare, remove hard stems and hard outer leaves, and rinse them well. Don't overcook these vegetables. Not only do they become mushy, they lose their nutrients quickly if overcooked.

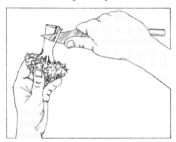

■ To ensure even cooking of broccoli stems over 1 inch in diameter, cut lengthwise slits in stem ends before cooking.

■ For brussels sprouts with the best flavor, look for tightly closed buds with fresh green leaves.

■ Speed the cooking time for brussels sprouts by marking an "X" with a knife on the bottom of each before putting it in the pot.

■ To soften and peel whole cabbage leaves for stuffed cabbage, core the cabbage head and freeze it for several days. Put the head into a large bowl of hot water, and the leaves will peel right off.

■ Prevent red cabbage from turning purple during cooking by adding a tablespoon of vinegar to the cooking water.

■ To retain the fresh white color of cauliflower while cooking, add the juice of half a lemon or lime to the cooking water.

BULB VEGETABLES

Garlic
Leeks
Onions
Scallions
Shallots

This group of vegetables is typically used to flavor other foods. Scallions, or green onions, are baby onions used raw or lightly cooked. Leeks, a versatile and mild-tasting member of the onion family, add a subtle yet distinctive flavor to recipes. Shallots, sort of a cross between garlic and onions, have a very mild flavor. The name "onion" actually refers to a wide variety of onions—pearl; white; red; yellow; Spanish; and Vidalia, a sweet onion grown in Georgia.

■ The easiest and fastest way to peel garlic cloves is to trim off the ends and crush the cloves with the bottom of a heavy saucepan or the flat side of a large knife. The peels can then be removed easily.

■ Avoid burning garlic, which makes its flavor very bitter.

■ Look for leeks with fresh tops that are no more than 1½ inches in diameter.

■ To clean leeks, cut two perpendicular slits, starting about three inches from the root end and running all the way through the stem end. Wash the vegetables under cold running water.

■ Fresh white onions peel quickly if you first immerse them in boiling water for a minute or two.

■ Soak onion rings in cold water for an hour to make them milder and more suitable for use in salads.

CUCUMBERS AND SQUASHES

Acorn squash
Butternut squash
Cucumber
Pumpkin
Summer squash
Zucchini

Characterized by their thick skins and many seeds, this group of vegetables is not as nutritious as most. Cucumbers, for example, are 96 percent water. Squashes vary in size and shape. Acorn squash has dark green fluted skin and yellow-to-orange pulp. Summer squash vary from dark green to yellow.

■ Wash cucumbers thoroughly in cold water to remove the waxy protective covering. Refrigerate whole cucumbers in a plastic bag for up to one week.

■ Choose summer squash that is no more than 5 inches in length. It can be steamed, fried, stuffed, or eaten raw.

■ Pumpkins can be used in ravioli, cheesecakes, relishes, and, of course, baked in a pie.

LEAFY VEGETABLES

Arugula
Chicory
Escarole
Boston lettuce
Iceberg lettuce
Radicchio
Romaine
Sorrel
Spinach
Swiss chard
Watercress

Select leafy vegetables that are crisp with no signs of withering. Leafy vegetables have a relatively short shelf life and should be eaten within two to three days. Wash them in plenty of cold water, drain them, and dry them with paper towels. If they are not to be eaten immediately, refrigerate them with two or three wet paper towels in a closed plastic bag to keep the leaves crisp.

■ Lettuce will rust more slowly if there is no excess moisture in its container. To keep your lettuce bag or vegetable compartment relatively dry, put in a few dry paper towels or  dry sponges to absorb excess water.

■ To core a head of iceberg lettuce, strip off any coarse outside leaves. Holding the head core end down, whack it onto the kitchen counter, and lift or twist out the core.

■ Wash spinach by plunging it into a bowl of water two or three times to get rid of any grit.

MUSHROOMS

All mushrooms are fungi, but the term "mushroom" is used to distinguish edible fungi from poisonous toadstools. Supermarkets stock many varieties of both fresh and dried mushrooms—crèpes (otherwise known as porcini), chanterelle, enokitake, portobello, and shiitake, to name just a few. The domestic white button mushroom, however, continues to be the most popular and widely available. Choose button mushrooms that have caps tightly closed around the stems. Do not peel mushrooms, and do not wash mushrooms until you are ready to use them. Wipe mushrooms clean with a damp paper towel—do not soak them in water. Cut off a small slice from the bottom of each mushroom, and they are ready to use.

■ Don't refrigerate mushrooms in a sealed plastic bag where they can become slimy very quickly. Use a brown paper bag instead.

■ To cut mushrooms into uniform sections, try using an egg slicer.

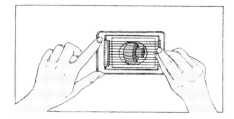

■ To maintain the whiteness and firmness of mushrooms while sautéing them, add a teaspoon of lemon juice to ¼ pound of melted butter.

PODS AND SEEDS

Corn	Peas
Fava beans	Runner beans
Green beans	Snow peas
Okra	String beans

Highly nutritious pods and seeds are staples in our diet. Because they retain their nutritional content when frozen right after picking, they are easily available year-round. If purchased fresh, these vegetables lose their nutrient value—and flavor—very quickly. Use them as soon as possible or refrigerate for one to two days.

■ When selecting fresh sweet corn, choose ears with green husks that are cool to the touch. If displayed without husks, look for developed kernels with good color.

continued on page 142

FRUITS MASQUERADING AS VEGETABLES

Fruit vegetables are technically fruits, but we treat them as vegetables. They include avocados, a wide variety of chilies, eggplant, peppers, and tomatoes. Although dissimilar, they share one important characteristic—they're more perishable than most vegetables.

AVOCADOS

Although they're loaded with vitamins, especially vitamin C, avocados are high in fat. Most avocados are sold when they're green and hard and must be ripened so that the skin is brown and the pulp is soft but not mushy. To test if an avocado is ripe, stick a toothpick in the stem end. If it slides in and out with ease, the avocado is ready to eat. To speed up the ripening of avocados, place them in a brown paper bag and store the bag in a warm place. Once ripe, you can retard spoilage by keeping them in the refrigerator.

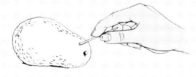

■ Peel the avocado and remove the pit immediately before serving. The flesh darkens very quickly.

■ For a perfect avocado half, cut the fruit in half lengthwise, pull the halves apart, and plunge a very sharp chef's knife into the pit. The pit will pull away cleanly with the knife. Remove the avocado halves from the shell with a spoon, or very gently with your fingers.

■ To keep an unused avocado half from turning dark, press the pit back into place before refrigerating.

CHILIES

The difference in flavor and hotness found among chili peppers depends on the variety. Chili peppers contain volatile oils that may burn your skin and make your eyes smart. When handling them, it is best to wear rubber gloves and avoid touching your face or eyes. Thoroughly wash any skin that comes in contact with chili oil.

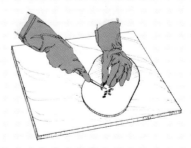

■ Canned chilies should be rinsed in cold water before using. Much of the "fire" is in the seeds and canning liquid.

FRUITS MASQUERADING AS VEGETABLES *continued*

■ The canners who pack chilies rate their hotness on a scale of 1 to 200—with 1 being the mildest. A jalapeno chili, hot enough to burn your mouth, bring tears to your eyes, and make your hair curl, rates only 15 on this scale!

■ Dried chilies can be found in markets that specialize in Mexican, Puerto Rican, and Spanish foods. The following are the most common:

Ancho chilies are large, full-flavored, and range from mild to medium-hot.

Mulato chilies are usually larger than anchos and have a more pungent flavor—usually medium-hot.

Pasilla chilies are slender, medium-size, and dark brown in color. Flavor ranges from mild to hot, and they are sold in dried and powdered forms.

Chipotle chilies are brownish red with wrinkled skin; dried, smoked, and often canned, this chili is very hot and has a distinctive smoky flavor.

EGGPLANT

Eggplant comes in a variety of shapes, colors, and sizes. The most common form of eggplant is dark purple. When purchasing eggplant, look for a firm eggplant that is heavy for its size, with tight, glossy, deeply colored skin. The stem should be bright green. Dull skin and dark spots are a sign of old age. Refrigerate unwashed eggplant in a plastic bag for up to five days. To remove the bitter juices from eggplant before cooking, cut it into slices or cubes. Sprinkle the eggplant liberally with coarse or kosher salt, and set the pieces on several layers of paper towels for 30 minutes. Rinse the slices or cubes quickly under cold running water, and pat them dry before cooking.

PEPPERS

Bell peppers have come a long way since they existed only in a single color—green. Now it's easy to find yellow, red, orange, purple, and brown bell peppers. Apart from their visual appeal, they each have their own distinctive taste. Green sweet peppers should be fresh looking, firm, thick-fleshed, and of bright color. Avoid peppers that are soft and dull looking. Keep peppers cool and humid and use within a few days for maximum freshness. Red sweet peppers are simply green peppers that have matured. Red peppers are high in vitamin C and are also a fair source of vitamin A and potassium.

■ Peppers will stay bright green during baking if you coat them with salad oil or olive oil before stuffing them.

■ To save time, roast a lot of red peppers at one time by using the just-lit coals of a barbecue. Char the peppers on all sides, then place them in a heavy plastic bag and seal for 10 minutes. Use a small, sharp knife or your fingers to lift off the skin, stem, and seeds of each pepper. Slice and store the peppers in a jar in the refrigerator. They'll keep for several weeks and can be used in hot vegetable dishes, in salads, or as an antipasto.

■ To roast peppers in the oven, put them on a rack in a broiler pan 3 to 5 inches from heat. Turn often until blistered and charred on all sides. Transfer to a plastic bag; seal the bag, and let it stand 15 to 20 minutes to loosen the skins. Remove loosened skins with a paring knife.

TOMATOES

From bite-size cherry tomatoes to hefty beefsteaks, tomatoes should be chosen for their color and aroma. Underripe tomatoes can be placed, stem side down, in a warm, sunny spot for a few days. They will soften and improve in flavor. Store ripe tomatoes at cool temperatures to slow down loss of vitamin C. Wash tomatoes just before using, and remove any stems that are present.

Sun-dried tomatoes are available in supermarket produce departments and come in two varieties. The oil-packed variety tends to be more expensive but benefits from being soaked in liquid, making them ready to use. The dry variety needs to be poached in liquid before being used (see package directions).

■ To hasten ripening, place an apple in a paper bag along with a tomato.

■ To peel tomatoes, place them, one at a time, in a saucepan of simmering water for about 10 seconds. (Add about 30 seconds if they are not fully ripened.) Then immediately plunge them into a bowl of cold water for another 10 seconds. The skins will peel off easily with a knife. Do not add more than one tomato at a time to the water or the temperature will drop rapidly and the tomatoes will stew before their skins can be removed.

■ To heighten the flavor when cooking tomatoes, add a pinch of sugar to the cooking water.

continued from page 138

■ To maintain maximum quality of fresh sweet corn if you can't serve it immediately, shuck the corn, wrap in plastic, and refrigerate.

■ A damp paper towel rubbed over corn on the cob easily removes the corn silk.

■ Snow peas (also known as sugar peas and Chinese pea pods) are translucent green pods. Choose fresh, crisp, thin pods in which the outline of the peas is barely visible. Keep peas refrigerated in plastic bags and use promptly.

■ The delicate flavor of okra is best if you choose 2- to 3-inch pods that are deep green in color, firm, and free of blemishes. You should be able to easily snap the pods and puncture them with slight pressure.

■ To easily shell peas, drop the pods in boiling water. The pods will split open and release the peas, and the pods will float to the surface.

ROOT VEGETABLES

Beet	Radish
Carrot	Rutabaga
Jicama	Turnip
Parsnip	

Root vegetables are a great source of vitamin A, as well as other vitamins and iron. Carrots are probably the most popular root vegetable in the United States—they are available year-round, store well, can be eaten

LEGUMES

The term "legume" is used to describe the dried seeds of pod-bearing plants. When combined with grains, they provide essential amino acids to form protein and thus are an important food for vegetarians and those restricting meat intake.

Store legumes in an airtight container or in their packaging for up to a year. Most legumes need to be rinsed and soaked before they can be cooked. To soak them, place them in a bowl of water for at least 8 hours. You may also use the quick-soak method: Add dry beans to a large pot. Cover them with water. Bring to a boil and continue boiling for 2 minutes, uncovered. Take them off the heat, cover, and let them sit for 1 hour. Beans will be ready to use.

Cooking times vary, and package directions should be followed carefully. The best way to cook legumes is to simmer them slowly and skim off any foam that collects on the surface. They are done when they can be easily mashed. Be careful not to overcook legumes—this makes them mushy and can affect their flavor.

- **Aduki beans** are small, red Japanese beans that can be cooked much faster than most beans and are considered to be easier to digest. They can be substituted for kidney beans in most recipes.

- **Black beans,** also called turtle beans, are very flavorful. They are often used in Latin American cooking and are great in tacos, burritos, soups, and stews.

- **Cannellini beans** are cultivated white beans, similar to kidney beans, which are used extensively in Italian cooking. Great Northern beans may be substituted.

- **Chickpeas,** also called garbanzo beans, are available canned as well as dried and are the basis for many Middle Eastern dishes, including hummus.

- **Dried peas** are great in soups and can be used in place of lentils in many recipes.

- **Fava beans** are Mediterranean beans with a nutty flavor. They make a rich addition to soups and stews. Unlike most beans, the skins of fava beans need to be removed after soaking to avoid a bitter taste.

- **Kidney beans** are available in white or red varieties. They can be used interchangeably with pintos and are available dried and canned. They are the usual basis for chili.

- **Lentils,** whether brown, green, or red, cook very quickly and don't have to be soaked. Most often used in soups and stews, lentils can be substituted for ground meat in various recipes.

- **Lima beans,** also known as butter beans and calico beans, are usually sold frozen or canned, although dried forms are available.

- **Pinto beans,** like kidney beans, are often used in Southwestern dishes and are usually the basis for refried beans.

- **Split peas** are most often used in soups. Like lentils, these do not require soaking before cooking.

- **Soybeans** are rich in protein, but they are seldom served cooked because they are difficult to digest. They are more often used to make various protein-rich sauces, soy milk, tofu, soy sauce, and even flour.

raw or cooked, and are very versatile, used in salads, stews, and even cakes. Purchase root vegetables when they are as fresh as possible, and avoid those that have any wrinkling. Small young root vegetables only need to be scrubbed to prepare them for eating or cooking. Larger root vegetables should be pared or scraped.

■ To keep beets from fading during cooking, leave an inch of stem attached and add a few tablespoons of vinegar to the water.

■ When you buy carrots, look to see that the bag contains smooth, well-shaped carrots of good orange color. If you buy fresh carrots that are not packaged, look for those with fresh green tops and brightly colored roots.

■ Because carrot tops can rob the vegetable of moisture during storage, slice off the tops before refrigerating.

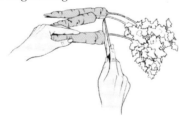

■ Jicama has a sweet, nutty flavor. It can be purchased in the produce section of most large supermarkets. Cut leftover jicama into julienned strips, and use them as dippers with your favorite dip.

■ Select small, young turnips for a mild, sweet flavor and crisp texture; older turnips can be woody and bitter.

SHOOT VEGETABLES

Artichokes	Celery
Asparagus	Endive
Bamboo shoots	Fennel

Most of the vegetables in this group are not highly nutritious. To maximize their nutrients, asparagus and artichokes should be only lightly steamed and never boiled. The rest can be eaten raw. Any sign of limpness in this group indicates an old vegetable. Refrigerate after purchase, and use quickly.

■ Cooking artichokes in iron or aluminum pots will turn the pots gray; use stainless steel or glass pots instead.

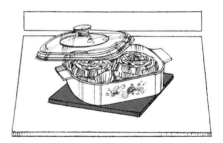

■ To keep artichokes from discoloring as you clean them, squeeze half a lemon into a bowl of cold water. As you clean each artichoke, rub it with the other half of the lemon, and then drop it into the water.

■ Select asparagus with firm, straight stalks and closed, compact tips. Always choose stalks that show the most green color. Open tips are a sign of over-maturity.

■ To maintain the moisture content of asparagus, cut a small slice off the bottom of each stalk, then stand all stalks upright in a container with an inch of water at the bottom and store in the refrigerator.

■ Avoid damaging the delicate tips of canned asparagus by opening the can from the bottom rather than the top.

■ Noted for its pleasant, flavorful sharpness, Belgian endive adds elegance to meals, either fresh in a salad or gently braised. Look for tightly furled stalks of creamy white color. The leaves should be pale yellow, not green, at the tips.

TUBERS

Potatoes
Sweet potatoes
Yams

Choose firm, smooth, clean tubers. They should be reasonably well shaped and free from cuts or bruises. Avoid greenish tubers and those with sprouts. Store tubers in a cool, dark place; do not refrigerate. Protect them from light, which can cause them to turn green and lose their vitamin C content.

■ Exposure to air turns peeled potatoes dark, so if you want to peel potatoes ahead of time, cover them with water and refrigerate.

■ To quickly peel sweet potatoes, boil them until just tender and drop them into cold water. The skins will slip right off.

■ To firm raw potatoes that have gone soft, immerse them in ice water for 30 minutes.

■ If you need to bake potatoes quickly, use baking nails. Insert a nail lengthwise in each potato; it will heat rapidly and then radiate heat to the inside of the potato, decreasing baking time by as much as 15 minutes.

■ To prevent potato pancakes from discoloring, add sour cream to the grated potatoes; you can also grate the potatoes into a bowl of ice water, draining before use.

COOKING METHODS

KNOW YOUR OVEN

While modern ovens have become more precise, cooking times can vary according to the oven. Although most people use a conventional oven, convection ovens have become popular in recent years.

In a conventional oven, the air does not circulate, and it's important to preheat the oven to the desired temperature and not to overcrowd the inside of the oven. With a convection oven, a fan circulates the hot air, which eliminates the need to preheat and allows more food to be baked or roasted at one time.

■ For even cooking in a conventional oven, allow 2 inches between pans and 2 inches between pans and the oven wall.

STEAMING

Using only a small amount of water in a pan on top of the range, this cooking method relies on the steam, rather than the heat of the water, to cook food. This method is great for vegetables, because they also retain more nutrients when steamed than when boiled.

■ If your oven doesn't have an indicator, allow 10 minutes for preheating before cooking.

■ If you want to use aluminum foil in the oven to catch spills, place it on the rack below the one used for baking to allow air circulation. Use foil only on the part of the lower rack that is directly under the pan; do not cover the entire rack.

BAKING AND ROASTING

Both baking and roasting involve cooking food with dry, hot air. Although similar to baking, roasting usually begins with a higher heat (400°F and above) to brown meats or vegetables. Then the heat is lowered to finish the cooking. Typically, one temperature is maintained during baking, and very often the meat is cooked in some form of liquid.

■ Meat will shrink less during roasting if it's cooked longer at a lower temperature.

■ A shallow pan is best for cooking a roast because it allows heat to circulate around the meat.

■ Dropping a few tomatoes in the pan will help tenderize a pot roast. Acid from the tomatoes helps break down the roast's stringy fibers.

■ It's best to baste a chicken only during the final 30 minutes of cooking. Sauce won't penetrate during the early cooking stages and may cause the chicken to brown too quickly.

■ Fish won't stick to the pan during baking if you lay it on a bed of parsley, celery, and onions. This vegetable bed also adds flavor.

BOILING, SIMMERING, AND POACHING

The important difference among boiling, simmering, and poaching is the temperature of the cooking liquid. Boiled foods are cooked in boiling liquid at 212°F. Simmered foods are cooked in gently bubbling liquid at 185–205°F. Poached foods are cooked in liquid that is hot but not actually bubbling (160–180°F).

■ Prevent boil-overs by inserting a toothpick horizontally between pot and lid so that steam can escape harmlessly.

■ Prevent steam from scalding your wrists and hands when you drain boiling water from a pot by first turning on the cold water tap.

■ When poaching a whole fish, wrap it in a length of cheesecloth for easy removal from the poaching liquid.

BROILING

Cooking food on very high heat under a broiler is the essence of broiling. Usually, meat is broiled on a wire rack over a pan. The high heat seals in the juices of the food and browns the outside, while the fat drips into the pan under the food.

■ If grease on your broiler catches fire, sprinkle salt or baking soda on the flames. Don't try to use flour as a fire extinguisher—it's explosive.

■ Broiling with gas is different from broiling with electricity. When you broil with gas, keep the oven door closed because gas flames absorb moisture and consume smoke. When you broil with electricity, keep the door slightly open so the oven can expel moisture.

■ To prevent chicken from drying out when broiling, brush it with lemon juice to keep it moist and add a touch of extra flavor.

■ Save time and effort when broiling sausages by putting the links on a skewer so you can turn them all with one movement. They'll all be evenly browned, too.

FRYING

To fry food, cook at high heat in a skillet on top of the range. Almost all foods to be fried require some liquid or fat to prevent them from sticking to the pan. Sautéing generally involves much shorter cooking times and is reserved for foods that cook very quickly.

■ When frying meats, be careful not to overcrowd the pan. If there are too many pieces in the pan, the meat will steam instead of brown.

■ To sauté food in butter, add the food just after the foam on the butter subsides.

■ Don't use the same vegetable oil for frying more than a few times. Old oil soaks into fried foods.

■ Chicken livers won't splatter during frying if you first perforate them with a fork. Puncture several holes in each.

■ When sautéing boneless chicken breasts or other chicken pieces, use a shallow skillet if you want the chicken to stay crisp. A deep pan creates steam, causing a buildup of moisture and a loss of crispness.

■ If you chill a chicken for an hour after flouring it for frying, the coating will adhere better.

■ To get the odor out of a pan used for frying fish, sprinkle the pan with salt, pour hot water in it, let it stand for a while, and then wash as usual.

STIR-FRYING

Follow these simple steps for successful stir-frying:

1. Prepare all the ingredients in advance, including cleaning, cutting, measuring, and combining.

2. Cut the meat and vegetables into uniform sizes and shapes to ensure even cooking.

3. Make sure the oil is hot before adding any food to the wok or pan. (The best oils to use for stir-frying are peanut, corn, or soybean.)

4. Add food that takes the longest time to cook first. Add food that requires little cooking time, such as mushrooms, at the end.

5. Stir the food often so that it cooks evenly on all sides.

COOKING FROZEN FOODS

■ Thaw frozen foods by placing the container under cold running water for a few minutes. Then place the container in a pan of lukewarm water until the food slips out easily.

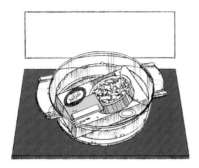

■ Most frozen vegetables should be cooked without thawing, but one major exception is corn on the cob. It should be thawed completely before cooking; otherwise you'll have to cook it too long and it will get tough.

■ If you have leftover tomatoes, freeze them for later use in stews and soups. Freezing makes them soft but won't affect their taste.

TIPS FOR COOKING PASTA AND RICE

PASTA

■ When buying pasta, make sure it's made from semolina rather than ordinary flour. Pasta made from semolina holds its shape better and doesn't become mushy.

■ When boiling water for pasta, add a teaspoon or so of cooking oil to prevent the pasta from sticking together (or to the pot).

■ There are several ways to prevent the pot from boiling over when cooking pasta. You can lay a large metal spatula across the top of the pot; rub shortening around the

rim before cooking; or add several teaspoons of cooking oil or a dab of butter to the cooking water.

■ For superior pasta, let salted water come to a boil, stir the pasta into the water, cover the pot, and turn off the heat. After the pasta sits for 10 to 15 minutes, it will be ready to eat.

■ To prevent cooked spaghetti from becoming sticky, run fresh hot water into the pot before draining.

■ If you're going to use pasta in a dish that requires further cooking, reduce the pasta cooking time by one-third.

RICE

■ If you've cooked too much rice, freeze it. When you're ready to use it, put rice in a sieve and run hot water through it.

■ For rice that's snowy white, add lemon juice to the cooking water.

■ If the rice you're cooking has burned slightly, remove the burned flavor by adding a heel from a loaf of fresh white bread and covering the pot for a few minutes.

■ When cooking rice, add a pinch of rosemary to the water instead of salt for a special flavor.

COOKING IN THE MICROWAVE

Microwaves are great time-savers, but cooking in a microwave is much different than cooking in an oven or on top of the range. Along with following the manufacturer's directions, keep these tips in mind:

■ Be sure to use nonmetal utensils in the microwave.

■ For microwave cooking, cut meats and vegetables in uniform sizes to make sure that they cook evenly.

■ Paper plates, cups, and napkins can be used in the microwave. But don't use foil-lined paper products, paper towels that include nylon or synthetic fibers, or newspaper.

■ When using plastic roasting or cooking bags in the microwave, discard the wire twist tie and use a plastic fastener or a piece of string instead.

■ To ensure that food cooks fully and evenly in the microwave oven, stir food and turn dishes periodically while they're cooking.

■ Remove large bones from meat before microwaving it because the dense bone may keep the area around it from cooking.

■ To get more juice from a lemon or other citrus fruit, pop it in the microwave on high power for 30 seconds.

■ Paper towels around sandwiches, rolls, or other baked goods will absorb moisture that would otherwise make the food soggy.

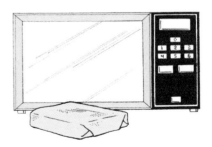

■ Potato chips that have lost their crunch can be placed on paper towels in the microwave oven and heated briefly. The towels will absorb moisture and restore the chips to crispness.

■ Thick-skinned foods, such as potatoes, squash, and tomatoes, trap steam during microwave cooking. Pierce the skins before cooking to allow steam to escape.

■ If your brown sugar has turned into an intractable lump, just place a piece of dampened paper towel in the box, close the box tightly, and put the whole thing in the microwave for 20 to 30 seconds on high to soften the sugar.

■ Ease the chore of peeling such foods as tomatoes or peaches. Heat for 30 seconds on high, then allow to stand for 2 minutes. The peel will slip off easily.

BARBECUING

The smoky taste of food grilled over an open fire isn't the only reason people love to barbecue, but it's one of the best. If you have a gas grill, you'll want to skip right to the "Grilling Techniques" section, but if you're grilling with coals, it can be tricky to get your barbecue burning just right. For **direct cooking,** arrange the coals in a single layer directly under the food. Use this method for quick-cooking foods, such as hamburgers, steaks, and fish. For **indirect cooking,** arrange coals to one side of the grill. Place a drip pan under the food at the other side. For more heat, divide the coals on either side of the drip pan. Use this method for slow-cooking foods, such as roasts and whole chicken.

GRILLING TECHNIQUES

■ Spray your barbecue grill with nonstick cooking spray so you'll be able to turn chicken pieces without tearing.

■ Watch foods carefully during grilling. Total cooking time will vary with the type of food, position on the grill, weather, temperature of the coals, and degree of doneness you desire.

■ Use tongs or a spatula to turn meat. A fork or knife punctures meat and lets the juices escape.

■ Use a meat thermometer to accurately determine the doneness of large cuts of meat or poultry.

■ Spice up the flavor of food on the barbecue by sprinkling the coals with fresh herbs that have been soaked in water.

- To tenderize pork chops or chicken pieces before barbecuing, boil them in a saucepan for 15 minutes, drain them, and then marinate them in barbecue sauce for 30 minutes. Then grill as usual.

- If you're cooking a variety of vegetables on skewers on the grill, make sure they all finish cooking at the same time by blanching or parboiling long-cooking vegetables (such as potatoes or carrot chunks) ahead of time.

- Add zip to skewered vegetables by brushing them with salad dressing instead of butter.

- Cook potatoes, carrots, or winter squash directly on the coals by first wrapping the vegetables thoroughly in foil. They'll take 30 to 45 minutes to cook.

CLEANUP

- A grill will steam-clean itself if wrapped in wet newspapers or sprayed with window cleaner while it's still hot.

- Wipe the grill with crumpled aluminum foil while it's still warm.

- A can opener makes a great scraper for cleaning barbecue grills; file a

---

GRILLING SEAFOOD

- Seafood generally cooks much faster than meats. Watch it carefully.

- If you use a marinade, remove excess before placing seafood on the grill.

- Use bacon strips to hold shrimp and scallops on skewers. Thread one end of the bacon on the skewer, add a shrimp or scallop, bring the bacon through the skewer again, add another shrimp or scallop, and continue until you reach the end of the bacon rasher.

---

notch in the end of the opener opposite the sharp point.

SAFETY TIPS

- Position the grill on a heatproof surface, out of the path of foot traffic and away from trees and bushes that could catch a spark.

- Make sure the grill's vents are not clogged with ashes before starting a fire.

- To avoid flare-ups and charred food when grilling, remove visible fat from meat.

- When you barbecue juicy meat, fat dripping on the hot coals can cause flames to flare up. Put out the flames by dropping lettuce leaves on the coals, or by squirting

MARVELOUS MARINADES

Marinades add unique flavors to foods and help tenderize cuts of meat. After food is removed from a marinade, the marinade may be used as a basting or dipping sauce. When used as a basting sauce, marinades should only be applied up to the last 5 minutes of grilling or broiling. This precaution is necessary because the marinade could have become contaminated with harmful bacteria from the raw food during the marinading process. The marinade must be cooked over the heat for a minimum of 5 minutes to ensure that the harmful bacteria are destroyed. If you wish to use marinade as a dipping sauce, place it in a small saucepan and bring it to a full boil.

- Turn marinating foods occasionally to let the flavor infuse evenly.
- The safest way to apply basting sauce is to brush it on the food before turning it over.
- Basting sauces containing sugar, honey, or tomato products should be applied only during the last 15 to 30 minutes of grilling. This will prevent the food from charring. Basting sauces made from seasoned oils and butters may be brushed on throughout grilling.

water on the coals with a spray bottle or turkey baster.

- Always serve cooked food from the grill on a clean plate, not one that held the raw food.

SALADS AND SALAD DRESSINGS

- Crisp up soggy lettuce by submerging it in a bowl of cold water and lemon juice and putting it in the refrigerator. After an hour, remove the lettuce from the refrigerator and dip it briefly in hot water, then in ice water to which you've added a dash of apple cider vinegar. Pat the lettuce dry.

- Another way to make lettuce crisp is to place it in a pan of ice water to which you've added slices of raw potato for about 15 minutes.

- Put washed salad greens in the freezer about 10 minutes before preparing the salad to give the greens extra crunch.

- For extra-crisp cucumber slices, soak them in salted ice water for

30 minutes. Just before serving, drain and rinse under cold water. Pat dry and toss with dressing.

■ Be sure that lettuce leaves are well dried before tossing, otherwise the salad dressing won't cling.

■ When dressing a salad with vinegar and oil, remember to pour the vinegar first. If you pour the oil first, the vinegar won't stick to the greens.

■ Don't pour vinaigrette dressing over salad greens until just before serving. Only shredded cabbage or tomatoes can stand a vinaigrette bath for up to an hour before serving without losing firmness.

■ Don't toss sliced tomatoes into your salad. Their water content will dilute the salad dressing. Add them on top at the last minute, or use whole cherry tomatoes.

■ You can keep your salads crisp if you invert a saucer in the bottom of the bowl to allow any liquid to drain and collect under the saucer, away from the greens.

■ If you want crumbled Roquefort or blue cheese for your salads, freeze it; it will crumble easily when scraped with a paring knife. (This does not work well with other cheeses.)

■ For extra-creamy salad dressings, place dressing ingredients in a slow-running blender and slowly add the oil.

■ If salt is used as a salad seasoning, it's best to add it at the last minute. If you add the salt ahead of time, the lettuce will wilt.

■ A crushed garlic clove rubbed on the inside of a salad bowl will heighten the taste of the salad ingredients.

SOUPS AND SAUCES

A soup is any combination of vegetables, meat, or fish cooked in a liquid. The stock—the strained liquid that is the result of cooking vegetables, meat, or fish—determines its flavor.

■ **Bisque** is a thick soup made from puréed shellfish, fowl, or vegetables and cream.

■ **Broth** (or bouillon) is the liquid resulting from cooking vegetables, meat, or fish in water.

■ **Chowder** is a thick, chunky seafood soup. It can contain any of several varieties of seafood and vegetables. The term is also used to describe any thick, rich soup containing chunks of food (corn chowder, for example).

■ **Consommé** is a rich clear broth made by straining all sediment out of the soup or seasoned stock.

■ **Fruit soup** is made of cooked puréed fruit combined with water, wine, milk or cream, spices, and other flavorings. Sugar is sometimes added. Fruit soups are served either hot or cold.

STOCK-MAKING BASICS

■ Begin with a good soup pot—one that is heavy and conducts and distributes heat evenly.

■ For meat stocks, place the meat and bones in a soup pot and cover them with cold water. Heat the water slowly to a boil without stirring. Use a ladle to remove the scum as it collects on the surface of the water. Add the vegetables and seasonings of your choice; add salt sparingly. Reduce heat and simmer gently, partially covered, for at least 2 hours. Strain the stock through dampened cheesecloth.

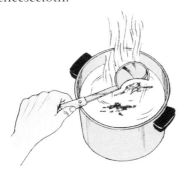

■ To remove the fat from stock, cover and refrigerate. The fat will solidify on the surface for easy removal.

■ When making stock, do not allow the liquid to boil very long, or the stock will become cloudy. Simmer instead.

■ Puréed leftover vegetables lend additional flavoring to stocks.

■ If you want rich brown beef stock, add beef bones that have been browned in the broiler.

■ To make a concentrated stock, reduce brown beef or chicken stock to a heavy, syruplike consistency, being careful not to burn the stock. Store it in the refrigerator or freezer, and break or cut off small pieces as needed to flavor soups or sauces.

■ When saving meat juices for stock, leave the fat in place on the surface. When the fat solidifies, it will seal in the flavor.

FREEZING SOUPS AND STOCKS

■ Before freezing, refrigerate the soup until the fat rises to the surface. Skim the fat, and discard bones, bay leaves, or any other ingredients that will not be eaten.

■ Divide the soup into portions to serve two, four, or more people.

■ To save freezer space, store soup in sealed plastic bags, stacking them in the freezer.

■ There's no need to thaw frozen stock before using. Just pop a frozen block of stock into a covered pan, and heat it gently.

■ If freezer space is tight and you want to store homemade stocks, simply cook down the stock until it's reduced by half, then freeze it. Restore the stock to its original volume by adding water.

■ To avoid scorching and boil-overs when cooking soup in a large stock pot, position two or three bricks around the burner so that the pot is elevated above the heating coils or the gas flames. Then simmer the contents as long as necessary over low heat.

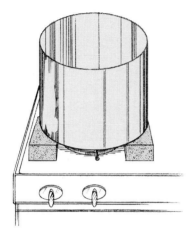

■ For tastier clam chowder, add the minced clams at the last moment and cook just long enough to heat. As a bonus, the clams won't become mushy.

■ To keep milk from curdling when you prepare tomato soup, add the soup stock to the milk, instead of the milk to the stock.

SAUCES

■ Brown sauce won't thicken if you add acids, such as citrus juice or vinegar, before the sauce has been reduced.

■ If brown sauce is too thick, thin it with more meat stock or 1 to 2 tablespoons of light cream.

■ To give your sauce an extra shine, whip in 2 tablespoons of cold butter just before serving.

■ Don't cover meat sauces while keeping them warm. Moisture will build up and dilute your sauce.

■ If a sauce begins to separate, add a little cold water. If the sauce begins to cool too quickly, alternate cold and hot water.

■ If you make béarnaise sauce several hours ahead of time, keep it in a tightly closed, preheated vacuum bottle.

■ If an egg-base sauce curdles, it's probably because it's been boiled. Keep the temperature moderate when making egg sauces.

GRAVIES

■ If a gravy is too salty, add several pinches of brown sugar to remove the salty taste.

■ If your gravy tastes burned, stir in a teaspoon of peanut butter.

■ There are two quick ways to darken gravy. The first is to mix

MAKING VINEGAR FROM SCRATCH

■ **Apple cider vinegar:** Plain apple cider can be made into vinegar if left to stand in an open bottle for about 5 weeks. The bottle should be kept at 70°F. It will first become hard cider and then vinegar.

■ **Chili vinegar:** Put 3 ounces chopped chilies into 1 quart vinegar, and store for 2 weeks in a capped bottle. Strain liquid after 2 weeks. For a spicier, stronger vinegar, let chilies steep longer.

■ **Cucumber-onion vinegar:** Boil 1 pint vinegar, and add 1 teaspoon salt and a dash of white pepper. Add 2 sliced pickling cucumbers and 1 small onion, sliced very thin, to vinegar mixture. Store in a capped glass jar for 5 weeks, then strain. Pour strained liquid into a recycled wine bottle, and cork it.

■ **Garlic vinegar:** Peel cloves from 1 large bulb of garlic, and add them to 1 quart vinegar. Steep liquid for 2 weeks, then strain and discard garlic. Use a few drops for flavoring salads, cooked meat, or vegetables.

■ **Hot pepper vinegar:** Pour 1 pint vinegar into a clean bottle with cap, then add ½ ounce cayenne pepper to it. Let mixture sit for 2 weeks out of direct sunlight. Shake bottle about every other day. After 2 weeks, strain and pour into a separate clean bottle for use.

■ **Raspberry vinegar:** Make a raspberry vinegar with 2 quarts water and 5 quarts red or black raspberries. Pour water over 1 quart washed red or black raspberries, and keep in airtight container. Let stand overnight, then strain and keep liquid (discard raspberries). Pour liquid over another quart of raspberries, then strain and discard raspberries. Add 1 pound sugar to strained liquid, and stir until dissolved. Let mixture stand uncovered for 2 months, strain, then use.

■ **Strawberry vinegar:** Combine a bottle of white wine vinegar with ½ cup fresh, washed, and stemmed strawberries. Cover, and let it sit at room temperature for 1 week. Remove fruit, and use vinegar.

■ **Tarragon vinegar:** Add ¼ cup tarragon leaves to a pint bottle of vinegar. Let stand, capped, for 2 months. Strain, and rebottle vinegar.

■ **White wine vinegar:** Add 2 pounds raisins to 1 gallon water. Let sit in a warm place for 2 months. Strain vinegar, then pour it into a bottle.

1 tablespoon of water with 1 tablespoon of sugar, heating the blend in a pan until the sugar browns and the water evaporates. Pour the gravy into this pan. The second method is to add coffee to the gravy; it will add color without affecting the flavor.

■ One way to make rich brown gravy for a roast is to put flour in a pie pan and let it brown in the oven along with the roast. When the meat is done, mix the browned flour with a little cold water and heat it with the meat juice.

ALL ABOUT BAKING

MEASURING INGREDIENTS

DRY INGREDIENTS

■ Always use standardized measuring spoons and cups.

■ Fill the correct measuring spoon or cup to overflowing, and level it off with a metal spatula or knife.

■ If a recipe calls for sifted flour, sift the flour before it is measured.

■ When measuring flour, lightly spoon it into a measuring cup and then level it off. Do not tap or bang the measuring cup—this will pack the flour.

LIQUID INGREDIENTS

■ Use a standardized glass or plastic measuring cup with a pouring spout. Place cup on a flat surface, and fill to the desired mark.

■ When measuring sticky liquids such as honey and molasses, coat the measuring cup with vegetable cooking spray before adding the liquid to make removal easier.

BREADS

In most breads, yeast is used to make dough rise. Quick breads rely on other agents—such as baking powder—to make them rise.

DISSOLVING YEAST

Dissolving yeast properly is the most important step in successful yeast breads and coffeecakes.

■ Dissolve the yeast with a small amount of sugar in warm (105° to 115°F) water or milk. The warmth and sugar cause the yeast to grow and multiply. Use a thermometer to check the temperature of the liquid.

■ After about 5 minutes the yeast will start to foam and bubble. If it doesn't, throw out the yeast mixture and start over.

■ Be sure to use yeast before its expiration date. It quickly loses its effectiveness as it ages.

■ Yeast doughs need to rise before baking to ensure proper volume and texture. Be sure to cover the dough, and set it in a warm (70° to 75°F), draft-free place.

KNEADING

Although bread dough starts out soft and sticky, it becomes smooth and elastic when kneaded. The purpose of kneading is to develop the gluten, a protein present in wheat flour that gives the bread structure. The gluten forms long elastic strands in the dough that trap carbon dioxide gas produced by the yeast. The trapped gas causes the bread to rise.

■ Knead bread dough on a lightly floured surface.

■ Always use the heels of your hands—not your fingers—to knead.

■ Push the dough away from you with the heels of your hands, then bring the far end down to fold the dough in half. Give the dough a quarter turn, and repeat the process, adding more flour as needed to prevent sticking.

■ Knead the dough until it is smooth, satiny, and springy when pressed with a finger (8 to 10 minutes). Air bubbles or blisters should appear just below the surface.

RISING

■ Shape the kneaded dough into a ball, and place it in a lightly oiled bowl. Turn the ball to coat the entire surface with oil. This prevents the bread from forming a crust that could hinder rising.

■ Cover the bowl with a cloth towel, and set it in a warm (70° to 75°F), draft-free place.

■ Let the dough rise until it has doubled in size, about 1 hour.

SHAPING AND SECOND RISING

■ After the dough has doubled, punch it down with your fist. This removes large air bubbles, giving the bread a fine, even texture.

■ Pull the edges of the dough to the center to form a ball.

■ Shape the dough according to the recipe directions, and place it on a greased baking sheet or in a greased loaf pan.

■ Cover the shaped loaves, and let them rise again in a warm place until they have doubled in size, about 1 hour.

BAKING

■ Place the bread on the center rack of a preheated oven.

■ The bread is done when it is golden brown, well rounded, and sounds hollow when tapped.

■ For a crisp crust, place a pan of water in the bottom of the oven during baking, or brush the top of the loaf with water.

■ For a softer crust, brush the loaves with softened butter immediately after baking.

COOLING AND STORING

■ Immediately remove the bread from the pan or baking sheet, and place it on a wire rack to cool.

■ Once the bread has completely cooled, wrap it in plastic wrap or place in an airtight plastic bag or container.

■ Store bread at room temperature; placing it in the refrigerator causes it to become stale faster.

■ Thaw unwrapped yeast loaves at room temperature for 2 to 3 hours; you can also heat them partially unwrapped in a 375°F oven for 20 minutes.

■ Allow a freshly baked loaf to cool for at least 3 hours on a wire rack before freezing. Place the loaf in the freezer on a flat surface for 2 hours or until it is solidly frozen. Wrap the frozen loaf in plastic wrap and then in aluminum foil. Label it with the date and the type of bread, and return it to the freezer. Bread can be frozen for up to 6 months. Thaw frozen bread in its wrapping at room temperature for 2 to 3 hours. Freshen the loaf by heating it in a 300°F oven for 20 minutes.

QUICK BREADS

These breads are quick to make because they rely on quick-acting leavening agents such as baking soda, baking powder, and eggs— rather than yeast—to make them rise. Quick breads include biscuits, scones, and muffins.

BISCUITS AND SCONES

■ When preparing biscuits, cut the shortening or butter into the dry ingredients with a pastry blender or two knives until the mixture forms coarse crumbs.

■ Mix the dough gently and quickly to achieve light and tender results. Overworking the dough makes the biscuits tough.

■ On a lightly floured surface, roll or pat out the dough to the desired thickness.

■ Press a floured cutter straight down through the dough; twisting produces lopsided biscuits.

■ For crusty biscuits, place them at least one inch apart on the baking sheet. For soft, fluffy biscuits, place them close together.

■ Scones are similar to biscuits, but the dough is richer due to the addition of cream and eggs. While the dough can be cut into any shape, scones are usually cut into wedges or triangles.

MUFFINS

■ For most muffin recipes, mix the dry ingredients together first to evenly distribute the baking powder and/or baking soda.

■ Combine the liquid ingredients, and add them all at once to the dry ingredients. Stir just until the dry ingredients are moistened. The batter should be lumpy; the lumps will disappear during baking.

■ Grease the cups of the muffin pan, or use paper baking liners, and fill

them ⅔ to ¾ full with batter. Pour water into any empty cups to prevent the pan from warping in the oven.

■ Muffins are done when the center springs back when lightly touched and a wooden toothpick inserted into the center comes out dry.

■ Remove muffins from their cups immediately after baking, and cool them on a wire rack.

■ Muffins will stay fresh in a sealed plastic bag for several days.

■ For longer storage, wrap and freeze. To reheat, wrap frozen muffins in foil and heat in a 350°F oven for 15 to 20 minutes. For best flavor, use frozen muffins within one month.

CAKES

Cakes are divided into two basic categories according to what makes them rise. Butter cakes rely primarily on baking powder or baking soda for height, while sponge cakes depend on the air trapped in the eggs during beating.

BUTTER CAKES

Butter cakes include pound cakes and yellow, white, spice, and chocolate layer cakes. These cakes use butter, shortening, or oil for moistness and richness and are leavened with baking powder or baking soda.

- Before mixing the batter, soften the butter so that it mixes easily with the sugar.

- Grease and flour the pans before mixing the cake batter so that the cake can be baked immediately.

- A butter cake is done when it begins to pull away from the sides of the pan, the top springs back when touched, and a cake tester or toothpick inserted into the center comes out clean and dry.

- After removing butter cakes from the oven, let them stand in their pans on wire racks for 10 minutes, or as the recipe directs. Run a knife around the edge of the cake to loosen it from the sides of the pan, and invert it on a wire rack. Turn the cake top side up onto a second rack to finish cooling.

SPONGE CAKES

These cakes achieve their high volume from beaten eggs. Sponge cakes do not contain butter, oil, or shortening. Angel food cakes are the most popular and can be fat-free since they use only egg whites, not yolks. Yellow sponge cakes are prepared with whole eggs.

- When preparing sponge cakes, be sure to beat the eggs to the proper stage. Handle the beaten eggs gently when folding the other ingredients into them to prevent them from losing air and volume.

- Sponge cakes are usually baked in tube pans. The center tube helps the heat circulate during baking and also supports the delicate structure of the cake. Do not grease the pan for sponge cake batters. The ungreased pan lets the batter cling to the sides as it rises.

- A sponge cake is done when it is delicately browned and the top springs back when lightly touched.

- Invert a sponge cake baked in a tube pan onto a funnel or bottle immediately after removing it from the oven. If it is cooled top side up, it will fall. Do not remove a sponge cake from the pan until it is completely cool.

TIPS FOR A FLAWLESS CAKE

- Some cake recipes specifically call for cake flour, which contains less protein than all-purpose flour and produces a more tender cake. Use cake flour if the recipe calls for it.

- Be sure to use the pan sizes specified in cake recipes.

- Place the cake pan(s) in the center of a preheated oven. Oven racks may need to be set lower for cakes baked in tube pans.

■ Let the cake cool in the pan on a wire rack for about 10 minutes, then loosen it from the side of the pan with a knife or metal spatula. Invert it on the rack, and let it cool completely before frosting or cutting.

■ Make sure the cake is completely cool before frosting it. Brush off any loose crumbs from the cake's surface.

■ To halve a cake horizontally, remove the cake from the pan, and place it on a flat surface. Measure the cake with a ruler, and mark a cutting line with toothpicks. Cut through the cake with a long serrated knife, just above the toothpicks.

■ To cut an angel food cake, use a long serrated knife and cut with a sawing motion.

STORING CAKES

■ Store single-layer cakes in their baking pan, tightly covered.

■ Store 2- or 3-layer cakes in a cake saver or under an inverted bowl.

■ Cakes with whipped cream frostings or cream fillings should be stored in the refrigerator.

BEATING EGG WHITES

■ Separate eggs while they are cold because the yolk is firm and less likely to break. Egg whites won't beat properly if any trace of yolk remains. Flecks of yolk can be removed with the moistened tip of a cotton swab.

■ Let the whites sit out at room temperature for 30 minutes before beating to achieve their highest volume.

■ For best results, use a copper, stainless steel, or glass bowl.

■ Add a pinch of cream of tartar and salt to the egg whites after they have been beaten slightly and are foamy; this will prevent them from collapsing.

■ When a recipe calls for sugar, add it slowly to the egg whites, beating well after each addition. If the mixture feels grainy to the touch, continue beating before adding more.

■ If the egg whites are to be folded into other ingredients, this should be done immediately after they are beaten.

■ Unfrosted cakes can be frozen for up to four months if wrapped well in plastic. Thaw them in their wrapping at room temperature.

■ Frosted cakes should be frozen unwrapped until the frosting hardens and then wrapped and sealed; freeze for up to two months. To thaw, remove the wrapping and thaw at room temperature or in the refrigerator.

■ Cakes with fruit or custard fillings do not freeze well because they become soggy when thawed.

COOKIES

Despite the multitude of flavors, shapes, and sizes, cookies can actually be divided into five basic types: bar, drop, refrigerator, rolled, and shaped. These types are determined by the consistency of the dough and how it is formed into cookies.

BAR COOKIES

Bar cookies and brownies are very easy to make—simply mix the batter, spread in the pan, and bake. These cookies are also quick to prepare since they bake all at once, rather than in batches on a cookie sheet.

■ Always use the pan size called for in the recipe. A smaller pan will give the bars a more cakelike texture, and a larger pan will produce a flatter, drier texture.

THE ABCs OF BAKING

■ Read the entire recipe before beginning to make sure you have all the necessary ingredients and baking utensils.

■ Remove butter, margarine, and cream cheese from the refrigerator to soften, if necessary.

■ Toast and chop nuts, pare and slice fruit, and melt chocolate before preparing cookie dough.

■ Measure all the ingredients accurately, and assemble them in the order they are called for in the recipe.

■ Use the pan size specified in each recipe, and prepare it as stated. The wrong size pan may cause a burned bottom or edges or a sunken middle.

■ Aluminum pans reflect heat and give a golden color to breads and cookies. For pies, use dark pans to absorb heat and keep the crust from getting soggy.

■ Oven temperatures can vary depending on the model and manufacturer, so watch your baked dish carefully and check for doneness using the test given in the recipe.

■ Adjust oven racks and preheat the oven. Check oven temperature for accuracy with an oven thermometer.

■ Most bar cookies should cool in the pan on a wire rack until barely warm before cutting.

■ To make serving easy, remove a corner piece first; then remove the rest.

DROP COOKIES

These cookies are named for the way they are formed on the cookie sheet. The soft dough mounds when dropped from a spoon and then flattens slightly during baking.

■ Space the mounds of dough about 2 inches apart on the cookie sheet to allow for spreading.

■ To easily shape drop cookies into a uniform size, use an ice-cream scoop with a release bar.

■ Cookies lift off a cookie sheet easily if you run a piece of dental floss underneath them.

REFRIGERATOR COOKIES

Refrigerator doughs are perfect for preparing in advance. Tightly wrapped rolls of dough can be stored in the refrigerator for up to one week or frozen for up to six weeks. These rich doughs are ready to be sliced and baked at a moment's notice.

■ Always shape the dough into rolls before chilling.

■ Before chilling, wrap the rolls securely in plastic wrap to prevent air from penetrating the dough and causing it to dry out.

■ Use gentle pressure and a back-and-forth sawing motion when slicing the rolls so the cookies will keep their shape. Rotating the roll while slicing also prevents one side from flattening.

ROLLED COOKIES

Rolled or cutout cookies are made from stiff doughs that are rolled out and cut into fancy shapes with floured cookie cutters, a knife, or a pastry wheel.

■ Chill the cookie dough thoroughly before rolling for easier handling.

■ Save trimmings and reroll them all at once to keep the dough from becoming tough.

■ To make your own custom cookie cutters, cut a simple shape out of clean, heavy cardboard or poster board. Place the cardboard pattern on the rolled-out dough, and cut around it using a sharp knife.

SHAPED COOKIES

These cookies can be hand-shaped into balls or crescents, forced through a cookie press, or baked in cookie molds.

■ Be sure to use the specific cookie press or mold called for in the recipe. The consistency of the dough may not lend itself to using a different tool.

■ To flatten cookies, use the bottom of a greased and sugared glass. Place balls of dough on the cookie sheet, then flatten with the glass.

TIPS FOR FLAWLESS COOKIES

■ Use shiny cookie sheets with little or no sides for best baking results.

■ Promote even baking by placing only one cookie sheet at a time in the center of a conventional oven. If you use more than one sheet at a time, rotate the cookie sheets from top to bottom halfway through the baking time.

■ Most cookies bake quickly and should be watched carefully to avoid overbaking. Check them at the minimum baking time, then watch carefully to make sure they don't burn.

■ Let cookie sheets cool between batches; the dough will spread if placed on a hot cookie sheet.

■ Most cookies should be removed from cookie sheets immediately after baking and placed in a single layer on wire racks to cool. Fragile cookies may need to cool slightly on the cookie sheet before being moved. Always cool cookies completely before stacking and storing. Bar cookies and brownies may be cooled and stored in the baking pan.

STORING COOKIES

■ Store soft and crisp cookies separately to prevent changes in texture and flavor.

■ Keep soft cookies in airtight containers. If they begin to dry out, add a piece of apple or bread to the container to help them retain moisture.

■ Store crisp cookies in containers with loose-fitting lids to prevent moisture buildup.

■ Store cookies with sticky glazes, fragile decorations, and icings in single layers between sheets of waxed paper.

■ As a rule, crisp cookies freeze better than soft, moist cookies. Rich, buttery bar cookies and brownies are an exception to this rule since they freeze extremely well.

■ Freeze baked cookies in airtight containers or freezer bags for up to six months. Thaw cookies and brownies unwrapped at room temperature.

ALL ABOUT CHOCOLATE

When a recipe calls for chocolate, you'll want to make sure you have the right chocolate on hand—semisweet, unsweetened, milk, white chocolate, or cocoa. It's not a good idea to substitute one chocolate for another.

Store chocolate in a cool, dry place. If chocolate gets too warm, the cocoa butter rises to the surface and causes a grayish white appearance, which is called a bloom. The bloom will not affect the chocolate's taste or baking quality.

Types of Chocolate

- **Unsweetened chocolate** contains no sugar. It is usually sold in 1-ounce squares.
- **Semisweet chocolate** is usually about 40 percent sugar. It is sold in squares or chips. Bittersweet chocolate contains even less sugar.
- **Milk chocolate** contains milk solids and is rarely used in baking.
- **White chocolate** is not really chocolate at all—it's cocoa butter with added sugar, milk, and flavorings. White chocolate is more delicate than other chocolates.
- **Unsweetened cocoa** is formed by extracting most of the cocoa butter from pure chocolate and grinding the remaining chocolate solids into a powder.

Melting Chocolate

Make sure the utensils you use for melting chocolate are completely dry. Be careful not to scorch chocolate when you melt it.

- **Double Boiler**—The safest method of scorch-free melting is to use a double boiler. Place the chocolate in the top of a double boiler or in a bowl over hot, not boiling, water; stir until smooth.

- **Direct Heat**—Place the chocolate in a heavy saucepan, and melt it over very low heat, stirring constantly. Remove the chocolate from the heat as soon as it is melted. Be sure to watch the chocolate carefully since it is easily scorched with this method.
- **Microwave Oven**—Place an unwrapped 1-ounce square or 1 cup of chips in a small microwavable bowl. Microwave on high 1 to 1½ minutes. Stir the chocolate at 30-second intervals until smooth.

PASTRIES

The only real secrets to tender, flaky pie crusts are to keep the ingredients cold and handle the dough as little as possible. Tough crusts are the result of overdeveloped gluten, a protein present in flour.

PREPARING PASTRY DOUGH

- If you use butter in your pastry dough, it must be chilled. Vegetable shortening and lard, though soft at room temperature, do not need to be chilled. Also make sure that the liquid you add is cold. Cold liquid, such as ice water, keeps the fat solid.

- Blend the flour and salt together, then cut the fat in quickly with a pastry blender, two knives, or your fingertips until the shortening lumps are the size of peas.

- Add cold liquids gradually, a tablespoon at a time, stirring lightly with a fork. The dough should be just moist enough to hold together with slight pressure and be gathered into a ball.

- To create a tender pie crust, add a small amount of acid, such as lemon juice, vinegar, or sour cream, to the pastry dough along with the liquid.

- Handle the pastry dough quickly; overworking it will make it tough. If the dough is difficult to handle, refrigerate it until firm.

- Wrap the ball of dough in plastic wrap, and refrigerate it for at least 1 hour. Chilling the dough makes it easier to handle and helps prevent shrinkage during baking.

- Flour the rolling pin and surface just enough to prevent sticking. Place the chilled dough on a lightly floured surface, and flatten it into a ½-inch-thick circle. Roll the dough with a floured rolling pin, pressing from the center toward the edge using quick, short strokes. Continue rolling until the dough is ⅛-inch thick and 2 inches larger than the inverted pie pan.

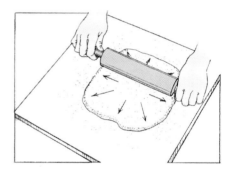

- Loosely fold the dough into quarters, and place the point of the folded dough into the center of the pie pan. Gently unfold the dough, and ease it into the pan; do not stretch the dough or it will shrink during baking.

BAKING PASTRY

- **Single-crust pies,** such as custard pies, are baked in an unbaked pastry shell. Others require the shell to be prebaked so that it does not become soggy. If the pastry shell is to be baked without the filling, prick the dough all over with a fork. Line the pastry with aluminum foil, waxed paper, or parchment paper, and spread dried beans or pie weights over the bottom to prevent it from puffing and losing its shape during baking. The pastry can be fully or partially baked in this manner. Cool it completely before adding the filling.

■ **Double-crust pies** are made by placing the filling (usually fruit) between two unbaked layers of pastry. Spoon the filling into the pastry shell, and brush the rim of the shell with water. Roll out the top crust, and place it over the filling. Press the pastry edges together to seal, then trim and flute. Cut a few slits or vents in the top crust to allow steam to escape. Before baking a double-crust pie, try glazing the top crust with milk or cream to promote browning.

STORING PASTRY

■ Refrigerate custard or cream pies immediately after cooling.

■ Fruit pies can be stored at room temperature overnight; refrigerate them for longer storage.

■ To freeze unbaked pies, do not cut steam vents in the top crust. Cover the top with an inverted paper plate for extra protection, packaging it in freezer bags or freezer wrap. To bake, do not thaw. Cut slits in the top crust, and allow an additional 15 to 20 minutes of baking time.

■ Baked pies can also be cooled and frozen. To serve, let the pie thaw at room temperature for 2 hours, then heat until warm.

■ Freezing is not recommended for pies with cream or custard fillings or meringue toppings.

■ Unbaked pie dough can be frozen in bulk for later use. Simply flatten the dough into circles, and stack the circles in a freezer bag with waxed paper separating each layer. Bulk pie dough must be thawed before using.

SOLUTIONS TO COMMON BAKING PROBLEMS

PROBLEM	SOLUTION(S)
QUICK BREADS	
BITTER TASTE	Distribute baking soda and baking powder evenly with other dry ingredients.
FAILURE TO RISE	Use fresh baking soda and baking powder.
TOUGH TEXTURE, TUNNELS, PEAKED TOPS	Avoid overstirring; batter should be lumpy.
RAISINS OR OTHER DRIED FRUIT SINK TO BOTTOM OF LOAF	Toss fruit lightly with flour before adding to batter.
LOPSIDED BISCUITS	Press floured cutter straight down into dough and do not twist.
YEAST BREADS	
BREAD IS HEAVY AND COMPACT	Liquid used to dissolve yeast may have been too hot or too cold; check temperature with a thermometer.
	Too much flour was added during kneading; do not exceed maximum amount called for in recipe.
BREAD IS CRUMBLY	Dough has risen too much. Let rise just until double for first rising and until nearly double for second rising.
CRUST IS TOO THICK	Oven temperature may be too low; use oven thermometer to check for accuracy.
BREAD HAS LARGE HOLES	Press or punch air bubbles out of dough thoroughly before shaping into loaf.
COOKIES	
UNEVEN BROWNING	Bake on only one rack at a time; use cookie sheets with little or no sides.
COOKIES SPREAD TOO MUCH	Allow cookie sheets to cool between batches before reusing.
CUT-OUT COOKIES ARE TOUGH	Save dough scraps to reroll all at once; handle dough as little as possible.
	Use just enough flour on board to prevent sticking.

PROBLEM	SOLUTION(S)
CAKES	
CAKES FALL IN MIDDLE	Avoid overbeating—too much air is incorporated into batter.
	Avoid opening oven door before cake sets.
CAKE PEAKS IN CENTER	Oven temperature may be too high causing cake to rise too quickly; use oven thermometer to check for accuracy.
CAKE IS DRY	Avoid overbeating egg whites.
	Avoid overbaking. Check cake for doneness at lower end of baking time range.
PIE CRUSTS	
PASTRY IS CRUMBLY	Add water, one teaspoon at a time.
	Add water gradually, stirring lightly after each addition.
PASTRY IS TOUGH	Avoid overworking dough; toss flour mixture and water together just until evenly moistened.
	Handle dough as little as possible.
CRUST SHRINKS EXCESSIVELY	Roll pastry from the center outward; roll to an even thickness.
	Avoid stretching pastry when transferring from rolling surface to pie plate.

WHEN YOU RUN OUT, SUBSTITUTE

If you don't have:	Use:
1 teaspoon baking powder	¼ teaspoon baking soda plus ½ teaspoon cream of tartar
½ cup firmly packed brown sugar	½ cup sugar mixed with 2 tablespoons molasses
1 cup buttermilk	1 tablespoon lemon juice or vinegar plus milk to equal 1 cup (Stir; let mixture stand 5 minutes.)
1 ounce (1 square) unsweetened baking chocolate	3 tablespoons unsweetened cocoa plus 1 tablespoon shortening
3 ounces (3 squares) semisweet baking chocolate	3 ounces (½ cup) semisweet chocolate morsels
½ cup corn syrup	½ cup granulated sugar plus 2 tablespoons liquid
1 tablespoon cornstarch	2 tablespoons all-purpose flour or 4 teaspoons quick-cooking tapioca
1 cup sweetened whipped cream	4½ ounces frozen whipped topping, thawed
1 cup heavy cream (for baking, not whipping)	¾ cup whole milk plus ¼ cup butter
1 whole egg	2 egg yolks plus 1 tablespoon water
1 cup cake flour	1 cup minus 2 tablespoons all-purpose flour
1 cup honey	1¼ cups granulated sugar plus ¼ cup water
1 teaspoon freshly grated orange or lemon peel	½ teaspoon dried peel
1 teaspoon apple or pumpkin pie spice	Combine: ½ teaspoon cinnamon, ¼ teaspoon nutmeg, ⅛ teaspoon each allspice and cardamom
1 package active dry yeast	1 packed tablespoon compressed yeast

Maintenance and Repair

A nicely maintained home, lawn, and garden take a lot of work. Many potential problems can be avoided with a scheduled maintenance program. However, it is a fact of life that things break down and require repair. The more you're prepared to fix problems on your own, the less expensive they are. The following pages contain a lot of information on how to take good care of your home and property and how to do common repairs.

BASIC TOOLS AND SUPPLIES

You don't need expensive power tools or even a full workshop of hand tools for many home repair and maintenance chores. To tackle most minor home repairs, you'll need an electric drill and between 12 and 15 hand tools.

When selecting tools, make quality a priority. Metal parts should be smooth and shiny and the tool should be well balanced. While you'll pay more for quality equipment, you'll have tools that are safer and more durable.

CHISELS
- **Wood chisel.** Wood chisels are used to remove wood and cut mortises.
- **Cold chisel.** Cold chisels are used to cut metal, such as bolts, and other hard materials, like brick or concrete.

MEASURING AND MARKING TOOLS

■ **Flexible measuring tape.** A measuring tape that is at least 1 inch wide and 25 feet long is suitable for most home uses.

■ **Folding rule.** Use the folding rule to measure straight edges and hard-to-reach areas.

■ **Level.** A level is used for finding correct horizontal and vertical readings when installing cabinets, appliances, or hanging wallpaper. A 30-inch level is adequate for most home repairs.

■ **Chalk.** Use chalk to mark a straight line over long distances.

HANDSAWS

■ **Crosscut saw.** A crosscut saw cuts across the grain of wood. A crosscut saw has five to ten (or more) teeth per inch to produce a smooth cut in the wood. It is used for plywood and hardboard panels and for cutting miters (angles).

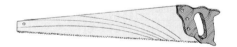

■ **Hacksaw.** A hacksaw is used to cut metal, plastic, and pipe.

For woodworking projects, you may also want a ripsaw, used to cut along the grain of the wood; a backsaw, used to make miter cuts and for trimming molding; a drywall saw, used to cut openings for pipes and electrical boxes; and a coping saw, which has thin, replaceable blades to be used for multiple projects.

HAMMERS

■ **Claw hammer.** A 16-ounce curved claw hammer with a cushioned grip is adequate for most home repairs.

A rubber mallet comes in handy when you're trying to unstick painted windows or have to do light hammering on surfaces that can be damaged. Other specialty hammers include a ball-peen hammer for metal work and a mason's hammer for brick and concrete projects.

SCREWDRIVERS

Every toolbox should have one set of high-quality screwdrivers. There are many types of screwdrivers, which vary depending on the screw head each is designed to fit. Following are the most popular screw heads:

■ **Standard head.** Also known as flat, slotted, or straight screwdriver. Make sure the tip is the correct width and thickness to snugly fit the screw head slot.

■ **Phillips head.** Also called cross or X-head screwdrivers, Phillips heads fit into a cross-shape recess in the screw or bolt head.

■ **Torx head.** Torx head (or similar designs called Robertson) screwdrivers fit into a hexagonal or square hole, which allows more torque for tightening or loosening the fastener.

WRENCHES

■ **Adjustable wrench** (6 to 10 inches long). This type of wrench adjusts to various widths to accommodate various bolt head and nut sizes.

For plumbing repairs, you may need a pipe wrench. To work with appliances, cars, and machinery, you'll need various sizes of open-end and box-end (or combination) wrenches, which must precisely fit on the nut or bolt. An Allen or hex-key wrench is necessary when tightening screws with Allen-type heads.

POWER TOOLS

■ **Electric drill.** A ⅜-inch drill is good for most projects. For flexibility, a cordless, reversible, variable-speed drill is helpful.

■ **Electric sander.** An orbital sander is the handiest for most small projects.

For woodworking projects, you'll want a circular saw and a saber saw, sometimes called a jigsaw. A circular saw, the power version of a crosscut saw or ripsaw, can be mounted and used as a small table saw. A saber saw, the power version of a keyhole and coping saw, can hold different blades and cut many materials, such as wood, plastic, and metal.

OTHER TOOLS

■ **Clamps.** These come in various sizes to hold materials together; start with several sizes of C-clamps and a set of bar clamps.

■ **Planes.** A jack plane is used to remove excess wood and bring the surface of the wood to trueness and smoothness; a smoothing plane is used to bring wood to a final finish. A block plane can do both, plus it is used to smooth and cut the end grain of wood.

■ **Router.** This is the power equivalent of chisels, files, planes, and saws and can cut dados, mortise joints, and step moldings. You can also use a router to trim plastic and laminate.

STORING AND MAINTAINING TOOLS

■ To protect tools, store them so they aren't subjected to moisture. Keep a thin coating of oil on metal parts, and wrap them in plastic wrap, or keep carpenter's chalk, which absorbs moisture, in the toolbox.

DO-IT-YOURSELF COATING FOR TOOLS

To make a rust-preventive coating for tools, outdoor furniture, and other metal objects, combine ¼ cup lanolin and 1 cup petroleum jelly in a double boiler over low heat. Stir until the mixture melts and blends completely, then remove from heat and pour into a clean jar, letting the mixture partially cool. Use the mixture while it's still warm, and don't wipe it off—just let it dry on the object. If there's any extra, cover the jar tightly, and rewarm the mixture before you use it again.

SELECTING NAILS

The easiest way to fasten two pieces of wood together is with nails, which are manufactured in a wide variety of shapes, sizes, and metals. Most commonly, nails are made of steel, but other types—aluminum, brass, nickel, bronze, copper, and stainless steel—are available for use where corrosion could occur. In addition, nails are manufactured with coatings—galvanized, blued, or cemented—to prevent rusting and to increase their holding power.

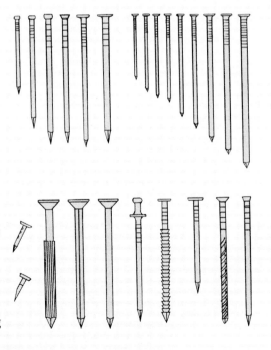

Nail size is designated by penny size, originally the price per hundred nails. Penny size, almost always referred to as "d," ranges from 2 penny, or 2d (1 inch long), to 60 penny, or 60d (6 inches long). Nails shorter than 1 inch are called brads; nails longer than 6 inches are called spikes.

The length of the nail is crucial in repair jobs. At least two-thirds of the nail should be driven into the underlying material.

SELECTING SCREWS

Screws provide more strength and holding power than nails. Like nails, screws are available with different coatings to deter rust. They are manufactured with four basic heads and different kinds of slots. Flat-head screws are almost always countersunk into the material being fastened so that the head of the screw is flush with the surface. Oval-head screws are partially countersunk, with about half the screw head above the surface. Round-head screws are not countersunk; the entire screw head lies above the surface. Filister-head screws are raised above the surface on a flat base to keep the screwdriver from damaging the surface as the screw is tightened.

Most screws have slot heads and are driven with slotted, or standard, screwdrivers. Phillips-head screws have crossed slots and are driven with Phillips screwdrivers. Screws are meas-ured in both length and diameter at the shank, which is designated by gauge number from 0 to 24. Length is measured in inches. At least half the length of the screw should extend into the base material.

Tip: To prevent screws from splitting the material, pilot holes must be made with a drill before the screws are driven.

For most home repair purposes, wood screws will suffice. Sheet metal screws, machine screws, and lag screws also come in various types. If you're trying to replace one of these screws, take an old screw with you to the hardware store.

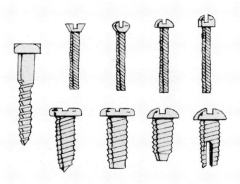

- A piece of garden hose slit open is handy for protecting the teeth of a handsaw between projects.

- If you hang tools on pegboard walls, outline each tool with an artist's brush so you'll know at a glance where each tool goes.

- Keep screwdrivers handy—slide the blades through the mesh in plastic berry baskets nailed to the shop wall.

- To retard moisture and rust, keep mothballs with your tools.

- Paint all tool handles with an unusual, bright color, or wrap reflective tape around them so they'll be easy to identify.

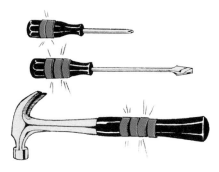

■ Rags will last longer if they're stored in an airtight container to keep them from drying out. Airtight storage also prevents spontaneous combustion, which can be very dangerous.

■ To sharpen shop scissors, use them to slice several pieces of sandpaper.

■ Clean tools without expensive cleaners. Pour a small amount of kerosene on the metal part of a tool and rub vigorously with a soap-filled steel-wool pad. Then wad a piece of aluminum foil into a ball and rub it on the surface. Wipe away the residue with newspaper, and coat the tool lightly with olive oil before storing. Caution: Kerosene is flammable; do not pour it or use it near an open flame.

■ Don't take a chance of hitting a thumb or finger when hammering a small brad, tack, or nail. Slip the fastener between the teeth of a pocket comb; the comb holds the nail while you hold the comb.

TIME-SAVERS

■ Wipe a thin coat of shaving cream on your hands before starting a messy task.

■ Pick up spilled nails, screws, or tacks with a magnet covered with a paper towel. When the spilled items are attracted toward the magnet, gather the towel corners over the pieces and then pull the "bag" away from the magnet.

■ Loosen a stubborn screw, bolt, or nut from a metal surface with a shot of penetrating oil. (Don't use this with a wood surface—it could absorb the oil.) If you don't have oil, use hydrogen peroxide, white vinegar, kerosene, or household ammonia. Caution: Kerosene is flammable; do not pour it or use it near an open flame.

■ Many rusted bolts can easily be worked loose by pouring a carbonated beverage directly on them.

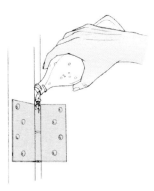

■ If a bolt repeatedly loosens due to vibrations, coat the threads with fingernail polish and reinsert it; it won't loosen again.

■ To fix a too-large screw hole, make a plug out of a cotton ball by soaking it in white glue and stuffing it into the hole. Let dry, then reinsert the screw.

■ You can also repair an enlarged screw hole by making a paste of sawdust and white glue. Fill the hole, let the glue dry, then reinsert the screw.

EXTERIOR MAINTENANCE

DOWNSPOUTS, FLASHING, AND GUTTERS

■ Inspect your gutters frequently. They should be cleaned in the autumn after all leaves have fallen and again in the spring. If you have heavy rains and lots of trees in your area, you'll want to clean them more frequently.

■ Clean gutters by hand using a whisk broom to remove leaves. Then use your garden hose to flush out the debris remnants. Observe the flow of water, and check for low spots or improper pitch.

■ When cleaning gutters, inspect each hanger for bent straps and

PATCHING HOLES IN GUTTERS

1. Remove all rust and loose metal by cleaning the area with a wire brush. Cover the bad spot with paint thinner.

2. Cut a patch from wire window screen material. The patch must be large enough to cover the hole and extend about ½ inch beyond it.

3. Coat the area around the hole with asphalt roofing cement.

4. Put the patch down over the cement, and press it in place.

5. Brush the cement over the screen.

6. When the first coat sets, cover it again with cement.

7. Tiny holes can be patched without the screen; the cement will fill in by itself, but you will have to apply several coats.

popped nails. If the house has a fascia or board trim, check the gutter's alignment with it. The gutter should rest firmly against the fascia for maximum support.

■ Use roof cement to patch any thin spots or gaps along a flashing joint, at a chimney, or along a valley.

■ Check the nails or screws in the straps holding the downspout to your house. These can work loose with use or age.

■ To keep downspouts clear, flush them frequently with a garden hose. If necessary, remove stubborn clogs by forcing the running hose down the downspout.

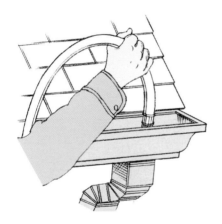

■ For best wear and protection, paint the outside of gutters with exterior house paint, and coat the insides with asphalt roofing paint, which will make them resistant to rust. When painting galvanized gutters, you'll first need to neutralize the zinc coating. If you don't, the paint will quickly peel. While commercial washes are available, an inexpensive and effective home remedy is to mix a 50/50 solution of warm water and white vinegar. Apply at least three coats of this solution to the gutters, allowing for drying time between coats, and rinse thoroughly before painting.

GATES AND FENCES

■ Use pressure-treated lumber for posts that will be sunk in the ground. While more costly, they will last many years.

■ Don't procrastinate on fence repairs; one weak post can bring down the entire fence.

■ Shore up a broken fence rail with a 2×4 scrap, securing it with galvanized nails.

■ Steady a wobbly post by driving a pair of stakes into the ground on either side of the post and bolting them down. You can also soak the ground with water, and then tamp the soil around the post hole.

■ Use galvanized steel T-braces, available at most hardware stores, to repair a rail. Level the rail, drill pilot holes into the post and rail, and secure with galvanized screws. Caulk the joint, then paint the braces to match the fences.

■ If a gate sags or won't close properly, replace its hinges with heavier ones. Make sure to use galvanized screws.

■ A slight sag in a gate can sometimes be repaired by shimming under the bottom hinge. Prop up the gate in the open position, remove screws from the post side of the hinge, and cut a thin piece of cedar shake to fit into the hinge mortise. Reattach the hinge by driving longer screws through the shim.

DECKS

■ Inspect your deck frequently for popped nails and loose railings or boards. Remove and replace any nails that have popped with coated screws, and immediately repair or replace loose railings to avoid hazards.

■ Use a mild household detergent in water to clean everyday dirt from a wood deck. Rinse thoroughly.

■ To remove stains caused by tree sap, use mineral spirits and rinse thoroughly.

■ To remove mildew, use a solution of 1 cup bleach to 1 gallon warm water. Flush the area with clear water, and allow it to dry.

■ Deck stains make routine cleanup much easier and preserve the life of the wood. Apply stains especially formulated for decks immediately over new wood, except for pressure-treated lumber, which should age for six months before being stained. The deck will benefit from a new coat of stain every one to two years. Follow the manufacturer's instructions for applying the stain. If your deck has been painted, you will have to remove the paint before a stain can be applied.

■ Avoid applying clear finishes, such as varnish or shellac, to wood decks. They don't withstand sun and moisture, and they must be removed if they start to peel.

OUTDOOR FURNISHINGS

■ Drilling holes in solid metal patio furniture will allow rainwater to drain. If water is allowed to collect, the furniture will rust prematurely.

- Waxing the ends and bottoms of wooden patio furniture legs helps protect against moisture that might be absorbed from standing rainwater.

- The metal edges of tubular patio chairs won't be able to cut through the rubber cups on the leg bottoms if metal washers are first inserted in the protective cups.

- Clean awnings in the direction of the seam, not against it, to prevent seam weakening.

ROOFS

The best way to preserve your roof is to inspect it annually for wear and make repairs as soon as possible. Once you have a leak, however, you have to know where it's coming from—the water may often travel before dripping into a room below.

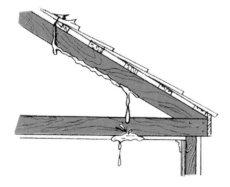

If there's an unfinished attic below a leaky roof, finding a leak isn't too difficult. Climb into this space, and look around with a flashlight—it's easier to see a leak in the semidark, so don't turn on a light.

When you find the leak, outline the wet area with chalk. If possible, push a piece of wire up through the leaky spot, so that it protrudes from the roof. This makes it easier to find the leak when you're working outside.

PITCHED ROOFS

- It's not necessary to replace a cracked shingle if all the pieces are still in place. Slide a piece of roofing felt or roll roofing under the shingle until it is behind the cracks. Drill holes for the new nails needed, then drive in the nails. Cover the nail heads with roof cement.

- When repairing shingles, use synthetic or fiber-impregnated cement.

- For emergency repair of a shingle, cut a patch to fit from a piece of sheet metal and slip it well under the shingle above the one you're repairing. Apply a coat of roof cement to the bottom of the patch, and tack it in place. Cover the tack heads with cement. When you return to make a more permanent repair, pry up the patch.

FLAT ROOFS

- A leak in a flat roof may be seen under the damaged spot, making the damage to the roof easy to see. But built-up roof layers often cause water to migrate laterally rather than straight down.

WORKING SAFELY WITH LADDERS

- Always open a stepladder to its fullest position, lock the spreader braces on each side in place, and pull down the bucket shelf.
- Make sure your ladder is in good condition. Replace any missing or broken rungs or discard the ladder.

- To keep your hands free while you're making repairs, make a holster for the nails and screws you'll need. Take a paper cup and make two vertical slits in it about 1 inch apart; the slits should be wide enough to slip your belt through.
- To avoid marring a paint job when leaning a ladder against siding, cover the top ends of the ladder with heavy woolen socks.
- When using an aluminum ladder, watch out for power lines: Aluminum conducts electricity.

- When positioning a ladder against a house or tree, it is safest to position it so that the distance from the base of the ladder to the house or tree is $\frac{1}{4}$ of the ladder's extended length. Otherwise the ladder may fall forward or tip backward.
- The best way for a lone worker to raise a ladder is to pin its feet against the base of the house and push the ladder up from the other end, hand over hand, until it is upright.

- Keep your hips within the ladder's rails. Extend the top two rungs higher than the place where you're working.
- Make sure your ladder has firm support at the top. If you place it against a window sash or close to an edge, a slight shift could cause you to fall.

■ Any water pooled in the leak area should be mopped up so that the surface is dry before attempting repairs.

SAFE ROOF REPAIRS

■ Roof repairs should be done on a sunny day when the roof is completely dry. A wet roof is slippery and very dangerous.

■ Adequate safety measures must be taken for any roof repairs. Always use safety ropes.

■ On steep roofs, use a ladder framework to provide secure anchoring.

■ Rubber-soled shoes provide the best traction when working on a roof.

■ The location of power lines should be kept in mind when working on a roof.

WALLS AND SURFACES

BRICK AND CONCRETE

■ To remove white powdery surfaces on brick or concrete, go over them with a stiff brush. Wet the surface with a weak 5 percent solution of muriatic acid and water, leaving it on for 5 minutes. Brush the wall, and rinse it immediately.

■ When you're pouring concrete steps, be sure to use solid objects as fillers; hollow objects buried in concrete—pieces of pipe, for example—have a tendency to float to the surface.

■ A smooth concrete surface is a hazard on outdoor steps. After the concrete has set but is still workable, run a stiff broom across the steps to roughen the surface.

■ When laying a brick patio, start from a corner of the patio near the house and work outward.

■ Laying a dry brick patio is simple. Dig out the area, edge with weather-resistant boards staked into place, and spread out a sand base 2¼ inches deep. Spray the base with water, tamp it down until it's at a 2-inch level, and let it

CAULKING

Caulking is a great way to repair minor holes in walls and joints between different materials. Gaps that measure more than ½ inch wide and ½ inch deep, however, are not good candidates for caulk.

∎ Remove all old caulk before applying new caulk.

∎ To use a caulking gun, pull out the plunger arm to disengage the notches and insert a tube of caulk, base first, so that the nozzle sticks out through the slot at the end of the gun. Turn the plunger arm, and push it in to engage it. Hold the nozzle at a 45-degree angle to the joint you want to fill.

∎ Use a steady movement to caulk. Don't try to smooth by smearing.

∎ Never caulk when the temperature falls below 50°F.

∎ Caulk when painting the house. Apply primer to the seams first, then caulk. Allow the caulk to cure as directed by the manufacturer, then apply a finish coat. Be sure to use a compound that will take paint.

∎ Plug a tube of leftover caulk with a large nail to keep it from drying out.

---

dry. Position the bricks, fitting them tightly and making sure they're level. Pour sand on the bricks, sweep it into the crevices, sprinkle with water, and repeat as necessary to fill any gaps.

∎ Put sand on top of asphalt sealer to prevent the sealer from sticking to your shoes.

∎ Small cracks in blacktop can be patched with sand and liquid blacktop sealer. Pour sand along the crack to fill it partway. Then pour the blacktop sealer into the crack over the sand, which will absorb the sealer quickly. Repeat until the surface is smooth.

SIDING

∎ Cracked, warped, or loose siding should be repaired immediately. Water works its way through such defects into the interior wall where rotting can take place undetected.

∎ If you don't have time for a thorough repair, seal splits with caulking compound and clamp them together by driving nails and clinching them over the boards.

∎ To remove mildew from siding, scrub the surface with a bleach and water solution (1 cup bleach to 1 gallon warm water). Flush the area with clear water, and allow it to dry thoroughly before painting.

- To replace an unstained shake or shingle, take replacement shakes or shingles from an inconspicuous area of the house, reserving the new shingles for that spot. This eliminates an unweathered patch in the repair area.

Interior Maintenance

WORKING SAFELY WITH ELECTRICITY

An electric shock is distressing, hazardous, and often fatal. Understanding the hazards and the precautions required by those hazards are mandatory for safe electrical work.

- Everyone in the family should know how to throw the master switch that cuts off all electrical current to the house.

- If there's a chance of contact between water and electricity, do not wade in water until the master switch has been shut off.

- Never do anything that would compromise the integrity of the conductor insulation, such as stapling an extension cord to a baseboard or to a wall. The staple can cut through the insulation and create a short circuit, which can start a fire.

- Examine all wiring, and discard any cord that has brittle insulation.

- Never work on an electrical circuit that is live or attached to an electrical source. Unplug the circuit, trip the circuit breaker, or unscrew the fuse before you begin.

- You should wait to work on a switched outlet or lighting fixture—even though you've flicked off the switch—until you have also deactivated the circuit.

- You should always assume that an electrical outlet or apparatus is energized until you prove otherwise with a circuit tester or by pulling a fuse or tripping the disconnect plug.

- Insulating your pliers by slipping a length of small-diameter rubber hose on each handle is a necessity when you work with electricity. Wrap other metal parts with electrician's tape. Insulate the shank of a screwdriver by slipping a section of rubber or plastic tubing over it. Be sure to cut the tubing so that it extends from the handle down to the blade.

- Use only equivalent replacement parts. That is, replace a controller with one that has the same function and rating. Don't replace a 10-amp appliance cord with one that is rated for 5 amps.

■ Stand on a dry board or wooden platform when working with a fuse box or a circuit breaker box. Also use a wooden stepladder rather than an aluminum one to minimize the risk of shock when working with electrical wiring.

■ You can save time by determining which circuits activate which outlets in your home; diagram or print the information on a card attached to your circuit breaker or fuse box. When your electricity fails, you'll be able to identify the problem quickly.

FUSES AND CIRCUIT BREAKERS

Fuses and circuit breakers are safety devices built into your electrical system—they prevent overloading of a particular circuit. Without fuses or circuit breakers, if too many appliances are operating on a single circuit, the cable would get extremely hot, melt, and possibly start a fire.

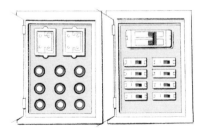

To prevent prolonged electrical overloads, fuses are designed to blow, and circuit breakers are designed to trip. Either device stops the flow of current to the overloaded cable. For example, a 15-ampere fuse should blow when the current passing through it exceeds 15 amperes. A fuse that blows or a circuit that trips is not necessarily faulty; it is doing its job properly, indicating that there is trouble in the circuit. Either there are too many devices plugged in or some malfunctioning device, such as an appliance with an internal short, is connected to the circuit.

A blown fuse must be replaced with a new one, while a tripped circuit breaker must be reset to restore power. Some circuit breakers flip to a neutral position and must be turned off before being turned on. Do not replace a blown fuse or reset a tripped circuit breaker until you have located and eliminated the cause of the trouble.

Caution: Never try to defeat this built-in safety system by replacing a fuse with one of a larger capacity.

HEATING AND COOLING

All climate-control devices or systems have three basic components: a source of warmed or cooled air, a means of distributing the air to the rooms being heated or cooled, and a control used to regulate the system (e.g., thermostat). The sources of warm air, such as a furnace, and cool air, such as an air conditioner, in a house often use the same distribution and control systems. If your house has central air conditioning, cool air probably flows through the

continued on page 190

MONTHLY HOME MAINTENANCE SCHEDULE

The following monthly schedule is a guide that should be adjusted for your climate, your home, and your lifestyle. Notice chores that can be done any time are relegated to the least active months. The important thing about a routine maintenance schedule is to get your chores completed so that minor maintenance won't become a major problem.

JANUARY

■ Change disposable filters on forced-air furnaces; wash permanent filters.

■ Clean dust from behind refrigerator compressor panel and move refrigerator away from wall to clean behind back panel; clean range according to manufacturer's instructions; clean sediment from washing machine hose lines and filters.

■ Check wood ladders for loose rungs; repair or replace any defective ladders.

FEBRUARY

■ Change disposable filters on forced-air furnaces; wash permanent filters.

■ Pour water into the sump pump to make sure that it's in good working order and that the float can rise and fall freely. Clean any sediment

accumulated on the strainer screen.

■ Check cords on appliances and extension cords for wear or fraying. Repair or replace any defective cords.

MARCH

■ Change disposable filters on forced-air furnaces; wash permanent filters.

■ Check window and storm-door screens for holes. Patch or replace the screens.

■ Inspect roof shingles or shakes for damage from winter storms; replace any missing shingles.

■ Inspect siding for popped nails and weathering; check brick for crumbling mortar.

APRIL

■ Change disposable filters on forced-air furnaces; wash permanent filters.

■ If needed, paint or stain the exterior of your home.

■ Wash windows and put up screens.

■ Change batteries in smoke alarms on the weekend that daylight saving time begins.

■ Check the exterior of your home for insect infestations.

■ Turn on outside faucets after the threat of a hard freeze has passed.

MAY

- Inspect outdoor furniture and barbecue for wear; make necessary repairs.
- Check deck, patio, walkway, and driveway for split wood or cracks.

JUNE

- Call a professional service person to inspect and adjust the central air conditioning. Install room air conditioners.

JULY

- Flush the hot water tank to remove accumulated sediment. (Be sure to shut off power to the water heater.) Follow the manufacturer's instructions for draining.

AUGUST

- Check the exterior for signs of weathering and to see if you need to make time to touch up peeling paint when cooler weather arrives.
- Patch any cracks in concrete sidewalks or driveways. Fill any cracks in asphalt drives.
- Improve drainage around your home to accommodate the expansion of wet soil when it freezes.

SEPTEMBER

- Have your furnace and chimney cleaned.
- Inspect the roof for any problems. If you have sky-lights, make sure to check that the flashing is intact.
- Store outdoor furniture.

OCTOBER

- Change disposable filters on forced-air furnaces; wash permanent filters.
- Change batteries in smoke alarms on the weekend that daylight saving time ends.
- Remove or cover window air conditioners.
- Check thermostat.
- Remove and clean screens before storing them for the winter.

NOVEMBER

- Change disposable filters on forced-air furnaces; wash permanent filters.
- Clean gutters and down-spouts.
- Put up storm windows.
- Put weatherstripping around windows and doors.
- Empty gas-power lawn mowers. Follow manufacturer's instructions for cleaning lawn mowers and sharpening blades.

DECEMBER

- Change disposable filters on forced-air furnaces; wash permanent filters.
- Make sure your electrical system is operating well before using holiday lights.

EMERGENCY BLACKOUT KIT

■ Candles or oil lamps and matches for area lighting

■ Flashlight, battery lantern, or other auxiliary light source

■ Correct and up-to-date circuit directory posted on main entrance panel door

■ Tool kit with appropriate tools for making electrical repairs

■ Circuit tester, preferably the voltage-readout type

■ Two replacement plug fuses of each amperage rating in use, preferably Type S

■ Four replacement cartridge fuses of each amperage rating in use

■ One replacement pull circuit breaker of a rating equal to the smallest size in use or one of each size in use

■ One replacement double-pull circuit breaker of each amperage rating in use

■ Selection of lightbulbs

■ One replacement duplex receptacle to match existing units

■ One replacement single-pole switch to match existing units

■ One replacement three-way or other special switches to match existing units

■ Wirenuts and electrician's tape

continued from page 187

same ducts that heat does and is regulated by the same thermostat. When a heating or cooling system malfunctions, any of these three basic components may be causing the problem.

DISTRIBUTION SYSTEMS

■ **Forced-air systems.** A forced-air system distributes the heat produced by the furnace or the coolness produced by a central air conditioner through an electrically powered fan, called a blower, which forces the air through a system of metal ducts to the rooms in your home. As the warm air from the furnace flows into the rooms, colder air in the rooms flows down through another set of ducts, called the cold air return system, to the furnace to be warmed. This system is adjustable: You can increase or decrease the amount of air flowing through your home. Central air conditioning systems use the same forced-air system, including the blower, to distribute cool air to the rooms and to bring warmer air back to be cooled.

■ **Gravity systems.** Gravity systems are based on the principle that hot air rises and cold air settles; they cannot be used to distribute cool air from an air conditioner. In a gravity system, the furnace is located near or below the floor. Warmed air rises and flows through ducts to registers in the floors throughout the house.

■ **Radiant systems.** Radiant systems function by warming the walls, floors, or ceilings of rooms, or, more commonly, by warming radiators in the rooms. These objects then warm the air in the room. Radiant systems cannot be used to distribute cool air from an air conditioner.

BASIC MAINTENANCE PROCEDURES

■ Make sure the unit is receiving power. Look for blown fuses or tripped circuit breakers at the main service panel. Some furnaces have a separate power entrance, usually located at a different panel near the main entrance panel. Some furnaces have fuses mounted in or on the unit.

■ If the unit has a reset button (marked RESET and located near the motor housing), wait 30 minutes to let the motor cool, and then press the button. If the unit still doesn't start, wait 30 minutes and press the reset button again.

■ Check to make sure the thermostat is properly set. If necessary, raise (or for an air conditioner, lower) the setting 5°.

TROUBLESHOOTING DOORBELLS AND CHIMES

If a doorbell or chime does not ring, follow these steps to determine which parts, if any, should be replaced:

1. Test the button. Remove the button, and touch the two wires together. If the bell rings, the button is defective.

2. Test the bell. Detach the wires at the bell or chime, and connect them to a spare bell. If the substitute bell rings when the doorbell button is pressed, the present bell is defective.

3. Connect the test bell to the transformer, and press the doorbell button. If the bell does not ring, the transformer is defective.

4. If the transformer is not receiving power, check to see that the circuit is turned on. Check for a loose connection at the transformer. Then trace and check all wiring to detect a break in the circuit. Replace the faulty wiring segment if the circuit is broken.

■ If the unit uses gas, check to make sure the gas supply is turned on and the pilot light is lit. If the unit uses oil, check to make sure there is an adequate supply of oil.

■ Clean or replace furnace filters at the beginning of the heating season and when necessary throughout the season (monthly or every other month). Use a new filter of exactly the same kind, material, and size as the old filter.

■ Clean permanent filters according to the manufacturer's instructions.

COOLING SYSTEMS

A professional service person should be called for any maintenance. There are some cleaning procedures, however, that will help your system function properly:

■ The condenser is located outside the house, where it accumulates dirt and dust, which need to be removed periodically. Cut away grass, weeds, or vines that could obstruct the flow of air to the condenser unit.

■ Clean the condenser with coil cleaner, available at refrigerator supply stores. Instructions for use are included.

■ Clean the fins on the condenser with a soft brush to remove accumulated dirt. You may have to remove a protective grille to reach them. Do not clean the fins with water, which could turn the dirt into mud and compact it between the fins. Be careful when cleaning the fins; they're made of light-gauge aluminum and are easily damaged. If the fins are bent,

straighten them with a fin comb, sold at most appliance parts stores.

■ Check the concrete pad under the condenser to make sure it's level; set a carpenter's level front to back and side to side on top of the unit. If the pad has settled, lift the pad with a pry bar or a piece of 2×4, then force gravel or rocks under the concrete to level it.

■ Protect condensers during the fall and winter with a condenser cover made to fit the shape of the unit or with heavy plastic sheeting, secured with sturdy cord.

SAFETY PROCEDURES

■ Before doing any work on any type of heating or cooling system, make sure all power to the system is turned off. At the main electrical entrance panel, remove the fuse or trip the circuit breaker that controls the power to the unit. If you're not sure which circuit that is, remove the main fuse or trip the main circuit breaker to cut off all power to the house. Some furnaces have a separate power entrance, usually at a different panel near the main entrance panel. If a separate panel is present, remove the fuse or trip the circuit breaker there.

■ If the fuse blows or the circuit trips repeatedly when the furnace or air conditioner turns on, there is a problem in the electrical system. Do not try to fix the furnace. Call a professional service person.

■ If the unit uses gas and there is a smell of gas in your home, do not try to shut off the gas or turn any lights on or off. Get out of the house, leaving the door open, and go to a telephone; call the gas company or the fire department immediately to report a leak. Do not reenter your home.

IMPROVING HEATING AND COOLING EFFICIENCY

■ Protect the thermostat from anything that would cause it to give a false reading. If the thermostat is in a draft, on a cold outside wall, or too close to a register, its accuracy will be compromised.

■ If you won't be home for a few days, turn the thermostat to its lowest setting. If there's no danger of pipes freezing or other household items being damaged, turn the heating system off completely.

■ If your home has rooms that are seldom or never used, close the vents in these rooms and shut the doors most of the time. Make sure the rooms get enough heat to prevent mildew from growing.

■ Avoid constant thermostat adjustments, as they can waste fuel.

■ One heating adjustment you should make, however, is a reduction in the thermostat setting before you go to bed every night. Cutting back for several hours can make a big difference in fuel consumption.

■ Aim the vents of room air conditioners upward for better air circulation; cold air naturally settles downward. On central air conditioning systems, adjust the registers so the air is blowing up.

■ If you have room air conditioners, close all heating system vents so the cool air isn't wasted.

PLUMBING

Plumbing actually refers to two complementary but entirely separate systems in your home—one system brings fresh water in and the other system takes wastewater out. Any cross-connection of these systems could jeopardize your water supply.

All water that enters your home is cold; it is piped through the cold-water trunk lines directly to all fixtures and appliances that use unheated water; offshoots to individual fixtures are called branches. Pipes that run vertically, extending upward, are called risers. One pipe

continued on page 196

TROUBLESHOOTING THE TOILET

Problem	Possible Cause	Solution
Water in tank runs constantly	1. Float ball or rod misaligned.	1. Bend float rod carefully to move ball so that it will not rub against side of tank.
	2. Float ball contains water.	2. Empty or replace float ball.
	3. Float ball not rising high enough.	3. Carefully bend float rod down but only slightly.
	4. Tank ball not seating properly at bottom of tank.	4. Remove any corrosion from lip of valve seat. Replace tank ball, if worn. Adjust lift wire and guide.
	5. Ballcock valve does not shut off water.	5. Replace washers in ballcock assembly or, if necessary, replace entire assembly.
Toilet does not flush or flushes inadequately	1. Drain is clogged.	1. Remove blockage in drain.
	2. Not enough water in tank.	2. Raise water level in tank by bending float rod up slightly.
	3. Tank ball falls before enough water leaves tank.	3. Move guide up so tank ball can rise higher.
	4. Leak where tank joins toilet bowl.	4. Tighten nuts on spud pipe; replace spud washers, if necessary.
	5. Ports around bowl rim clogged.	5. Ream out residue from ports.
Tank whines while filling	1. Ballcock valve not operating properly.	1. Replace washers or install new ballcock assembly.

Problem	Possible Cause	Solution
Tank whines while filling (cont.)	2. Water supply is restricted.	2. Check shutoff to make sure it's completely open. Check for scale or corrosion at entry into tank and on valve.
Moisture around fixture	1. Condensation.	1. Install foam liner, tank cover, drip catcher, or temperature valve.
	2. Leak at flange wax seal.	2. Remove toilet and install new wax ring seal.
	3. Leak at bowl-tank connection.	3. Tighten spud pipe nuts; replace worn spud washers, if necessary.
	4. Leak at water inlet connection.	4. Tighten locknut and coupling nut; replace washers and gasket, if necessary.
	5. Crack in bowl or tank.	5. Replace bowl, tank, or entire fixture.

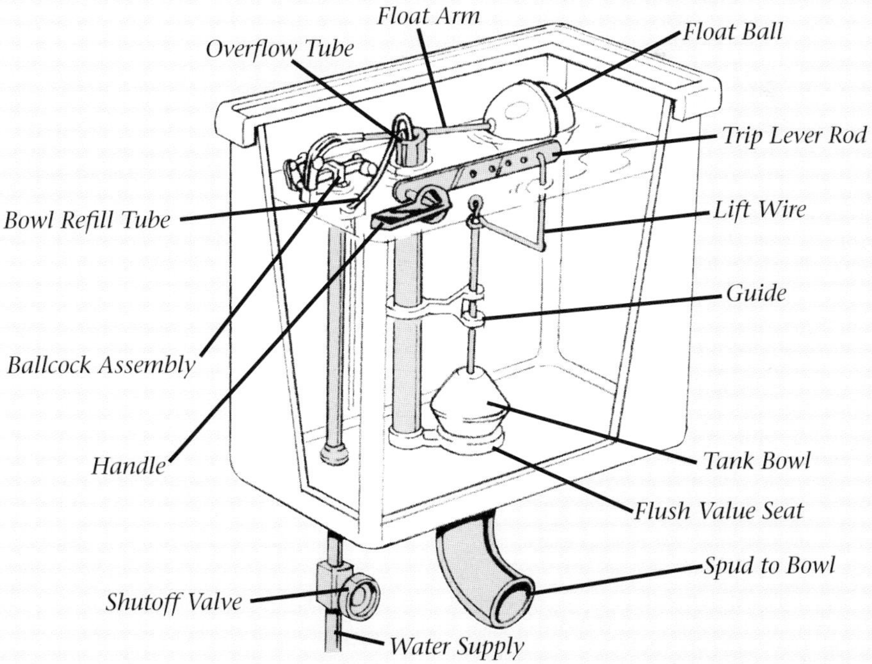

Float Arm

Overflow Tube

Float Ball

Trip Lever Rod

Bowl Refill Tube

Lift Wire

Guide

Ballcock Assembly

Handle

Tank Bowl

Flush Value Seat

Spud to Bowl

Shutoff Valve

Water Supply

continued from page 193

carries water to your water heater, while a hot water line from the water heater carries water to all the fixtures and appliances that require hot water.

PLUMBING ESSENTIALS

■ Some fixtures have individual supply shutoff valves so you do not need to close the main shutoff to repair them. It's a good idea to make sure everyone in the family knows the location of the main

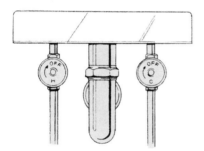

shutoff valve in your house, as well as how to use it. This could prevent flooding and minimize damage if a pipe bursts.

■ Turn off the water supply before attempting any repair.

■ Check with your local plumbing code official before you add or change any pipe in your house.

DRAINS

■ For better suction when plunging a clogged drain, cover the rubber cap of the plunger with water and plug the fixture's other openings with wet rags.

■ Unclog a moderately clogged drain by pouring ½ cup baking soda followed by ½ cup vinegar into the drain. Caution: The two ingredients interact with foaming and fumes, so replace the drain cover loosely. Flush after 3 hours.

■ Fix greasy drains with this treatment: Pour in ½ cup salt and ½ cup baking soda, followed by a teapot of boiling water. Allow to sit overnight, if possible.

FAUCETS

■ If a dripping faucet is getting on your nerves before the plumber arrives or before you have time to fix it yourself, tie a 2-foot-long string around the nozzle, and drop the string's end into the drain. As the faucet drips, the drops will run silently down the string.

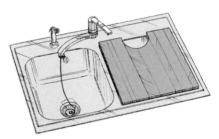

■ You can avoid having the teeth of a wrench scar a plumbing fixture during installation by first wrapping the fixture with a double coating of plastic electrical tape.

PIPES

■ The easiest way to thaw a pipe is to wrap and secure a heavy towel or a burlap bag around it to concentrate and hold heat against it. Pour the hottest water you can obtain over the towel. Be careful because most of the water will run off the towel onto you or the floor. A properly positioned pan or bucket can save you a scalding mess.

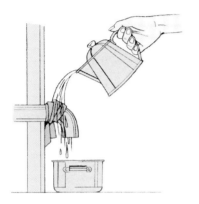

■ If a water pipe is banging against a wall and causing noise, silence it by wedging the pipe off the wall with a wood block and clamping the pipe to the wedge with a strap.

■ A good way to clean copper pipe before sweat-soldering is to wrap a strip of emery cloth around the pipe and move it back and forth as if you were buffing a shoe.

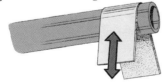

■ Most amateur plumbers are so proud of their first sweat-soldered joints that they immediately turn on the water. Allow the joint to cool a bit because the sudden

cooling effect of rushing water could weaken the joint and cause it to crack.

■ If a pipe springs a leak, you should consider replacing an entire section rather than just patching the leak. A pipe that is compromised to the point of leaking in one place will often start leaking in other places.

■ Drainpipes must be pitched so that the downward flow will carry out the waste. The maximum degree of pitch is ¼ inch per foot, though ⅟₁₆ to ⅛ inch is better.

VALVES

■ To keep the water shutoff valve in good working order, you should make a habit of turning it off and then on again twice a year.

■ When shutting down your water system, you should remember to open all the faucets and outdoor hose spigots to drain. Flush the toilet, and sponge out remaining water from the tank. Drain water out of fixture traps.

DOORS

■ For better control when lifting a door off its hinges, remove the bottom pin first. When replacing a door on its hinges, insert the top pin first.

■ If hinge screws on a door are loose because the holes have become enlarged, try using longer screws.

Or fill the holes with pieces of wood toothpick dipped in glue. When the glue dries, reinsert the screws.

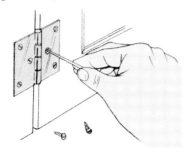

■ Cardboard shields will protect the finish on a door when you clean and polish door hardware. Fit the shields around the metal parts, holding them in place with masking tape.

■ If you need to plane the bottom of a door because it scrapes the threshold or the floor, you can do so without removing the door. Place sandpaper on the threshold or floor, then move the door back and forth over this abrasive surface.

■ To remove ¼ inch or more from a door, score with a utility knife to prevent chipping and finish with a circular saw.

■ Before you replace a door that you have planed, seal the planed edges. If you don't, the door will swell and stick again.

FLOORS

■ If you have a squeaky hardwood floor under tile or carpet, you may be able to eliminate the squeak without removing the floor covering. Try to reset loose boards by pounding a hammer on a block of scrap wood in the area over the squeaky boards. The pressure may force loose nails back into place.

■ To silence squeaky hardwood floors, try using talcum powder as a dry lubricant. Sprinkle powder over the offending areas, and sweep it back and forth until it filters down between the cracks.

■ Fill dents in a hardwood floor with clear nail polish or shellac. Because the floor's color will show through, the dents will not be apparent.

FLOOR COVERINGS

■ Sometimes bulges or curled seams in a linoleum or vinyl floor can be flattened by placing aluminum foil over them and "ironing" them with your steam iron. (The heat will soften and reactivate the adhesive.) Position weights, such as stacks of books, over treated areas to keep them flat until the adhesive cools and hardens.

■ To remove a resilient floor tile for replacement, lay a piece of aluminum foil on it, pressing down with an ordinary iron set at medium. The iron's heat will soften the mastic, and you can easily pry up the tile with a putty knife.

■ Make a perfect floor patch from scrap flooring by placing the scrap piece over the damaged area so that it overlaps. Tape it to hold it in place. Cut through both layers at the same time to make a patch that is an exact duplicate.

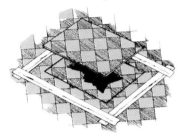

■ To patch a small hole in a resilient floor, take a scrap of the flooring and grate it with a food grater. Mix the resulting dust with clear nail polish, and plug the hole.

■ Laying resilient floor tile is easier if the room temperature is at least 70°F before you start because tile is more pliable at higher temperatures. Try to keep the room temperature at the same level for about a week after laying the tiles, and then wait at least a week before washing the floor.

REPAIRING A BURN HOLE IN CARPET

If a burn goes all the way to the backing but the backing isn't burned, the carpet can be repaired by removing the charred fibers and inserting new ones.

■ Carefully cut out the burned fibers, then pull the stubs out of the backing with tweezers. Clean out the entire burn area so that the woven backing is exposed in the hole.

■ To fill the hole, ravel fibers from the edge of a scrap piece of carpet; you'll need enough individual tufts of yarn to place one tuft in each opening in the backing. If you don't have a scrap piece, use tufts from an inconspicuous area of the carpet, such as the back of a closet.

■ Apply a little latex adhesive to the exposed backing.

■ Use a carpet tuft-setting tool to insert the new fibers. Fold each fiber in half to form a V, and place the folded tuft into the tuft-setter. Set the tip of the tuft-setter into the opening on the backing, and strike the handle lightly with a hammer. When you lift the tuft-setter, the fiber will stay in the carpet backing.

■ Set fibers across the entire burn area, one at a time. The repair area should match the rest of the carpet in density and depth; if a tuft doesn't match in height, you can adjust it by pulling it up a little with tweezers. You can also tap it down again with the tuft-setter.

■ When the hole is completely filled, cut any protruding fibers flush with the rest of the pile.

ADHESIVES

Follow the manufacturer's instructions for projects, or use the following chart to determine what kind of adhesive you need for a particular job.

MULTIPURPOSE ADHESIVES

■ **White glue.** White glue is usually sold in plastic squeeze bottles for use on porous materials such as wood, paper, cloth, and pottery. It is not water-resistant. Clamping for the entire curing time is required.

■ **Epoxy.** Epoxies are sold in tubes or cans. They consist of two parts: resin and hardener, which must be mixed for use on metal, ceramics, some plastics, and rubber. Clamping is required for about 2 hours.

■ **Cyanoacrylate.** Also called super or instant glue, cyano-acrylate is similar to epoxy but is a one-part glue. It forms a very strong bond and is recommended for use on metal, glass, ceramics, some plastics, and rubber. Clamping is not required.

■ **Contact cement.** A rubber-base liquid sold in bottles and cans, contact cement is recommended for bonding laminates, veneers, and other large areas. Clamping is not required.

■ **Polyurethane glue.** This high-strength glue is used for wood, metal, ceramics, glass, most plastics, and fiberglass. Clamping is usually required.

■ **Silicone rubber adhesive or sealant.** Silicone rubber glues and sealants are used for gutters and on building materials. They are highly durable and waterproof. Clamping is not required.

■ **Household cement.** This fast-setting, low-strength glue is used for wood, ceramics, glass, and paper. Clamping is usually not required.

■ **Hot-melt adhesive.** Hot-melt glues are sold in stick form and used with hot-glue guns for temporary bonds of wood, metal, paper, and some plastics. Clamping is not required.

WOOD GLUES

■ **Yellow glue.** Also known as aliphatic resin or carpenter's glue, this yellow liquid is used for general woodworking and is more water-resistant than white glue. Clamping is usually required for the entire curing time. Yellow glue does not accept wood stains.

■ **Plastic resin glue.** Plastic resin glue is recommended for laminating layers of wood and for gluing structural joints. It is water-resistant but not waterproof. Clamping is required.

■ **Resorcinol glue.** This glue is waterproof and forms strong and durable bonds. It is recommended for use on outdoor furniture, kitchen counters, structural bonding, boats, and sporting gear. It is also used on cork, fabrics, leather, and some plastics. Clamping is required.

ADHESIVES FOR CERAMICS AND GLASS

■ **China and glass cement.** Many cements are sold for mending china and glass. These cements usually come in tubes and have good resistance to water and heat. Clamping is usually required.

■ **Silicone rubber adhesive.** Only silicone adhesives made specifically for glass and china are recommended. They form very strong bonds, with excellent resistance to water and temperature extremes. Clamping is usually required.

METAL ADHESIVES AND FILLERS

■ **Steel epoxy.** This two-part compound is heat- and water-resistant. It is used for patching gutters and gas tanks, sealing pipes, and filling rust holes.

■ **Steel putty.** This metal putty consists of two putty-consistency parts that are kneaded together before use. It forms a strong, water-resistant bond and is recommended for patching and sealing pipes that aren't under pressure. It can also be used for ceramic and masonry.

■ **Plastic metal cement.** Plastic metal is a one-part adhesive and filler. It is moisture-resistant but cannot withstand temperature extremes. It is used for metal, glass, concrete, and wood.

PLASTIC ADHESIVES

■ **Model cement.** Usually sold in tubes as "model maker" glues, model cement is used for most plastics. Clamping is required until set.

■ **Vinyl adhesive.** Vinyl adhesives form a strong, waterproof bond on vinyl and on many plastics, but don't use them on plastic foam. Clamping is not usually required.

■ **Acrylic solvents.** Solvents are not adhesives as such; they act by melting the acrylic bonding surfaces, fusing them together at the joint. They are recommended for use on acrylics and polycarbonates. Clamping is required.

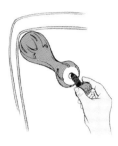

FURNITURE

REPAIRING FURNITURE

■ You can treat scratches on natural wood or antique finishes by polishing them with a mixture of equal amounts of turpentine and boiled linseed oil.

■ Paper stuck to a polished table can be lifted after saturating the paper with cooking oil.

■ Cabinet or dresser knobs can be tightened by dipping its screw or screws in fingernail polish or shellac and reinserting the knob. When the polish or shellac hardens, the screws will be set and the knobs will be tight.

■ Wooden drawers can be unstuck by rubbing contact surfaces with a bar of soap or a candle.

■ Decals easily lift off painted furniture if sponged with vinegar.

■ If loose cane on a rattan chair is snagging your clothing or stockings, tame it with clear tape, or blunt it by dabbing on clear nail polish.

■ If a chair wobbles because one leg is shorter than the others, steady the chair by forming an appropriately shaped piece of wood putty to "extend" the short leg. When the putty dries, sand and stain it to match the leg and glue it in place.

REUPHOLSTERING FURNITURE

■ When you reupholster furniture, put fabric scraps in an envelope and staple the envelope to the underside of the piece. That way you'll have scraps for patching.

■ When using ornamental tacks for upholstery, push extras into the frame in an inconspicuous spot so you have replacements if needed.

■ To hammer decorative furniture tacks without damaging their heads, place a wooden spool over each tack and pound on the spool.

■ When examining a sample of upholstery fabric, fold the sample and rub the backs together to make sure that the backing is firmly bonded to the fabric.

■ Test whether a fabric is likely to "pill" by rubbing it with a pencil eraser to see if bits of fabric appear.

STAIRS

■ Stairs are put together with three basic components—the tread, the riser, and the stringers (the side supports). In most cases, squeaks are caused by the tread flexing against the riser or the stringer. Have someone walk up and down the stairs to locate the squeak.

■ Try eliminating squeaks in stairs by using packaged graphite powder or talcum powder in a squeeze bottle. Apply along the joints in the problem area.

■ To stop squeaks at the front of a stair tread, drive pairs of screw-shank flooring nails, each pair angled in a V, across the tread and into the top of the riser below it.

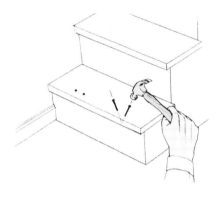

DRYWALL

■ To save your arm muscles when installing ceiling drywall, construct two "deadman" supports. Use floor-to-ceiling 2×4s, including T-bars at the tops. They will support the panels while you do the final positioning and securing.

■ Instead of carrying large drywall sheets into the house and possibly damaging them while navigating awkward corners, cut them to fit before bringing them inside.

■ To ensure that a nail stays in a stud, drive another drywall nail

PATCHING PLASTER

■ To fill a crack in a plaster wall, remove loose plaster with a putty knife. Make sure to widen the opening slightly in a V-shape.

■ Clean the loose plaster, and dust from the crack with a vacuum cleaner attachment.

■ Mix a thick paste of plaster of paris, and then wet the crack thoroughly.

■ Pack plaster of paris into the hole to its full depth, and smooth the surface with a scraper or trowel.

■ Let the filled crack dry until the plaster turns bright white—at least 24 hours.

■ Sand the patch lightly when the plaster is dry, using medium- or fine-grade sandpaper wrapped around a wood block.

■ Prime before painting the wall.

■ Large cracks have to be replastered at least twice (once with perlitic plaster, then with plaster of paris) to make the surface smooth.

REPAIRING A LARGE DRYWALL HOLE

■ Cut a scrap piece of drywall into a square or rectangle a little bigger than the hole or damaged area.

■ Set the patch against the damaged area, and trace around it lightly with a pencil.

■ Cut out the outlined area with a keyhole saw. Keep your saw cut on the inside of the traced line so that the hole will be the same size as the patch.

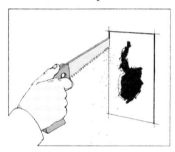

■ Make a backing board about 6 inches longer than the long dimension of the hole.

■ Insert the backing board coated with panel adhesive into the hole, and hold it firmly against the inside of the wallboard. Fasten the ends of the board to the drywall with drywall screws driven through the walls at the sides of the hole.

■ Countersink the screws below the surface of the drywall.

■ To hold the patch in place, spread panel adhesive on the back of the drywall patch and around its edges.

■ Set the patch into the hole, and adjust it so that it's exactly even with the surrounding wall. Hold it in place until the compound starts to set.

■ Let the patch dry at least overnight.

■ Fill the patch outline with seam tape and at least three coats of joint compound. Cover the exposed screw heads with drywall compound. Let dry overnight.

■ Sand lightly and then prime.

through the wall into the stud; set the new nail about 2 inches above or below the old one. Pound it flush with the wall, then give it one more light hammer whack to "dimple" the drywall around the nail head. Cover the nail head and hole with drywall compound and then lightly sand when dry.

WINDOWS AND SCREENS

WINDOWS

■ Applying a reflective vinyl coating on the inside of your windows will protect your furniture upholstery or drapery fabric from the fading effects of strong sunlight and help keep your home cooler in the summertime.

■ To free a window that's been painted shut, use a scraper, knife, or spatula to cut the paint seal between the sash and the window frame. Then, working from the outside, insert the blade of a pry bar under the sash and pry gently in from the corners. Lever the bar over a block of scrap wood.

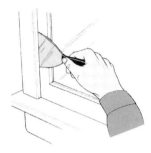

■ To remove cracked glass from a window without excessive splintering, crisscross the pane on both sides with several strips of masking tape, then rap it with a hammer. Most of the pane will be held together.

■ When installing a new window-pane, speed up the process by rolling the glazing compound between the palms of your hands to form a long string the diameter of a pencil. Lay the "string" along the frame, over the glass, and smooth it in place with a putty knife.

REPAIRING WALLPAPER

Make sure to save extra wallpaper for patching. Tape a piece or two on a closet wall so that it will correspond in color density and pattern to the paper on the wall.

To repair a section of damaged wallpaper, tear, don't cut, a patch from a new piece that's been weathered. Because less-defined torn edges blend with paper already on the wall, the patch will be virtually invisible. Don't remove the damaged wallpaper; simply paste the patch directly over the surface. Caution: This will not work on vinyl or foil wallpaper.

■ To make dried-out putty workable again, sprinkle it with a few drops of raw linseed oil and knead it until it is soft and pliable.

■ If you try to open a window and it refuses to budge, tap a hammer on a block of wood at various places on the sash.

■ To cover a clear bathroom window without putting up curtains, make the glass opaque by brushing on a mixture of 4 tablespoons Epsom salts and ½ pint of stale beer.

SCREENS

■ To keep aluminum screens from pitting, clean them outdoors (never indoors) with kerosene. Dip a rag in the kerosene and rub both sides of the mesh and the frames, then wipe off the excess. This is a particularly good rust inhibitor for older screens. (Caution: Kerosene is highly flammable. Never pour or use kerosene near an open flame.)

■ To repair a small tear in a wire screen, fold the wire strands back into place. If the hole doesn't close completely, brush clear nail polish sparingly across the remaining opening. Let the nail polish dry, and reapply until the hole is sealed. (Be careful not to let any polish run down the screen; immediately blot any excess.)

■ If there's a clean cut or tear in a window screen, stitch it together. Use a long needle and fishing line, strong nylon thread, or fine wire. Zigzag stitch across the cut, being careful not to pull the thread or wire so tight that the patch puckers. After stitching, apply clear nail polish to keep the thread or wire from pulling loose.

■ To close a large hole in a window screen, cut a patch from a scrap piece of screening that is the same type as the damaged screen. Zigzag stitch the patch into place, and then apply clear nail polish to the stitching.

WOODWORKING

■ To prevent dimpling a wood surface when removing a nail with a hammer, protect the surface with a small block of wood or a shim.

■ To prevent a saw from binding when ripping a long board, hold the initial cut open with a nail or wedge. Move the nail or wedge down the cut as you saw.

■ Check that wood is smooth after sanding by covering your hand with a nylon stocking and rubbing it over the surface. You'll be able to detect any remaining rough spots.

■ Lubricate a saw blade frequently by running a bar of soap or a candle stub over its sides.

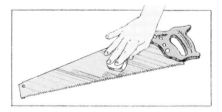

■ To avoid splitting a narrow section of wood with a screw, predrill a hole. Then the wood won't crack when you insert the screw. With hardwoods, you should also wax the screw threads.

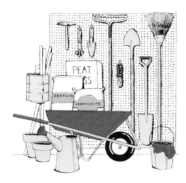

LAWN AND GARDEN

- **Bow saw** for trimming trees.
- **Flexible hose,** with length depending on the size of your property.
- **Gloves.** While thin cotton gloves are good for working with plants, wear thick gloves for pruning.
- **Hoe.**
- **Rakes,** both leaf and soil types.
- **Shovel.**
- **Spading fork or pitchfork**.
- **Small spade.**
- **Sprayer.**
- **Trowel.**
- **Wheelbarrow.**

TIPS ON GARDEN TOOLS

- Invest in quality tools; cheap tools increase your work and break under stress. Make sure the sizes and weights of your tools suit you.

- Select tools with handles made of hickory or ash, with the grain running straight along the full length of the handle.

- Make sure blade shanks are reinforced.

- Keep tools in good condition by storing them carefully and protecting them from the weather.

- Periodically sharpen the blades on shovels and hoes.

- Paint the handles of your small garden tools a bright color— anything but green—so that you can easily find them.

LAWNS, SHRUBS, AND TREES

Outside jobs are more than just keeping up appearances. Regular maintenance of your lawn and landscaping will actually minimize work. A neglected lawn soon goes to seed and begins to erode, and getting the lawn back into shape takes a lot of work. Fortunately, keeping up a lawn and landscaping elements is neither time-consuming nor expensive. Keep the following tips in mind to reduce maintenance time:

■ Don't try to grow grass in deep shade. Substitute with hardy groundcovers.

■ Plant shrubs and trees native to your area, because they will require less time and effort.

■ Plant for the future. Some trees and shrubs grow fast and spread. Don't plant them too closely, otherwise you'll have transplant work down the road.

■ Mulch flower beds to retain moisture and deter weeds.

LAWNS

■ The kind of grass that grows best in your area is determined by the climate, moisture, and soil. If you're planning to sow or sod a new lawn, find out what kind of grass seed is the most successful.

■ To help new grass grow in your yard, mix seeds with 2 tablespoons cold, strong tea, and store in the refrigerator for 5 days. Spread the seed on newspapers to dry another 2 days, then apply to the lawn.

■ Water only when the lawn needs it. Overwatering or everyday shallow watering isn't as good as deep-watering, because it causes shallow root systems that require frequent watering.

■ Do not allow leaves to remain on your lawn all winter because they will mat down and smother the grass.

■ As hot weather approaches, set your lawn mower blade higher; longer grass will provide shade protection for the roots.

SHRUBS AND TREES

■ Avoid buying shrubs with cankers, leaf rot, spots, insects, or other problems. Shrubs that are already weak won't have much chance of surviving a transplant to your yard.

■ Transplant balled-root shrubs into a hole that is 8 inches wider and 6 inches deeper than the balled roots of the plant.

■ Remove any twine or wrap from a shrub or tree that you intend to plant. Plastic and metal won't rot and may strangle the roots.

■ When you plant or transplant a bare-root shrub or tree, be sure to spread out the plant's root system in the hole and cover the roots with topsoil or a rich soil mixture.

OUTDOOR GARDENS

To a large extent, climate and soil dictate the composition of gardens. While you can't change the climate, you can modify the soil. And with a few tricks, you can even grow plants and vegetables that may be only marginally hardy in your area.

The United States is divided into zones according to climate conditions

PRUNING SHRUBS AND TREES

Most shrubs and trees benefit from a pruning that allows more air and light into dense growth and rids the shrub or tree of weak branches.

■ Keep your pruning shears sharp; dull blades cause bruising and ragged cuts.

■ Use the appropriate tool for the branch or limb to be pruned. Too large or too small a tool can make ragged cuts.

■ Make all cuts as close as possible to the base of the branch being removed without damaging the ridged collar where it attaches to the larger limb.

■ Prune most shrubs and trees—with the exception of trees that exude sap and early spring flowering species—in the winter when they are dormant. Spring flowering trees, such as lilacs, should be pruned after bloom.

■ Cut damaged or dead limbs anytime during the year.

■ If a tree or shrub needs heavy pruning (when as much as a third of the plant's live tissue will be removed), do the pruning in stages over a two- or three-year period.

■ Make sure that any limbs will not fall onto power lines when cut.

for gardening purposes. Trees, shrubs, and plants—the ones that do best in a given location because of the light, water, temperature, and soil conditions—are then assigned to these various zones. If you're attempting to grow a plant in a nonnative area, you'll have to consider how to adjust your soil and protect plants from temperature extremes that would otherwise kill them.

SOIL TESTING AND PREPARATION

Soil types vary from the extremes of dry, nutrient-poor sand to 90 percent rocks held together with 10 percent soil. Most soil conditions fall somewhere between these extremes. To find out what kind of soil you have, try this test: Take a small handful of moist garden soil and hold some of it between your thumb and the first knuckle of your forefinger. Gradually squeeze the soil out with your thumb to form a ribbon. If you can form a ribbon that stays together for more than 1 inch, you have a heavy clay soil. If a ribbon forms but holds together for between ¾ to 1 inch, you have a silty clay loam. If the ribbon breaks into shorter pieces, the soil is silty. If a ribbon doesn't form at all, the soil is sandy.

This test will tell you the general type of soil that is adequate for many gardens. To determine soil content for vegetable or flower gardens, you'll want to have your soil professionally tested. To obtain a soil sample to use for this test, take several slices of soil from the area where you are planning a garden bed. Dig 4 to 6 inches down before taking the samples, and mix them all together. Collect samples for each type of garden—i.e., lawns, vegetables, flowers—separately.

One test will be a pH test that reads for acidity or alkalinity. A pH test result between 6.0 and 7.0 is ideal for most plants and requires no adjustment. A result below 6.0 indicates the soil is acid—good for rhododendrons and azaleas but not for most other plants. Ground limestone can be applied to reduce soil acidity. A pH test result of over 7.2 means the soil is too alkaline for most plants. To solve this problem, add powdered sulfur or iron sulfate.

A complete test will also provide information about the nutrients and percentage of organic matter in your soil. Both of these results will help determine whether and how to fertilize your soil.

After testing your soil, keep these other tips in mind:

■ Adjusting the nutrient and pH levels in soil will not improve its consistency. To correct soil texture, add one of several conditioners, such as leaf mold, compost, manure, and peat moss.

■ For flower and vegetable gardens, thoroughly turn and loosen the soil to about a 6-inch depth, removing any rocks.

■ When cultivating the soil in your garden, remember that good soil is slightly lumpy. If you work it until it's too fine, it will pack hard when it rains or blow in a strong wind.

■ Work the soil before planting root crops. If they have to negotiate lumps, stones, or other obstacles, vegetables such as carrots and parsnips will grow forked or distorted instead of straight.

■ If your soil is poor, but you still want to grow vegetables, consider

 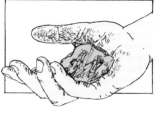 

Soil may vary from light sand to heavy clay. A rough test can be made by squeezing a wettened sample in your hand. If it falls apart easily, it's primarily sand (left); if it forms a solid, sticky glob, it's primarily clay (center). The ideal growing medium is somewhere between the two (right).

container gardening in pots, hanging baskets, and raised beds.

PLANNING THE GARDEN

■ Avoid setting your plants in the shade of buildings and large trees. In addition to blocking sun from your garden bed, trees will also compete for the available soil nutrients and moisture.

■ If you garden in containers or raised beds, remember that your plants will dry out faster than those in a regular garden bed.

■ Try to position tall plants on the north and northeast side of the garden so they don't overshadow other plants.

■ Vegetables grown for their fruits—tomatoes, peppers, and eggplants, for example—need a minimum of 6 to 8 hours of direct light per day. If they don't get enough light they may produce a leafy green plant but little or no fruit.

■ Save garden space by interplanting. For example, plant fast-growing lettuce between your tomato seedlings. By the time the tomatoes need the space, the lettuce will have been harvested.

■ To make sure you plant seeds in straight rows, make a simple planting guide with two stakes and a string stretched between them. Or use the handle of your rake to make a trench in which to plant the seeds.

WATERING

■ Early morning watering lets the sun dry leaves quickly, preventing the spread of fungal diseases that thrive in moist conditions.

■ Water gently, because a sharp jet of water can wash away the soil and expose the roots. Use a nozzle that breaks the force of the water at the end of the hose.

■ Always soak the soil thoroughly when watering. A light sprinkling can do more harm than no water at all because it promotes shallow root growth.

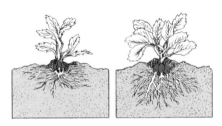

FERTILIZING

■ Remember that phosphoric acid encourages root growth and fruit production; nitrogen is necessary for leafy growth; and potassium promotes root growth and disease resistance. A good fertilizer contains these ingredients in fairly equal proportions.

■ Apply fertilizer at the rate suggested on the product label.

■ One way to supply fertilizer quickly is by spraying a solution directly on the plant foliage with a sprayer or watering can. Buy

LAWN AND GARDEN MAINTENANCE SCHEDULE

WINTER

- Order seed catalogs.
- Prune deciduous trees and shrubs.
- Start perennial seeds in seed trays indoors under lights.

EARLY SPRING

- Rake up leaves and debris that have accumulated during the winter.
- Remove top layer of winter mulch.
- Loosen turf with a leaf rake to remove matted material without disturbing grass.
- Reseed bare lawn patches.
- Plant container-grown and bare-root perennials.
- Work the soil in the vegetable garden.
- Apply superior dormant oil sprays to control insects when tree buds just begin to show new growth.
- Check trees and shrubs for winter damage. Prune where needed before buds begin new growth.
- Prune roses as new growth begins.
- Transplant shrubs and small trees while plants are still dormant.
- Plant hardy vegetable plants.

LATE SPRING

- Apply fertilizer to lawns and beds of spring bulbs in May to avoid early spring diseases.
- Fertilize shrubs and plants.
- Fertilize vegetable garden.
- If the spring is dry, be sure to water shrubs and plants.
- Mulch flower beds and shrubs.
- Stake plants if needed.
- Transplant perennial seedlings.
- Thin new growth in flower and vegetable gardens.
- Plant warm-season annual flowers and vegetable transplants after the danger of frost has passed.

SUMMER

- Keep weeds under control in vegetable and flower gardens.
- Keep shrubs and plants watered if the summer is dry.
- Check trees, shrubs, and plants for insect infestations and disease, and eliminate them, if necessary.
- Prune late-flowering shrubs and trees.
- Pinch off dead flowers.

EARLY FALL

- Divide and replant perennial flowers.
- Plant new trees and shrubs, except in areas with extreme winter temperatures.
- Reseed or sod new lawns.
- Fertilize lawns, shrubs, and trees.
- Remove dead branches from deciduous trees and shrubs.
- Cut back stems of flowering plants—except hardy plants—after the first frost.

LATE FALL

- Clean out all old vines, stalks, stems, and rotten fruit.
- Harvest vegetable garden.
- Rake remaining leaves and shred for winter mulch.
- Plant bulbs; dig up dahlia and canna roots, gladiolus, and other bulbs that do not survive the winter.
- Use hand pruners to cut back dead stems on perennials that die down. Leave only 2 to 3 inches of stem.
- Continue deep-watering perennials until the ground has frozen solidly.
- Apply winter mulch to perennial beds when the ground is frozen hard.
- Drain and store hoses.
- Clean and store tools.

fertilizers that are formulated for this purpose, and follow the manufacturer's instructions to avoid burning the foliage.

SEEDS AND SEEDLINGS

- Keep seed packets in the refrigerator or some other cool place until you're ready to plant the seeds.

- Seeds won't germinate if they're planted too deep. Follow this guide: Small seeds should be planted ¼ to ½ inch deep; medium seeds ½ to 1 inch deep; and large seeds 1 to 1½ inches deep. Very tiny seeds can just be pressed into the soil.

- Never transplant seedlings directly into the garden from indoors. They must be hardened off by being exposed gradually to outdoor conditions: Put the containers outside during the day, and bring them in again at night for a couple of weeks before setting the seedlings out.

■ Plastic jugs—such as milk jugs—with the bottoms removed make good insulators to protect young transplants from cold night temperatures.

■ Unless plants are thinned, you'll get a poor crop because individual seedlings will be fighting each other for space, moisture, and nutrients. Always thin as directed on the seed packet.

COMPOSTING

■ A 3- to 4-foot-tall compost pile is the most efficient size.

■ To start a compost pile in the fall, use leaves that have been shredded. Don't use large whole leaves, such as oak leaves, which take years to deteriorate.

■ Keep vegetable and fruit peelings, tea and coffee grounds, garden plants, weeds, and grass clippings in a plastic bag and empty them onto the pile when the bag is full. Apply more leaves over the scraps.

■ Water the pile when dry; turn it periodically to accelerate decomposition.

■ Compost is ready for garden beds when it is dark and crumbles easily. It should smell woody, not rotten.

■ Never start a compost pile when there is the danger of attracting rats, and never put scraps or bones from animal matter, including meat, poultry, and fish, in the compost pile.

PEST CONTROL

■ Use insecticidal soap on plants to control pests. You may also make a homemade insecticide by mixing 2½ tablespoons of biodegradable detergent to 1 gallon of water and using it to spray both sides of the plant leaves. After an hour, spray or hose them down with clear water.

■ Slugs like to feed on gardens primarily at night or on cloudy, damp days. To combat them, fill a spray bottle with half vinegar and half water. Search out slugs at night, and kill them by squirting them directly with the solution.

■ You can also kill slugs by sprinkling them with a heavy dose of salt. Wait 5 minutes, then sprinkle them again.

HERB GARDENS

■ Low-growing herbs, such as thyme, marjoram, and chives, should be planted where they won't be overshadowed by other plants. They make a delightful edging for a flower bed or a path.

■ Coriander, tarragon, and dill grow to a height of 2 feet or more, so plant them against a wall or toward the back of a flower bed that backs onto a fence or wall.

■ Certain herbs spread so fast that they'll take over the garden unless you control them. Wild marjoram, tarragon, and mint are perennials that flare out in all directions from season to season. Restrict them with a sunken section of stovepipe that confines their roots; a large coffee can with both ends removed works well, too.

VEGETABLE GARDENS

■ To protect your corn crop from birds, tie paper bags over the ears.

■ Peas don't like hot weather; harvest them before the summer heat gets too intense.

■ Harvest radishes when they're 1 inch in diameter; larger radishes are tough.

■ When buying tomato plants for the garden, look for plants that are short, stocky, and bright green in color. Be sure not to plant your tomatoes until the soil is warm and the danger of frost has passed.

GARDENING WITH INDOOR PLANTS

All plants need light, water, and nutrients in varying degrees to grow properly. While it's easy to kill succulents, like cacti, with too much water, other plants will die quickly if they dry out. Flowering plants need lots of light and fertilizer to bloom, while many plants prefer diffuse light. Consequently, the first rule of

MAKE YOUR OWN POTTING SOIL

To make a suitable potting soil for most houseplants, mix together 4 cups black soil or potting soil, 4 cups leaf mold or peat moss, 4 cups coarse sand, 2 to 4 cups activated charcoal, and 1 tablespoon steamed bone meal. This mix should be "cooked" in the oven so that it reaches 180°F for 30 minutes before use. Allow soil mix to cool before planting.

For plants with very fine roots, adjust the recipe by decreasing the black soil and sand to 3 cups each and increasing the peat moss to 6 cups.

To make potting soil for cacti, decrease the black soil and leaf mold or moss to 2 cups each, and increase the sand to 6 cups.

indoor gardening is to know the individual needs of your plant.

■ Choose plants that will fit your household; consider issues such as light and humidity, as well as tolerance of pets, children, and how much time you want to spend tending to them.

■ Plants that are highly tolerant of indoor growing—and even careless owners—include:

Bamboo palm (*Chamaedorea erumpens*)
Burro tail (*Sedum Morganianum*)

Chinese evergreen (*Aglaonema* 'Silver King')
Crown of thorns (*Euphorbia* 'Milii')
Norfolk Island pine (*Araucaria heterophylla*)
Philodendron (*Philodendron Selloum*)
Ponytail palm (*Beaucarnea recurvata*)
Pothos (*Epipremnum aureum*)
Rubber plant (*Ficus elastica*)
Sago palm (*Cycas revoluta*)
Spider plant (*Chlorophytum comosum*)
Swedish ivy (*Plectranthus australis*)
Split-leaf philodendron (*Monstera deliciosa*)
Wax plant (*Hoya carnosa*)

■ Some plants are poisonous if eaten. Among the more common ones are:

Azaleas (*Rhododendron species*)
Daffodils (*Narcissus species*)
Dumb cane (*Dieffenbachia species*)
Heart-leaf philodendron (*Philodendron species*)
Hydrangea (*Hydrangea macrophylla*)
Ivy (*Hedera helix*)
Spurges (*Euphorbia species*)
Yew (*Taxus species*)

LIGHTING

■ To test how much light your plants will get in a given location, place a sheet of paper where you want to put a plant, and hold your hand a foot above the paper. If your hand casts a crisp shadow, you have bright light. If the shadow is fuzzy but recognizable, you have filtered light. If all you get is a blur on the paper, the location is shady.

■ Plants grow toward light (this process is called phototropism). Keep a plant standing straight by periodically turning the pot.

■ Give newly potted plants a little less light for the first few days.

WATERING

■ If you're not sure whether a houseplant needs watering or not, poke your index finger 1 inch into the topsoil. If the soil is moist, don't water; if it's dry, do.

■ Water houseplants slowly and thoroughly until the water runs out of the bottom of the pot. If the plant is in a saucer, empty the saucer after the plant finishes draining.

■ Plants originating in deserts and dry areas like to be drenched and permitted to dry out.

■ Water bulb houseplants, such as cyclamen, from the bottom. Fill a pie pan with water, and let the plants sit in it for awhile.

■ Water that has been sitting for some time is best for watering plants. It will have reached room temperature (some plants dislike cold water).

■ Plants don't like softened water. If you have an ion exchange water softener, get your plant water from the tap before it goes into the softener.

■ A dried-out houseplant can be revived by sinking the pot in tepid water until air bubbles come out. Next time remember to water before the soil shrinks away from the edge of the pot, which indicates that the root ball has dried out.

■ There's nothing you can do to save an overwatered plant that has rotted; however, you can clip healthy leaves or stems and root them to start new plants.

■ Slip shower caps over the bottoms of hanging planters to catch the overflow when watering. The caps can be removed after an hour or so.

DRAINAGE

■ Any container used as a plant pot must have drainage holes. If you're recycling a container such as a yogurt cup or margarine tub, make holes in the bottom and stand the pot on a saucer.

■ Use pieces of plastic foam for a lightweight drainage layer in the bottom of a hanging planter.

■ Sand or perlite added to your plant mix will improve drainage.

FEEDING

■ Usual signs of nitrogen deficiency are stunted growth, pale yellow lower leaves, and rusty brown edges.

■ Usual signs of phosphorus deficiency are slow growth and spindly stems, although these could also indicate a lack of adequate light.

■ Potassium deficiency is usually indicated by scorched edges on leaves, weak stems, and shriveled seeds or fruit.

■ It's best to fertilize plants periodically, once a month, but give your plants a breather from fertilizer from January to March, which is the usual dormancy period of plants.

■ Don't fertilize a plant that is sick or droopy or plants that have been recently purchased or repotted.

■ Unflavored gelatin dissolved in water is a nitrogen-rich plant food. Use one envelope of gelatin to a quart of liquid, and water the plants with this mixture (freshly made) once a month.

REPOTTING

■ Repot plants only when needed.

■ If you have plants that need to be brought in and potted for the winter, line the pots with plastic. Leave some excess plastic over the edge of the pot, and punch a couple of holes in the bottom for drainage. In spring, when it's time for transplanting, lift the soil and the plant out of the pot by the plastic.

TENDING PLANTS WHILE YOU TRAVEL

■ Houseplants that like to be evenly moist will survive your absence for a couple of weeks if you water them well and put them on a tray of wet gravel inside a large, clear, plastic dry-cleaning bag (a terrarium tent).

■ Before going away, put water in the bathtub and set your large plants on top of bricks; the bricks should be placed on end with the tops just out of the water. Cover the plants and tub with a sheet of clear plastic, and set your bathroom light on a timer to give them 12 hours of light a day.

■ As an alternative when you go on vacation, set all your house-plants on old towels folded in a few inches of water in the bathtub. The plants will absorb the water as they need it.

■ Succulents, such as cacti, will survive your absence if you water them well and move them out of direct light before you leave.

■ Self-watering pots and plant waterers that work by means of wicks, gravity, or capillary action should be used only with plants that prefer to be evenly moist or wet.

■ When reusing old pots, free them of pests or disease by washing them in hot water and soaking them overnight in a solution of 1 part chlorine bleach to 8 parts water. Rinse well.

WORKING WITH SEEDLINGS

■ Use a cardboard egg carton for a seedling nursery. Fill with loam and your plant seeds. When the seedlings are ready to be transplanted, plant the shell and the plant. The carton will decompose and enrich the soil.

■ To speed up seed germination, place seed trays on top of your refrigerator, where the 72°F–75°F emitted heat will promote steady growth.

■ Use a mister to water delicate seedlings.

TIME-SAVERS

■ Clean the leaves of a houseplant quickly with a feather duster.

■ If you love indoor plants but don't want to invest a lot of time and effort in taking care of them, select large, mature, established plants.

They usually need less attention than young plants that are just getting started.

■ To cut down on the time you spend on your indoor garden, choose plants that have similar water, light, and temperature requirements.

■ Pinch new shoots at the growing points to encourage branching. Palms are an exception to this rule; it's fatal to pinch back palms.

PEST CONTROL

INSECTS

■ Keep ants away from your home with a concoction of borax and sugar. Mix 1 cup sugar and 1 cup borax in a quart jar. Punch holes in the jar's lid, and sprinkle the mixture outdoors around the foundation of your home and around the baseboards inside your house. The ants are attracted by the sugar and poisoned by the borax.

■ If you have cockroaches, sprinkle borax powder in the kitchen and bathroom cabinets. Avoid sprinkling where children and pets could be affected.

■ If there's a hornet, wasp, bee, or other flying insect in your house and you have no insect spray, kill it with hair spray.

- If your home becomes infested with fleas, vacuum rugs thoroughly before spraying, and throw out the dust bag at once.

- Change the water in a birdbath every 3 days to help reduce the mosquito population.

- The presence of carpenter ants indicates another problem. Because they're fond of damp wood, you should check your pipes, roof, and windowsills for water leaks.

- Centipedes prey on other bugs, so the presence of centipedes in your house may indicate the presence of other insects as well.

- You can distinguish termite damage from other insect damage by examining any holes you find in wood. Termites usually eat only the soft part of wood, leaving the annual rings intact.

- If you live in a multiunit building, any pest control measures you take individually will be ineffective in the long run simply because insects can travel from one apartment to another. To eliminate bugs completely, the entire building should be treated at one time.

RACCOONS AND RODENTS

- Raw bacon or peanut butter makes good bait for a mousetrap. Make sure a mouse will have to tug the trap to remove the bait. If you're using peanut butter, dab some on the triggering device and let it harden before setting the trap. If bacon is your bait, tie it around the triggering device.

- If a raccoon sets up housekeeping in your attic or chimney, chemical repellents—such as oil of mustard—are temporarily effective. (The smell may bother you as much as it does the raccoon.) Your best bet is to let the animal leave, and then cover its entrance hole with wire mesh so that it cannot return.

- To keep rodents out of your house, seal every opening they could squeeze through. Some need less than ¼ inch of space. Put poison in deep cracks or holes, and stuff them with steel wool or scouring pads pushed in with a screwdriver. Close the spaces with spackling compound mixed with steel wool fragments.

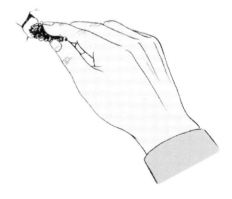

Organizing Your Home

D o you spend too much time chasing lost papers and rummaging through overstuffed closets for missing items? Chances are your household needs to be better organized. Structure comes easily to some people, but others seem to have no idea how to organize their day, let alone a week. If you fall into the latter category, the good news is there are plenty of tricks to help you get organized. It's not that difficult, nor does it take a lot of time. And although there's no guarantee that an organized household won't face a crisis now and then, you'll be much better prepared to cope with the inevitable emergencies that crop up.

MANAGING TIME

Missed appointments and slapdash meals aren't simply the result of hectic schedules—they're the consequences of disorganization. To efficiently manage time, papers need to be where you can find them, agendas must be set and followed, and items needed for daily life should be on hand. The following gives you some helpful ideas of how to accomplish these goals without wasting too much time in the process.

ORGANIZING HOUSEHOLD PAPERS

Chasing papers wastes time and energy. And when bills aren't paid or permission slips aren't turned in, the price for disorganization is paid in late fees and lost field trips. If your idea of organizing your papers is stacking them on the dining room table, try some of the following hints:

■ Designate one area of your home, even if it's only one drawer, for filing business papers, bills, letters, and clippings.

■ Set up a filing system for your important papers and receipts. This can be as simple as an accordion file or a file cabinet that can do double duty as an end table. Use the categories in "Creating a Filing System" to organize your files.

■ Use a "Miscellaneous" file for items that don't easily fit into a category, but be sure to go through this file when it fills up. You'll find that new categories will stand out, and unneeded items will be easily recognizable.

CREATING A FILING SYSTEM

WHAT TO FILE:

■ Banking—check registers, extra checks, passbooks, canceled checks

■ Car titles, insurance policies, maintenance records, payment stubs

■ List of all credit cards with numbers and telephone numbers; credit card statements

■ Guarantees and warranties, including instruction pamphlets

■ House records—insurance policy and mortgage papers; list of home improvements and receipts; lease and renter's insurance policy, if renting

■ Investment records—401(k), mutual fund, and broker statements

■ Medical records—immunizations, insurance forms, insurance payments, prescriptions

■ Life insurance policies

■ Tax records—copies of tax records for previous years and receipts for deductible expenses you plan to claim in next year's return

■ Copy of will (keep another copy at your attorney's office)

WHAT TO STORE IN A SAFE-DEPOSIT BOX:

■ Personal papers, including birth certificates, marriage license, passports, military service records, divorce decrees

■ House deed and title

■ Financial holdings, including savings bonds, bank certificates of deposit, stock certificates

■ List of valuables (include room-by-room videotape of home, if possible)

■ Keep your mail in one location in the house, and open up and file everything at least once a week. If you can't file papers on a regular basis, use a folder labeled "To File" to temporarily store items. Be sure to set aside time to file these items.

■ Hang a basket near the front door and keep your keys in it, so you'll always know where they are. Also use this basket for bills and letters that need to be mailed. When you grab your keys, you'll remember the mail.

■ For households with children, keep a special clipboard in a prominent place for all those permission slips and other school documents that are easily mislaid.

■ Instead of using an address book, try using index cards stored in a file box. Along with names, addresses, and phone numbers, you'll have room to keep track of birthdays, anniversaries, and even presents you've given in recent years. If someone moves, substitute an updated card.

■ Review your filing system periodically and toss out items you no longer need, such as last year's utility bills or warranties on discarded items.

USING LISTS AND PLANNERS

■ Use a large wall calendar to keep track of appointments, meetings, birthdays, and other events.

■ Make lists, both daily and weekly, to make sure you remember what needs to get done. Checking off the items will give you a sense of accomplishment as well as remind you of what you still need to do.

■ Create a weekly "Family Chore List" where family members can sign up for chores. This gives everyone some say in what they're going to do and also shares the responsibility of getting things done.

■ Use a yearly planner to set long-term goals, such as saving money or planning vacations.

SETTING PRIORITIES

■ Use the time of day when your energy level is highest to do your least favorite chore. You'll find you can get through it much more easily. Wind down the day with one of your favorite activities.

■ If you have trouble getting started in the morning, get organized the night before. Lay out your clothes, measure the coffee, and set the breakfast table before you go to bed.

■ Set realistic goals. Don't try to cram too much into one day or even one year. If you find yourself constantly behind schedule, keep a notepad with you and write down everything you do for a few days. Then look at the list objectively to determine whether you've attempted to do too much.

■ Separate a major project into manageable parts. For example, spend an extra hour each month thoroughly cleaning a room, instead of trying to do "spring" or "fall" cleaning.

■ Get the family involved in day-to-day chores. If school activities and homework prevent older children from carrying out weekday chores, get them involved for an hour or two on the weekends.

MANAGING A HOME OFFICE

A home office can be as small as a folding file or as large as a room. If you're running a business out of your home, you'll obviously need much more space and equipment than a family looking for a corner to file papers and tend to correspondence. The important thing to remember about creating a home office is to make it suit your family's needs. For example, if your children need to use a computer, you'll want to set up space that can be shared—not a corner in your bedroom. Likewise, equipment and supplies should be selected for versatility.

CREATING OFFICE SPACE

■ Use a wall or part of a wall to set up an office. If you're extremely short on space, mount shelves on the top portion of a wall to store files and use a table that can be folded down.

■ Use a screen to set off a corner of a room and create office space. While not ideal, it may be the best space you can find.

■ Find a niche—under the stairs, on a landing, or in an odd-size room or hallway. Use a roll-down window blind to enclose the niche when not in use.

■ Convert a closet into an office with a folding door. If there is no power inside the closet, have it wired to provide good lighting and an electrical outlet. This works particularly well in a guest room closet. Keep a portable wardrobe hanger on hand for guests when they arrive.

■ Replace a double bed with a sofa bed in an extra bedroom to allow space for your office.

OUTFITTING A HOME OFFICE

Equipment is almost secondary to some of the intangibles that a home office must have to work properly. Along with good lighting, make your office a place that you like. This doesn't require a lot of space. In fact, sometimes it's easier to plan a small space than a large area. If your office ends up looking like a sterile cubicle in a high-rise, you're not going to want to spend time there.

■ If you intend to outfit a room, draw up a floor plan before purchasing equipment. Use a 1-inch scale, and draw in windows and doors. Then plot various design arrangements for such items as your desk and computer.

CARING FOR COMPUTERS

■ Try not to position your computer in a carpeted room. Static from the carpet may damage the computer's circuits. If you must keep the computer in a carpeted room, buy an antistatic mat or use an antistatic spray to reduce buildup on the carpet.

■ Occasionally wipe your keyboard with a clean, lint-free cloth. You can use an antistatic cleaning fluid if necessary, but spray it on the cloth, not on the keyboard.

■ Air must circulate freely around the computer to avoid building up heat. Never block the slots that allow cooling air to circulate.

■ Smoke, humidity, and dust can harm your computer. Try to keep the appliance clear of such conditions. Cover the keyboard, printer, and peripherals when not in use.

■ Be sure to use three-prong electrical outlets for your computer. The three-prong plug grounds the equipment.

■ When you buy a computer, check your homeowner's insurance policy to find out if you're covered if your computer is stolen or damaged.

■ Plan your work space so you have room to keep items such as the phone within reach while still retaining space to jot notes.

■ Make sure you allow room for file cabinets to open. They're deeper than a desk.

■ Use bulletin boards to hold reminders, calendars, and a "To Do" list. Put the board where you can see it easily.

MANAGING SPACE

Some people manage to work quite well in disarray, but most of us find that crammed closets and cluttered countertops and tables hide more than they store. When it comes to closets and shelving, you have two options: You can either do it yourself or call in a professional organizer. Most professional organizing companies are limited to dealing with closets or garages, leaving the rest of the house up to you. Other companies may help with custom cabinetry for dens, kitchens, or bathrooms, and their professional designers can help with pricing and selection of materials. No one, however, can help with the principles of organizing. The good news is that you don't need carpentry skills to maximize the efficiency and organization of storage areas. With a little ingenuity, you can easily make basic organizing principles work for you.

GETTING STARTED

Start with the principle of first things first. If you're running out of room in your home, first determine whether you're storing too many items.

■ Apply the one-year rule to possessions in your home: If you haven't worn or used something over the last year, store it in the basement or attic. If it continues to gather dust, give it away or discard it.

■ Be ruthless about old clothes and paperback books that you don't intend to read again. They'll serve a much better use if given to a charity or library book sale than they will cluttering up your closets and shelves.

■ Store out-of-season clothes in basement closets or boxes. The time you'll spend doing this twice a year is much less than the time you'll spend trying to find clothes in a cluttered closet every day.

■ Make sure your coat closets and bedroom closets are used only for clothes worn regularly, not for storing infrequently used items.

■ Go through your kitchen drawers and cupboards and get rid of items that you don't use. Throw out junk, donate anything that might be useful to someone else, and store things that you rarely use elsewhere (such as in the cellar or basement).

TIME-SAVERS

■ Keep a seam ripper (with the safety cap on) near your favorite reading chair. It's perfect for clipping recipes and coupons from newspapers and magazines.

■ Help your children learn to make their beds by marking the centers of sheets, blankets, and spreads with an appliquéd design or colored thread. Even a young child will see that when the little line of teddy bears is in the middle of the bed, the sheet is on straight.

■ Put compartmented hanging closet organizers for shoes all around the house. They're ideal for storing sweaters, underwear, socks, needlework supplies, and many other household items.

■ Keep extra clothespins in the coat closet, and have your family use them to clip together gloves, boots, and sneakers so that you waste less time rummaging through piles of partnerless items. If your child takes a clothespin to school in his or her tote bag, it can be used to clip boots or gym shoes together for easy retrieval at the end of the day.

■ Assign a color to each family member and color-code items, such as backpacks, umbrellas, ponchos, coat hooks, storage boxes, and lunch boxes.

■ Label film as soon as it's developed with place, date, and any other information needed for identification.

■ Go through the "junk" drawer. Chances are you'll find something you are ready to throw out.

■ Evaluate each of the areas you plan to organize and determine which is the most troublesome. Make it a goal to begin with that area.

■ Manufacturers display a constant stream of new products and gadgets for organizing. Don't be swayed or confused by advertising or the many products on the market. Decide what you need for the space you're organizing and then search for the product or materials that will do the job.

■ If you have an estimate from a professional organizing company, compare it with the cost of doing it yourself. Nearly every product and accessory is available to the everyday consumer. Doing it yourself will reduce labor costs, but be sure to include the cost of any tools or special equipment required. Also, remember that when existing structures are removed, holes, scratches, and other unsightly conditions will be left behind. It demands less time and less energy if the closet or storage area is patched, prepped, and repainted before the new system is installed. Don't forget to add this extra expenditure to the total budget for the project.

MAXIMIZING CLOSET STORAGE

The key to success in organizing is to have a clear, well-conceived plan, whether the plan is your own or a scheme designed by a professional organizer. If you're adding a new closet or putting in a closet system and you don't plan the space well, you'll simply end up with space that will become as cluttered as your old closet. In their haste to get going, many people tend to disregard the planning stage. If you don't have a plan, you'll probably end up taking everything out of the closet and facing a mound of stuff with no idea how to organize it.

■ Draw an exact replica of your closet, including positive and negative features, and include all dimensions.

■ Assess your wardrobe and other storage items to see what needs to be stored. Keep in mind that you want to store like items together, such as all blouses in one section and all slacks in another.

■ Take advantage of all your closet space. Check whether your closet can accommodate a main clothes-hanging rod high enough to allow another rod to be installed beneath it. Hang the shorter rod at least 36 inches from the floor for slacks and shirts.

■ Be sure to plan on hanging clothes rods at least 1 foot from the back

MEASURING YOUR GARMENTS

Measure the lengths of your garments from the top of the closet rod to the bottom edge of the garment itself. This tells you how much vertical space is required for slacks, dresses, or suits, so they can hang without obstruction. Also consider the type of hanger your clothes hang from; this can alter your closet design.

The following is a list of average lengths for various garments. This should provide a basis for comparison as you measure your own clothes. Fashions with extremely short or long tails are the exception to these averages. They should not take precedence over the lengths of the majority of your clothes.

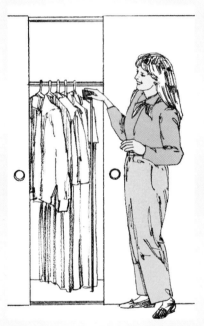

Man's suit/sport coat	40 to 42 inches
Man's shirt	39 inches
Man's or woman's slacks (folded over a hanger)	26 inches
Man's or woman's slacks (hanging from cuffs)	46 inches
Woman's blouse	30 to 34 inches
Woman's suit skirt (street length)	34 inches
Woman's dress skirt	38 inches
Woman's blazer/suit jacket	32 to 34 inches
Dress	45 to 50 inches

of the closet to avoid crushing garments. Allow at least a 3-inch minimum clearance for rods hung under shelves so you can remove hangers freely.

■ To avoid crowding, allow 1 inch of horizontal space per garment; allow 2 to 3 inches of horizontal space for each suit, sport coat, and blazer or jacket, depending on the bulk of the shoulder padding. Based on these allocations, when categories of clothes are hung together, you can easily figure out how much space you need. For example, 12 skirts would occupy 12 inches of horizontal space, and

3 suits would occupy 6 to 9 inches of horizontal space.

■ Plan for hooks, shelves, or hanging bins to transform the inside surfaces of closet doors into useful storage space.

■ Assign your clothes and accessories to specific locations inside your closet. Since different clothes and accessories possess different characteristics, you cannot treat them as one entity. Individuals have personal preferences for storing clothes, and people come in different sizes, shapes, and proportions. Determine what needs to be hung on hangers, hung from hooks, or stored on shelves or in baskets. Everything should be allotted rod space, shelf space, floor space, or space on a specialty rack.

QUICK TRICKS FOR YOUR CLOSET

■ For simple remodeling, consider adding a second shelf above the existing one. This can be a good place for little-used, bulky items that take up space.

■ Consider an overdoor shoe rack, which holds 18 to 21 pairs of shoes, for the inside of a closet door. Shoes in their boxes on the shelf occupy more space.

■ Install two rows of hooks on your closet doors—one down low for a child to use, another higher up for you to use.

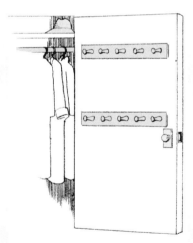

■ Use sturdy boxes stacked on their sides to make compartmented shelf space—you can see at a glance what's stored in the boxes.

ACCESSORY STORAGE

■ Divide larger spaces into smaller segments that more closely resemble the size and shape of the items they hold. This eliminates the stacks and piles of garments and accessories that are so common in closets.

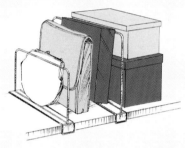

■ Acrylic shelf dividers provide an adaptable and easy way to segregate a whole shelf into specifically assigned storage compartments. These dividers are perfect for handbags, sweaters, and hats.

■ If drawers are your only recourse for sweater storage, roll the sweaters rather than folding them. Place the rolled edge up, and align the sweaters in the drawer single file from front to back or side to side so that each sweater is visible and handy.

■ Avoid using a belt ring—your belts get jumbled. Use a belt rack that provides an ample number of hooks for the placement of individual belts and that can be installed on the side or back walls of your closet.

■ A style of tie rack that has hooks for each individual tie and that can be installed on a closet wall is the best type to use. You can see the full complement of ties by extending their arms outward for easy selection and access. Afterward, the arms fold back into the unit, and the unit slides back into its original position.

■ Store jewelry in containers that are scaled to their size— jewelry boxes, bags, pouches, chests, and cases. Hang necklaces from padded hooks.

■ When it comes to closets, men and women aren't equal. Men's shoes take up more room, and jackets tend to be bulkier. Don't assume a particular storage piece works equally well and that each and every shoe rack on the market will serve all sizes. Be sure to examine any potential purchase of closet materials to make certain it can accommodate your size.

continued on page 234

EVALUATING CLOSET SYSTEMS

While cost is usually a factor, most closet systems fall into one of the following categories. The final decision to install one system rather than another depends on how much the system can be adapted to your needs.

SEPARATE SHELF/ SEPARATE ROD SYSTEM

This traditional style of closet is typically seen in most older homes where the closet hasn't already been renovated. Both the shelf (or shelves) and the closet rod are usually either metal or wood. The shelf is supported on each side wall and along the back wall by strips of wood that are nailed to wall studs. The shelf itself isn't permanently attached; it can be lifted off the wood strips and removed from the closet. The rod is either separate from or fused with the hardware, which is attached to strips of wood installed on the side walls. When these wood strips are removed, holes are left in the wall.

Advantages: Since no extra amenities, such as racks for shoes, ties, or belts, are included in the structure, you have the freedom to place them where you want them.

Disadvantages: At least a small degree of carpentry skill is required. The system must be installed between two supporting walls.

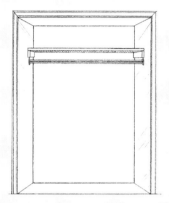

MODULAR SYSTEMS

Modular systems consist of presized cubicles and shelves with structural dividers, giving more definition to the closet space. They are still a separate shelf/separate rod system but with an upscale appearance. The structural dividers enable you to create compartments to confine your belongings to a specific area in your closet with a wood, metal, or plastic-coated metal rod.

Advantages: When modular systems can be modified or custom-designed to your own specifications to match the size of your closet and its possessions, they are definitely worth looking into. Some of these systems provide a wide variety of features that makes them very flexible.

Disadvantages: The structural dividers eat into your closet, reducing the actual space you have available for storing your belongings. This isn't a problem when you have a closet of reasonable size and dimensions, but it can be critical in a smaller closet where every inch counts. The preconstructed modular systems offer only a limited number of sizes and shapes, forcing you to accept someone else's concept of where things should be placed or hung in your closet. These systems seldom match up exactly with your individual needs. Accommodating a modular system to closets that are especially small or oddly shaped will be particularly difficult.

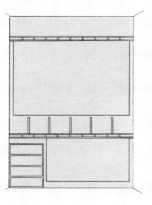

VENTILATED CLOSET SYSTEMS

These systems are constructed from metal rods covered with a vinyl or epoxy chip-resistant coating. The diameter of the rod inside the coating is the most important factor to consider: The smaller it is, the less sturdy and dependable the system will be. Take your time investigating the hardware used for installing these systems; some of it isn't reliable. Purchase only those systems with the attached wall "anchor" and not the ones that only supply an unsheathed screw. Precise measurements are a must, and a bit of know-how in handling a drill is helpful.

Advantages: Ventilated systems save space, because the overhanging front edge actually becomes the closet rod, extending a mere 2 inches below the shelf itself. All other closet systems require at least 4 to 6 inches for the same service. Ventilated systems allow the corner area of your closet to hold hanging garments, something no other system can do. These systems can resolve the problems presented by unusual wall configurations that otherwise would just be wasted space.

Disadvantages: Ventilated systems have vertical struts built into the front edge every 12 inches for added stability. These struts prohibit sliding your hangers the full length of the clothes rod. However, if your closet is properly organized, there should be no reason

EVALUATING CLOSET SYSTEMS *continued*

to shove the hangers aside. Ventilated systems need support braces every 12 to 24 inches, and these also prohibit sliding your hangers the length of the rod. Newer versions have corrected this problem by redesigning the brace so it is secured at the top of the shelf, leaving the rod area clear.

PREPACKAGED KITS

These kits actually come in a box containing the necessary pieces to assemble a ventilated system yourself.

Advantages: If you find a kit that fits your specific needs, it's certainly less trouble to carry home just one box. Kits include instructions to guide you through the installation process.

Disadvantages: For any given closet, there are a limited number of possible configurations, restricting the number of possi-

ble designs. You might see an unassembled kit designed precisely as you would like your own finished closet to be, but that kit may not be suitable for your closet's size and shape. Choosing a kit becomes a hit-or-miss proposition; you're lucky when all the pieces fit and disappointed when they don't.

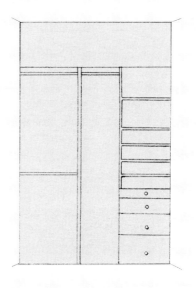

continued from page 231

■ Allow for any irregularities. A closet with a sloped or low ceiling, plaster or brick walls rather than drywall, windows inside the closet, vents, or other unusual structural components will restrict the materials that you may be able to use. The shape and size of your closet may also limit the location

and installation of any organizing materials you buy.

■ Plan for grids on the sides of closets to store belts, bags, and scarves that take up little space but lots of shelf room.

■ If you have obstacles inside your closet—air ducts or space taken by water heaters—utilize the space by storing objects that fit the space.

For example, if you have a narrow space between the closet wall and an air duct, fit it with shelves, hung on the wall, and store items such as bags and shoes.

■ The position of the door can be either a hindrance or a help because it determines whether the adjoining wall space (on the inside of your closet) is accessible or large enough to be used in some way. The wall space on either side of the door and above the door can often supply usable space. For example, extra wall space can be used to install boots on hooks.

■ Take advantage of cubbyholes, which work well for keeping stacks of sweaters contained and categorized or for keeping handbags and purses in an upright and standing position for easy access. This method allows you to clearly see each item without digging through various layers. This also opens up shelf space inside the closet.

■ Don't forget about the back of the door. The inside of the closet door works well for belts, scarves, necklaces, and other articles meant to hang. Laundry bags are not appropriate here. Any type of storage rack that is bulky or protrudes is going to get in the way, or it could brush against the clothes inside the closet when the door is closed.

MAXIMIZING EXISTING STORAGE

■ Most new homes, and many old homes, have enclosed staircases, which hide valuable space. These can often be opened to create closets, niches, or even shelf space.

■ Create a storage area by enclosing the underside of the staircase that leads to your basement. This can be a good space for a pantry, holiday decorations, or even children's toys.

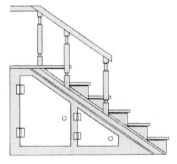

■ Put the space under a stairway to work. Construct a wheeled, wedge-shape container that fits into the farthest area under the steps.
■ Ready-made shelves can be installed just about anywhere to create storage for books and decorative items, toys, glassware, china, and just about anything that will fit on a 6- or 12-inch ledge. If you intend to store heavy items, make sure the brackets are securely anchored.

- A hallway that's wide enough can double as a storage area if you line the walls with shelves or shallow cabinets.

- Create a "closet" by storing bulky items such as golf clubs, skis, and camping equipment behind a decorative folding screen in a little-used corner.

BATHROOM

- Hang a wicker basket on the bathroom wall for storing towels, tissues, soap, bath toys, and other incidentals.

- Make your shower rod do double duty. Attach extra hooks to hold a back brush and a net bag for bath toys and washcloths.

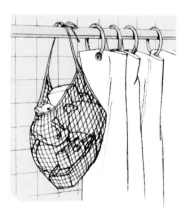

- Erect shelves in the space beside the vanity, behind the door, or over the toilet. Such shelves offer convenient storage without intruding on floor space.

- Consider installing over-the-door towel racks, or place hooks on the inside of the bathroom door for towels and bathrobes.

BEDROOM

- Add more storage space in your bedroom by building a headboard storage unit. You can place books, lamps, or a radio on top of the unit and store extra linens and blankets on the inside.

- Use flat roll-out bins for under-the-bed storage. They can hold bed linens, sewing supplies, and infrequently used items.

- For a double-duty ottoman, build a plywood box with a hinged cover. Paint the outside, or cover it with fabric. Add a thick cushion for comfortable sitting, and store your magazines in style.

KITCHEN

- An efficient kitchen saves both time and steps. Make sure your kitchen offers an efficient and effective work triangle. The work areas should be between 4 and 9 feet from one another. Shorter

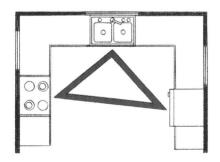

BUILDING BETWEEN-STUDS SHELVING

If your home is built with studs and drywall, you can add cabinets or shallow shelves between the studs anywhere you need them. Because they are recessed and don't project into the wall, they won't take up any space. Although these cabinets or shelves will be narrow in depth, they can be used for any of the following: a pantry in the kitchen, paperback shelves in bedrooms and family rooms, a second medicine cabinet or towel storage in the bathroom, shelves for stuffed animals in a child's room, or storage for hanging long tools, such as shovels and rakes, in the basement or garage. To build either a shelf space or cabinet, use the following tips:

■ Locate the studs with a stud finder. Make sure that no plumbing pipes or electrical wires are behind the space.

■ Lay out the dimensions of your planned storage on the wall. To avoid cutting through studs, plan your storage between the studs.

■ Turn off the power to the room you're working in.

■ Using a keyhole saw or saber saw, cut the wall opening along the layout lines. Go slowly and watch for electrical and plumbing lines. Then remove the drywall or plaster.

■ If you're creating storage wider than the space between two studs, you'll have to cut out the stud in the middle.

■ Cut two 2×4s to fit the top and bottom of the opening and nail them into the studs.

■ To finish an open storage unit, line the enclosure with wallboard or wood, and paint or wallpaper the opening. Ready-made laminated shelves are easy to install and easy to clean, but you can also make your own shelving. Trim the front edge with molding to hide the joints.

■ To make an enclosed recessed cabinet, you will need to buy a door the size of your opening and install a magnetic hinge inside a side panel.

distances mean you are too cramped; longer ones mean you must take tiring extra steps. If you're not remodeling, consider moving the refrigerator or the range if your kitchen is extremely inefficient.

■ Store dinnerware and cutlery near the dishwasher so that it can be emptied quickly and easily.

■ Keep placemats flat and out of the way by hanging them on a clipboard hung from a hook inside a cabinet or pantry door.

■ Free up counter space by putting your microwave on a shelf above the counter.

■ To make the most of available space when storing tapered glassware, position every other glass upside down.

■ Hang your sharp knives inside or on the side of a high cabinet to save drawer space and keep them out of the reach of children.

■ To economize on drawer space, arrange wooden spoons and other

GARAGE STORAGE

■ Hang as many items as possible on the walls to maximize floor space.

■ Install shelves or cabinets on the top half of the garage's front wall. Make sure you install them high enough so that the hood of your car can tuck under the shelves.

■ Install a platform across the garage ceiling joints to create a large storage place for infrequently used items.

■ Store nails and screws in glass or plastic baby food jars.

■ Use a metal garbage can to store yard tools with long handles. Hooks can also be attached to the outside of the can for hanging smaller tools. You can lift the whole can and move it to whichever part of the yard you're working in.

utensils bouquet-style in a handsome pitcher or canister.

■ If you lack drawer space for kitchen linens and towels, store them in baskets on the counter.

■ If you don't have cabinet space for your pots and pans, put a small wooden ladder—painted to match your kitchen—in a corner and place the pots and pans on the steps.

LAUNDRY ROOM

■ Add shelves in the laundry room to hold colored plastic baskets— one color for each family member. When you take clean clothes out of the dryer, sort each person's clothes into their basket. Family members can then pick up their baskets and fold and put away their own clothes.

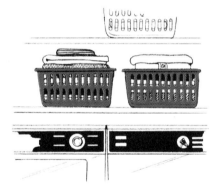

■ Keep two large paper bags near your washing machine or dryer. As you notice items that need mending or should be discarded, store them in the appropriate bag until you're ready to deal with them.

Paint and Wallcoverings

Keeping up a home is a never-ending chore. It seems as though you've just finished one job when another one pops up. Chores such as painting or papering walls will always entail a lot of work, but they can be made more manageable if you understand certain basic rules and techniques. Just a few routine procedures can save you time and help you do a more efficient job in the process.

EXTERIOR PAINTING AND STAINING

No one realizes how big their house is until they start to paint it. Exterior painting is a job that requires time, energy, and patience. Doing the work yourself can save a lot of money. Depending on how old the previous coat of exterior paint is, however, you may have a major job of scraping, sanding, and washing.

TOOLS AND MATERIALS

- Exterior paint or stain, stir sticks, and a container for mixing paint

- Primer suitable for paint or stain

- 3- or 4-inch-wide brush and 1½- to 2-inch-wide brush; buy brushes suitable for paint or stain

- Extension ladder or scaffolding

- Putty knife, wire brush, and scraper

- Sandpaper block or orbital sander and sandpaper

- Caulking gun and high-grade exterior caulk

- Nail set and hammer

- Garden hose, scrub brush, pail, and detergent or pressure sprayer

- Drop cloths and rags

Measure your home to determine how much paint or stain you will need. Multiply the average height of the house (distance between foundation and eaves and soffit area) by the distance around the foundation to get the surface area. A gallon of exterior paint usually covers about 500 square feet; stain coverage varies. Usually a gallon of paint for trim is sufficient for large homes. Be sure to check the manufacturer's estimate for coverage and consider how many coats of paint or stain you are applying. Ask your paint dealer for help in verifying your calculations.

■ Select paint or stain appropriate for your home's surfaces. Don't try to put alkyd paint on a surface previously painted with latex paint. Likewise, stain cannot be used over paint, although you can restain a house in a different color by using a stain primer and a solid stain.

■ Paint the downspouts and gutters to match the siding. Galvanized gutters must be specially treated before they can be painted; commercial products are available.

PREPARING SURFACES

Thorough preparation is the key to a good paint job. It could take you two or three times as long to prepare the surfaces as it will to paint, but if you bypass the preparation stage, you'll be repainting very quickly.

■ Scrape all loose paint with a wire brush or paint scraper, and sand

surfaces. Washing before you scrape will loosen paint chips and make scraping easier.

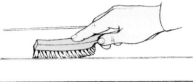

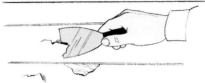

■ Correct any problems or defects in the previous paint job. (See "Paint Troubleshooting Chart," page 243, for guidance.)

■ Use a hammer to reset loose nails.

■ Tightly nail any loose boards.

■ Caulk around windows, doors, and chimneys with an exterior caulk that accepts paint or stain.

■ Replace any loose glaze in windows.

■ Tie back and cover shrubs and trees that would impede your movements; cover light posts and sidewalks. This step is particularly important with stains, which are thin and tend to spatter much more than paint.

■ If your house isn't too dirty, wash it with a garden hose to remove dust; for caked-on dirt, use a scrub brush or sponge and a pail of warm water with a strong household detergent. For a major job, rent a high-pressure sprayer to

SELECTING THE RIGHT EXTERIOR COAT

Most of the coatings listed below can be applied with an airless sprayer as well as a brush, roller, or painting pad. But if you want to spray, read the labels carefully or ask your paint dealer if you're buying a sprayable coating. Latex paints require only water to thin them enough for spraying. With alkyds, oils, and other types of paints, you'll have to purchase the appropriate solvents to dilute them.

Type	Characteristics/Uses	Applications
Acrylic	A type of latex; water-thinned, water cleanup. Fast-drying and suitable for any building material, including masonry and primed metal.	Brush, roller, pad, spray. Comparable to regular latex paint.
Alkyd	Similar to oil paints but dries faster. Solvent-thinned, solvent cleanup. Use over oil and alkyd coatings.	Brush, roller, pad, spray. Smooths out more readily than latex but more difficult to apply.
Latex	Most popular exterior paint. Excellent durability. Water-thinned, water cleanup. Mildew-proof; may even be applied over damp surfaces. Do not use over oil paints unless specified by the manufacturer.	Brush, roller, pad, spray. Except when spraying, don't thin; apply thickly with little spreadout.
Oil	Extremely durable but dries slowly. Solvents must be used for cleanup. Least popular.	Brush, roller, pad, spray on very dry surfaces. Insects and rain are dangers due to lengthy drying time.
Marine	Excellent durability on wood, some metals. Expensive. Solvent cleanup.	Brush recommended due to thick, gooey consistency.
Primer	Seals raw wood, bare metal. Also use over old, worn finishes. Provides good bonding for top coat. Use primer formulated for top coat.	Brush, roller, pad, spray. Easier than top-coat painting. Porous surfaces may drink up lots of primer.
Stains	Water- or solvent-thinned; both types durable. Choice of transparent, semi-transparent, solid-stain pigmentation.	Brush, roller, pad, spray.

remove grime and peeling paint. Scrape peeling paint; sand to feather the edges.

■ Loosen downspouts, light fixtures, and other accessories for easier painting.

APPLYING PAINT OR STAIN

■ The best time to paint is in late spring or early fall on a dry day that is not too sunny. Temperatures below 40°F and direct hot sun can ruin paint jobs.

■ Make sure all surfaces are dry. Do not paint within 24 hours of a heavy rain, and do not paint when rain is forecast.

■ Apply primer to bare spots, and allow them to dry thoroughly.

■ Mix all the paint or stain you will be using in a large container and stir carefully. This will avoid a color change in the middle of a wall. Then pour what you need into a smaller can for easier work.

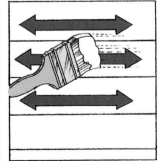

■ Use a 3-inch brush to paint clapboard siding. Dip the bristles in the paint, and coat the underside edges of four or five clapboards to a length of 3 feet. With a fully loaded brush, paint the face of each board, using short strokes to cover the surface. To finish, level the paint with smooth, horizontal strokes. For shingles and shakes, use the same

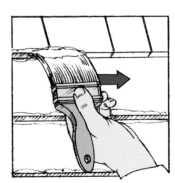
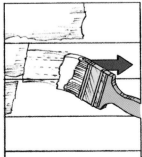

PAINT TROUBLESHOOTING CHART

Problem	Possible Cause	Solution
Peeling	Paint curls due to wet wood; interior moisture vapor; dirty, glossy surface.	Scrape, sand, prime, repaint. Install siding/soffit vents outside, exhaust fans inside.
Wrinkling	New paint sags and droops. Paint applied too thickly.	Scrape, sand, prime, and repaint. Stir new paint and brush out thoroughly.
Alligatoring	Paint dries into islands. Either due to incompatible paints or painting too soon over still-wet coat.	Scrape, sand, prime, and repaint with a compatible coating.
Blistering	Surface blisters caused by underlying moisture or solvent from paint applied on hot day.	Sand smooth, repaint. Install vents. Paint on mild days.
Chalking	Powdery residue stains on sidewalks, foundations. Inferior paint or porous undercoat to blame.	Wash down surface, let dry, repaint with nonchalking coating.
Mildew	Discoloration of exterior surface due to growth of fungus, usually black/green stains.	Scrub off with chlorine bleach or fungicide, let dry, repaint with mildew-resistant formula. Trim back tree branches, shrubs.
Running sags	Wavy paint surface. Paint applied too heavily.	Sand smooth, repaint. Brush out paint to a consistent thickness.
Paint won't dry	Inferior paint.	Patience or removing and repainting. Test paints on small areas before painting entire house.

technique but apply the paint vertically.

■ Paint from top to bottom to avoid dripping paint on freshly painted areas. Do the walls first, followed by the trim.

■ Use a solid extension ladder set firmly against the house. The top of the ladder should stick up above the roof. Make sure the ladder is on firm footing, with about one-quarter of its length out from the foundation of the house. Make sure both extension hooks are firmly locked on the supporting rungs. When moving the ladder, watch for power lines.

■ Use a brush specifically made for stain, and avoid getting too much stain on the brush. Use broad, horizontal strokes, and try to come to a natural ending point—like a corner—to prevent lap marks.

USING AN AIRLESS SPRAYER SAFELY

Airless sprayers are fast and efficient because they supply pressures of up to 3,000 pounds per square inch to cover a large area quickly. This force moves the paint at 100 to 200 miles an hour through the spray tip. All that power can be dangerous. Consequently, treat an airless sprayer with care, follow the manufacturer's instructions to the letter, and take the following precautions to prevent accident or injury:

■ Keep the spray gun's safety lock on when you're not painting.

■ Make sure the spray gun has a trigger guard and a safety shield around its tip.

■ If the spray tip becomes clogged, do not try to clear it by pressing your finger on it while the paint is being sprayed. Keep your fingers away from the tip when the sprayer is operating.

■ Never point the gun at anyone else or allow anyone to point it at you.

■ Always turn the sprayer off and disconnect it from its electrical source before you clean the gun or the sprayer's filters. Even then, if you have to clean the tip, squeeze the trigger to release any built-up pressure in the hose.

■ Work in a well-ventilated area, wear a painter's mask to avoid inhaling fumes, and don't smoke or work around open flames. If you're working outside, don't leave containers of solvents sitting in the hot sun.

■ Never leave the sprayer within reach of children or pets.

■ Stir the paint or stain frequently to keep pigment from settling.

INTERIOR PAINTING

TOOLS AND MATERIALS

■ Interior paint, stir sticks, and a large container for mixing paint

■ Primer suitable for paint

■ A 9-inch-wide roller and paint tray; extension handle if painting high walls or ceilings

■ A 1- or 1½-inch sash brush for window frames; a 2-inch brush for baseboards and moldings

■ Tall stepladder or scaffolding

■ Putty knife, wire brush, and scraper

■ Sandpaper block or orbital electric sander and sandpaper

■ Spackling compound

■ Nail set and hammer

■ Bucket, sponge, and household detergent

■ Drop cloths and rags

SELECTING PAINTS

Interior paints are available in both latex and alkyd bases. The main advantages of latex are that it dries quickly, has little odor, and requires only soap and water for cleanup.

Alkyd paints are often used on wood trim and doors for increased durability. A wide variety of finishes is available in both types of paints—flat, satin, semigloss, and high-gloss. While high-gloss is the most durable and washable, it must be sanded or "deglossed" when it's time to repaint. Flat paints are the least durable; reserve them for walls and ceilings that won't need to be scrubbed.

A gallon of interior paint will cover about 450 square feet. For estimating purposes, figure 400 square feet of coverage per gallon of paint. To determine the amount of paint required to cover a room, figure the area of the walls (length×height for each wall in the room), then divide by 400. With this method, a gallon of paint will cover a 10×10-foot room with 9-foot ceilings with one coat. Two coats will take two gallons. A rough-textured wall takes more paint than a smooth wall. To be on the safe side, estimate about 350 square feet of rough-textured wall per gallon.

CHOOSING COLORS

Even those who decide on white walls and ceilings can be overwhelmed by the many options among "white" paints. To select color, think about the mood and atmosphere you want to create, the colors in furniture and carpets, and the light in your rooms.

■ Color is much more intense on four walls than on a small 1-inch paint chip. Choose a lighter shade of a

INTERIOR PAINTS

Type	Characteristics/Uses	Applications
Acoustic	For acoustic ceiling tile. Water-thinned, water cleanup.	Spray (preferable) or roller.
Alkyd	Solvent-thinned, solvent cleanup. Don't apply over unprimed drywall.	Brush, roller, pad.
Cement	For concrete, brick, stucco. Some contain waterproofing agents. Must be mixed just before use.	Brush.
Latex	Most popular. Water-thinned, water cleanup. Gloss, semigloss, satin, flat. May be used over most surfaces but not on wallpaper, wood, or metal.	Brush, roller, pad.
Oil	Slow-drying, strong odor. Coverage may not be as good as synthetic paints. Solvent cleanup, solvent-thinned.	Brush, roller, spray.
One-coat	Water- or solvent-thinned. Costs more than regular latex or alkyd. Surface must be sealed first. Excellent covering power.	Brush, roller, pad.
Polyurethane/ Urethane	Expensive. Can be used over most finishes, porous surfaces. Extreme durability. Solvents, primers vary.	Brush.
Texture	Good for covering surface defects. Premixed or mix-at-home types. Application slow. Permits surface design of choice.	Brush, roller, pad, trowel, sponge.

color you like or have the paint mixed to one-half of the color.

■ Bring home paint chip samples and look at them in various kinds of light.

■ If you're in doubt about a color, buy a quart of paint and paint one wall. Wait until it dries and look at it in various lights to make sure it's what you want.

■ Color can saturate your eyes. When mixing paint, look away at a white surface for several minutes to allow your eyes to adjust so that you can judge the color accurately.

TAKING A BREAK

Although not difficult, painting can be tiring. It's worth taking a break to rest your muscles, especially those in the shoulders, neck, arms, and back. To keep your break easy, try the following tips:

■ Try not to stop in the middle of a wall or the ceiling. You'll lose the wet edge and risk visible lap marks when the paint dries.

■ Use all the paint in your tray, particularly if it's latex; otherwise it will dry out quickly.

■ If you want to take a short break or if you're interrupted in the middle of a painting job, wrap a plastic bag or aluminum foil around your brushes and rollers just tight

enough to keep the air out but loose enough to avoid crushing the bristles on brushes or the pile on rollers.

■ Leave brushes on a flat surface or hang them up. Do not leave your brush standing up in the can. The bristles may bend or paint may be drawn up into the top of the brush.

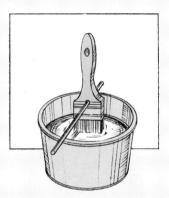

■ Leftover paint should be poured back into the can and the cans should be sealed. Wipe the rim of the can first with the tip of the brush, then with a paper towel. Drape a cloth over the lid, and lightly hammer it down.

PREPARING SURFACES

■ Patch any holes or cracks in plaster walls; prime them before painting.

■ Use a hammer to reset any popped nails in drywall. Fill the "dimple" created by the hammer with spackling compound, let it dry, and sand lightly.

■ Sand woodwork and any surfaces before using high-gloss paint.

■ Dust thoroughly, including ceilings.

■ Use masking tape to separate areas where different paints will be used, such as on window frames and trim. Use a spoon to press the tape

PAINTBRUSH TIPS

- Before getting paint or stain on the brush, condition it. For latex paints, dampen the brush with water; remove the excess moisture by gently striking the metal band around the handle's base over the edge of your palm and into a sink or pail. For alkyd paints, soak the brush for a day in a can of linseed oil. The brush will last longer and be easier to clean.

- Never dip a brush more than one-third of the length of the bristles into the paint.

- Clean latex paint and stain off brushes with a mixture of household detergent and water. Rinse thoroughly.

- Clean alkyd paint and stain off brushes with mineral spirits or paint thinner. Use a specially designed "comb" to get the thinner completely through the brush.

- An empty coffee can with a plastic lid makes a perfect container for soaking brushes. Just make two slits in the center of the plastic lid to form an "X," push the brush handle up through the "X," and replace the lid. The lid seals the can so the solvent can't evaporate, and the brush is suspended without the bristles resting on the bottom of the can.

tightly to the surface to keep paint from seeping under it. Remove the tape before the paint is dry. With latex paints, wait only 30 minutes to remove tape. With alkyd paints, wait 2 or 3 hours.

- Before painting a ceiling, turn off the light fixture, loosen it, and let it hang down. Then wrap it in a plastic bag for protection against paint splatters. Bring in a secondary light source.

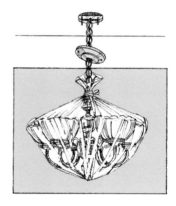

- Move as much furniture as possible out of the room or to the center of the room. Cover it and the floor with drop cloths.

- Glue paper plates to the bottom of paint cans to serve as drip catchers. The plates move along with the cans and are more convenient than newspapers.

- If you don't want to—or can't—remove hardware when painting adjacent areas, coat the hardware with petroleum jelly before painting. Any paint that gets on the metal by accident can be easily wiped off.

■ If your wall switch cover plate was painted over and you need to remove it, avoid flaking any paint by cutting around the plate's edge with a razor blade. Remove the screws, and lift off the plate.

PAINTING CEILINGS

■ Paint the ceiling before painting the walls. You'll not only eliminate the risk of spattering paint on the walls, it gets the worst job over first.

USING A PAINT ROLLER

■ Moisten the roller with water or thinner, depending on whether you're using latex or alkyd paint. Roll out the excess on a piece of scrap lumber, craft paper, or a paper grocery bag. Don't use newspaper because the roller could pick up the ink.

■ Fill the well of the roller pan about half-full and set the roller into the middle of the well.

■ Lift the roller and roll it down the slope of the pan, stopping just short of the well. Do this two or three times to allow the paint to work into the roller. Then dip the roller into the well once more and roll it on the slope until the pile is saturated.

■ If the roller is overloaded, it will drip on the way to the wall and have a tendency to slide and smear—instead of roll—across the surface.

■ Work on a 2- or 3-foot-square area at a time. Roll on the paint in a zigzag pattern without lifting the roller from the wall or ceiling, as if you're painting a capital "M" or "W." Without lifting the roller, fill in the

blanks of the letters with more vertical zigzag strokes.

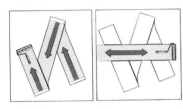

■ Finish the area with light strokes that start in the unpainted area and roll into the paint. At the end of the stroke, raise the roller slowly so that it leaves no mark.

■ Always start with a roller stroke away from you. On walls, the first stroke should be up. If you roll down on the first stroke, the paint may puddle under the roller and run down the wall.

■ Be careful not to run the roller so rapidly across the wall that centrifugal force causes it to spray paint.

■ Avoid bumping the roller into the walls as you paint the ceiling or into the ceiling as you paint the walls. The roller may leave a ridge of paint each time it touches the ceiling or wall.

CUTTING-IN CORNERS

To neatly paint up to a line where two edges or colors meet, called "cutting in," use a trim brush with beveled bristles. Paint five or six strokes perpendicular to the edge of the ceiling or the wall. Next, smooth over these strokes with a single, long stroke, painting out from the corner first and then vertically. Where the wall and ceiling meet, use downward strokes on the wall followed by smooth horizontal strokes. On the ceiling itself, cut in strokes toward the center of the room, away from the wall. Then paint a smooth horizontal stroke on the ceiling that follows the direction of the wall. Even if you're using the same color of paint on adjoining surfaces, follow this method of cutting in with 1-inch-wide borders rather than just plopping a loaded brush directly into a corner. This will prevent drips, sags, and runs.

Beading, another cutting-in approach, can practically eliminate the need to use masking tape to protect one painted area from another. Use a beveled trim brush with long bristles. Press the brush lightly against the surface, then as you move the brush, add just enough pressure to make the bristles bend away from the direction of your brushstroke. Keep the brush about $\frac{1}{16}$ inch away from the other colored surface. The bent bristles and the pressure will release a fine bead of paint that will spread into the gap.

■ Maintain a wet edge at all times to avoid creating lines or ridges.

■ When painting a ceiling with a roller, it's not necessary to try to keep the roller strokes all the same length; the lines won't show when the paint dries.

■ Use a zigzag pattern, starting about 3 feet out from one corner; work across the narrow dimension of the room in 3-foot-square areas.

PAINTING WALLS

■ Paint an entire wall before taking a break so that the painted portions won't lose their wet edge.

■ Always stand back when done and check for any missed spots or smears. Using a movable light

PAINTING PRECAUTIONS

- Water-thinned or solvent-thinned, paint ingredients are poisonous and should be kept away from children and pets. Antidotes are listed on can labels.

- Work in well-ventilated areas at all times, even if you're using odorless paints. They still contain fumes that may be harmful if inhaled. Wear a painter's mask when painting indoors. Also wear one outdoors if you're using an airless sprayer. Do not sleep in a room until the odor has dissipated.

- Do not smoke while painting, and, if possible, extinguish all pilot lights on gas appliances. Shut off gas to the unit first.

- Toxic paint chemicals can be absorbed through the skin. Wash up as soon as possible.

- When painting overhead, wear goggles to keep paint out of your eyes. Chemical ingredients can cause burns to sensitive eye tissue.

source, walk along the wall to detect any missed or thin areas.

- Paint in sections from top to bottom or from side to side. If you're using an extension handle, it's more convenient to start in one higher corner and go all the way across the room, so you won't have to change the handle on your roller as often.

- Where you don't have enough room to do the zigzag pattern—over and under windows and above doors—roll the paint on horizontally.

- Use a 4-inch roller or a paintbrush between windows and around doors.

PAINTING TRIM

- Trim can be painted before or after walls. If you paint trim after walls, take care to avoid touching the walls. If you paint trim first, mask it before painting walls.

- Use spackling compound to repair any holes in trim.

- Sand glossy wood trim to allow the next coat to adhere.

- Run a bead of quality interior caulk between moldings and walls. Wet your finger and smooth the caulk into the gap, avoiding the creation of ridges. Allow to dry thoroughly before painting.

PAINTING WINDOWS

- Some painters prefer to use painter's tape on windows; others believe that the time it takes to get the tape on just right (on the glass and butted up to the seal) isn't worth the time. Whether you use painter's tape or not, paint smoothly and avoid getting too much paint on the window.

■ To paint double-hung windows, raise the bottom sash more than halfway up and lower the top sash until its bottom rail is several inches below the bottom sash. Paint the bottom rail of the top sash and on up the stiles (or sides) as far as you can go. Paint all the surfaces of the bottom sash except the top edge.

■ Next, reverse the position of the sashes—top sash up to within 1 inch of the window frame, bottom sash down to within 1 inch of the sill. Paint the formerly obstructed surfaces of the top sash and the top edges of both sashes.

■ Next, paint the window frame, working from top to bottom, including the sill.

■ When the paint is dry to the touch on the sashes, move them both down as far as they will go and paint the exposed jambs. (Don't paint metal jambs.) Let the paint dry, then raise both sashes all the way and paint the lower jambs.

PAINTING DOORS

■ Flush doors—those with smooth, flat surfaces—can be painted with either a brush or roller.

■ For doors that are not flush, begin by painting the inset panels at the top of the door. Paint all the panels and the molding around them, working your way from top to bottom.

■ No matter what type of door you are painting, finish the entire door without stopping. Otherwise, the paint marks may show.

■ If possible, remove doorknobs, the plates behind them, and the latch plate at the top of the door.

■ If you can't remove doorknobs, protect them by wrapping the knobs with aluminum foil or by slipping plastic sandwich bags over them.

■ Paint the top rail, middle rail, and bottom rail (the horizontal rails) with back-and-forth strokes. Paint the stiles (the vertical rails) with up-and-down strokes.

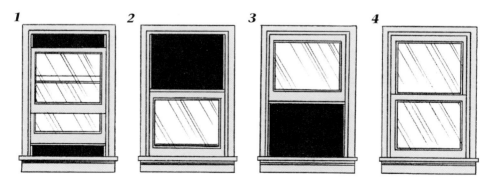

1   2   3   4

- Paint the top edge of the door with a light coat. Over time, paint can build up on the top edge, causing the door to stick.

- Paint the door's hinge edge and latch edge. Paint the bottom edge of the door or it may warp from moisture infiltration.

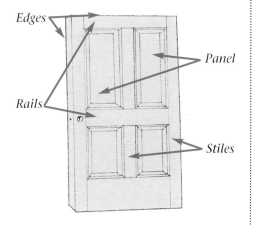

Edges

Panel

Rails

Stiles

PAINTING STAIRWAYS

- When painting stairs, paint alternate steps so that you'll have a way out. When those dry, paint the others.

- Where appearance isn't important, steps will be safer if you sprinkle a little silica sand over the wet paint (so that they'll be less slippery) and edge them with luminous paint (so that they'll be more visible).

PAINTING CABINETS AND CUPBOARDS

- Remove all obstructions, including handles, hinges, pulls, knobs, latches, and drawers.

- If the hinges have pins that can be removed easily, take off the doors until the cabinet and cupboard interior surfaces have been painted and dried.

- Paint interiors before exteriors in the following order: 1) inside back wall; 2) inside top; 3) side walls; 4) bottom; 5) top and edges of shelves.

- Work from the top down to paint the exteriors.

- Stand drawers on newspapers and paint only their fronts. Do not paint the exterior sides or exterior bottoms of the drawers.

- Be sure to let all pieces dry thoroughly before putting them back together.

CLEANUP AND STORAGE

- Begin cleaning as soon as possible. Fresh paint comes out easily from brushes and pans but once dry, it's almost impossible to restore them.

- To avoid having to clean a paint roller pan, use a disposable plastic pan liner.

- To clean a paint roller after its first use, roll it as dry as possible, first on the newly painted surface and then on several sheets of newspaper. Then slide the roller from its support and clean it with water or a solvent, depending on the type of paint used.

■ Mark paint cans with the level of paint, the color, and where they were used.

■ Remove paint splatters from your hair by rubbing the spots with baby oil.

■ To get paint drips off hardwood, ceramic tile, or resilient flooring, wrap a cloth around a putty knife and gently scrape up the paint. Then wash the areas with warm, soapy water.

WALLCOVERINGS

While painting is easier, covering your walls with paper, fabric, or even paneling lends a more decorative touch. Papering walls is the least expensive and easiest way to achieve a new effect in a room, although it is not recommended that novices begin with silkscreened paper that has not been precut.

WALLPAPERS

TOOLS AND MATERIALS

■ Appropriate adhesive for nonprepasted coverings

■ Paste brush and bucket for wall covering that must be pasted

■ Water tray for prepasted coverings

■ Sponge

■ Plumb line

■ Tape measure

■ Scissors and utility knife

■ Putty knife or scraper

■ Seam roller

■ Vinyl or nonvinyl smoothing brush, depending on whether you're using a vinyl covering

■ Screwdriver to remove screws from outlet and switch covers

■ Pasting table (optional)

ESTIMATING NUMBER OF ROLLS

Wallpapers (used generically to refer to paper, vinyl-coated, vinyl, burlap, and grass cloth) are sold in rolls that are between 15 and 54 inches wide. Regardless of the width, a single roll contains about 36 square feet. With trimming and waste, you can safely estimate about 30 square feet of coverage from a roll of wallpaper.

To calculate how many rolls you need for a room, find the perimeter of the room by measuring the length of each wall and adding the measurements together. Then measure the height. Multiply the first figure by the second and then divide by 30. The result will be the number of rolls you need. For example, in a 9×11-foot room, the perimeter equals 40 feet (9 + 9 + 11 + 11). With 8-foot ceilings,

REMOVING OLD PAPER

- Strippable paper has a smooth, plasticlike texture that allows the paper to be stripped from the walls. You'll simply have to sponge off any remaining adhesive.

- "Peelable" papers are just that—you can peel them off, but a papery surface will be left on the walls. This is easily removed with commercial wallpaper remover.

- If thick, old paper or layers of paper don't come off the walls easily, use a putty knife or scraper to score the old paper and allow the wallpaper remover to get under to the adhesive. Be careful not to slash into the actual wall to avoid making repairs. Make slits 8 to 10 inches apart, and sponge remover into the holes. Let set and use a wide drywall knife or putty knife to scrape off the paper when it starts to look soft.

- For major removal jobs, you may want to rent a wallpaper steamer. When removing old wallpaper with a steamer, save the ceiling for last. As you work on the walls, steam rising from the applicator will loosen the ceiling paper. Much of it will start sagging from its own weight, and peeling it off will be easy.

you would multiply 40 by 8 to get the total square footage of 320 square feet. Dividing this number by 30 equals 10.6, which means you'll need 11 rolls to wallpaper the room.

If you are covering a ceiling, multiply its width by its length to determine the surface area in square feet and divide the number by 30.

To make sure your estimates are accurate, ask your wallpaper dealer to check your figures, and don't scrimp. If you are using a patterned wallpaper, you'll need extra paper to accommodate the inches of paper that are lost in order to match the pattern. You'll also want some extra paper in case you make a mistake or need to make repairs later.

CHOOSING A WALLPAPER

Color, pattern, and texture aren't the only things to consider. In some rooms, like a child's bedroom, kitchen, or family room, durability is critical. A nonwashable wallpaper might be appropriate for a dining room that is reserved for special meals, but walls that will be exposed to regular doses of fingerprints and spills should be covered with durable, scrubbable vinyl.

Fabric-backed solid vinyls tolerate the most abuse. They're more washable than painted surfaces and resistant to scuffs and scratches. Vinyl-covered paper is slightly less durable; it is usually considered washable but not scrubbable. Printed papers, flocked papers, foils, grass cloths, and hand-painted papers should be reserved for rooms that won't be subject to much abuse.

You'll also want to consider whether a wallpaper needs a liner, whether it can be used on rough walls, and whether it is prepasted or must be pasted. Prepasted papers have a dry, factory-applied adhesive on the back that becomes sticky when moistened with warm water. Other wallpapers require an appropriate paste solution that must be applied to the back of the paper.

- If you're planning your first attempt at hanging wallpaper, choose a covering that's easy to work with—pretrimmed, vinyl-coated paper with a simple pattern.

- Small and random patterns are much easier to match than stripes and large patterns.

- Vertical patterns tend to make the ceiling seem higher; horizontal patterns do the opposite.

- A large room will seem cozier if covered with a large, bold pattern; small patterns with lots of light background open up a room.

- To raise the height of the room or to draw attention to the ceiling (particularly if it has decorative moldings), choose a simple pattern and use a more strongly patterned or colored border at the top of the walls.

- Pay attention to texture. Shiny surfaces, such as foils, attract light and tend to "cool" a room; heavier textures, such as burlap and grass cloth, absorb the light and "warm" the room.

- The reflective surface of foil wallpaper tends to emphasize small bumps or imperfections on the wall surface. To minimize irregularities, use a lining paper under these wallpapers.

- Color is uniform on machine-printed rolls cut from one continuous run, but it may differ from previous or subsequent runs. Because of this, wallpaper manufacturers assign lot or run numbers to each roll. When you buy machine-printed paper, make sure to get rolls that have the same lot number on them.

PREPARING SURFACES

■ Turn off the power and remove electrical cover plates and all fixtures on the walls. Keep the power off while you're hanging paper.

■ Strip or scrape old paper from the walls.

■ Sand any bumps and fill any holes with spackling compound, dry, and then sand smooth.

■ Wash walls to remove any built-up dirt or grime.

■ Plan your first strip. Choose an inconspicuous corner, preferably behind a door. It's almost inevitable that the pattern won't match perfectly as you return to the start.

HANGING WALLPAPER

■ Use a 4-foot level or chalk line to mark where your first strip of paper should hang. Remember that few walls are perfectly plumb (vertically level). If you begin by hanging your first strip in the corner without establishing a level line, the last strip may be seriously out of plumb.

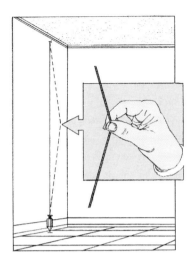

■ Cut the first strip of wallpaper 4 to 6 inches longer than the height of the room, then place it pattern side up on the pasting table.

■ To use prepasted paper, position the water tray under the place you plan to begin and fill the water tray about two-thirds full. Roll the cut strip so the pattern is on the inside and soak in the tray as directed by the wallpaper manufacturer. Remove the paper from the water and gradually unroll it.

■ To hang prepasted paper, trim the paper to length (leaving 4 to 6 inches for minor adjustments) and roll the paper loosely with the pasted side out. Then place the roll in a tray of warm water. Allow it to soak for one minute and slowly unroll it from the tray. Any areas that did not get wet in the soak will get a coating of water as you pull it from the tray.

HANGING BORDERS

Borders provide an easy, inexpensive way to dress up a room. You can hang them over wallpaper or painted walls. Border paper is available in various widths—usually between 2 and 8 inches—in a wide variety of designs. It can be hung under the ceiling molding to attract attention upward; slightly below the ceiling to make a tall room seem lower and cozier; at chair-rail height in a breakfast room or children's room; or around a door or window as a decorative "frame."

Wallpaper borders are sold by the yard. To find out how much you need, add up the distance all around the room in feet, then divide by 3 to give you the yardage. You will want to make sure that it's perfectly level, because any "wave" in the border will show up immediately.

If you're hanging the border around a window or door, be sure to miter the corners for a neat edge. Overlap the border strips at the corner with each strip extending past the other about 1 inch. Use a sharp utility knife to make a 45-degree cut through both papers. Remove the waste from the top border, then lift the other side and remove the waste from below.

■ Before hanging each length of paper, be sure to "book" it. When booking, lay the paper out on a clean surface, pasted side up. Then fold it in half, top-to-bottom, so the pasted sides of the paper are in full contact. (Be careful not to crease the fold area.) Allow each roll to book about 5 minutes.

■ To use nonprepasted covering, mix adhesive according to directions. Use a brush to apply the paste to the center of the strip, and work outward. Follow the manufacturer's instructions on how much paste should be used. When finished, book it—fold the pasted side of the paper toward the middle from each short edge. (Be careful not to crease the fold area.) Allow each roll to book approximately 5 minutes.

■ For nonprepasted papers, unfold the top half of the strip and position in place as suggested above. Then pull the other half of the paper out from under it before fully smoothing it on the walls.

■ Place the first strip of wallpaper near the top edge and along the plumb line. Use the wallpaper brush to smooth the paper on the wall, gradually working your way to the sides and down. Make sure the bottom is aligned before trimming the top with a utility knife.

■ To place each strip correctly, match the pattern near the top edge, set the paper against the wall next to the previous strip, and slide it to butt exactly against the already pasted paper.

■ Correct small mistakes in placement with the smoothing brush. Poorly set strips can be peeled off and repositioned.

■ Foil wallpapers are easily damaged, so instead of using a smoothing brush on them, pat them in place with a sponge or folded towel. Bond the seams in the same way.

■ Paper over all outlet openings, and simply trim the paper at these holes with a utility knife when you're finished papering the room. The switch and outlet covers will hide any ragged trims.

■ To work around a door, window, or other opening, set the precut short strip in place above the opening, handling it just as you would a full-length strip.

■ To paper around corners, make sure the strip doesn't fit exactly into a corner but goes beyond it by at least an inch. If your strip does end up in a corner, it's unlikely that your pattern will match because corners are rarely plumb.

■ Blisters result from excess adhesive. Use a smoothing brush to work them out to the sides of the strip. While small blisters may disappear as the adhesive dries, large blisters are unlikely to disappear. After about 2 hours, use a pin to puncture

the blister. Gently squeeze out the trapped adhesive with your thumbs.

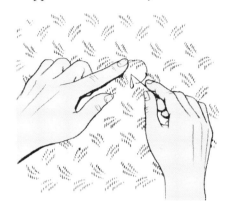

■ To repair loose seams, lift the seam and use an artist's brush to apply adhesive under the seam.

PANELING

If you're looking for a way to cover deteriorated walls or give any area a new look, consider installing manufactured wall paneling. Large but lightweight sheets of paneling go up fast, and once they're up, the job is usually over because most paneling requires no finishing.

On existing walls, remove the molding and trim and check for high or low spots by moving a board against the wall and watching for any gaps as you draw it along. Build up any low spots with joint compound, and sand down any high spots. If the walls are badly cracked or uneven, install furring strips on which to attach the paneling. (Furring strips are 2×4s that are nailed or glued to the wall, with pieces of cedar shingle under them to even up low spots.)

TIME-SAVERS

- If there are stubborn grease spots on walls that you're going to paper, seal them with clear nail polish or shellac so that the grease won't soak through the new wallpaper.

- Wallpaper a ceiling with the strips positioned crosswise—they're shorter and more manageable. Accordion-fold each strip, pasted area against pasted area, and unfold it as you go along, supporting the paper

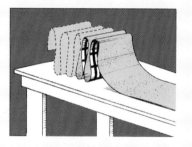

with one hand and smoothing it onto the ceiling with the other.

- When papering over wall anchors or places where you plan to reposition shelves or pictures, insert toothpicks in holes left by screws or picture hooks. As you cover these sections, force the toothpick points through the paper to mark reinstallation points for screws or hooks.

- Use a razor or small, pointed scissors to make tiny cuts to allow paper to lie flat next to openings and tight corners.

- If you don't have a seam roller to tame a loose wallpaper seam, rub the seam with the back of a spoon.

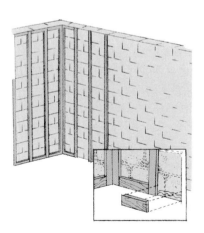

You'll need to compensate for the increased thickness of the wall at

electrical wall switches and outlets. Electrical codes will prohibit leaving a gap between an existing box and its coverplate, as this would expose the cable connections to combustible materials. Pull the receptacles from the existing boxes (without removing the wires) and install insert-type box extensions. These extensions look like standard boxes but don't have backs in them. As they are slightly smaller than standard boxes, they can be inserted into existing boxes. Front flanges keep them from going in too far. With the extensions in place, mount the receptacles and coverplates normally.

After the panels have stabilized to the humidity and temperature in the room for 48 hours, lean them against the walls where you want them. When you have the panels arranged the way you want them, number them.

Measure the distance from floor to ceiling at several different points. If the panels have to be cut for height, you can cut all of them the same, provided the height varies by no more than ¼ inch. If the variance is more than ¼ inch, you should measure the height for each panel and cut it to fit. If you are using ceiling moldings, leave a ¼-inch gap at the ceiling line. There should also be a ¼-inch gap at the floor, which will be concealed by the baseboard.

Because few corners are plumb, place the first panel in a corner next to the wall and check for plumb with a level. Get the panel plumb and close enough to the corner so that you can span the space with a scribing compass. Then run the compass down the corner, with the point in the corner and the pencil marking a line on the panel. Cut the panel along the marked line using a saber saw equipped with a fine-tooth blade. Install the first panel so that it is plumb. If it isn't, the error will compound itself with each additional panel you install.

If you plan to nail the panels, use nails of a matching color. You can use 3d finishing nails to attach the panels to furring strips. If you must go through wall material to reach the studs, be sure to use nails that are long enough to penetrate about 1 inch into the studs. Drive nails about every 6 inches along the edges of the panel and about every 16 inches across the center. Check frequently to make sure you are nailing into the furring strips.

If you are using panel adhesive, it is applied with a caulking gun. Run a ribbon of adhesive down all the furring strips or, if there are no strips, along the perimeter and in the pattern of an "X." Nail the panel in place at the top and bottom with a pair of nails.

When you come to a door or window, use one of the large sheets of paper that came between the sheets of paneling to make a pattern. Tape the paper in place, press it against the door or window frame, mark it with a pencil, and cut it to fit with scissors. Use this pattern to transfer the marks to the panel; then cut with a fine-tooth crosscut hand-saw or with a saber saw equipped with a fine-tooth blade.

To make cutouts for electrical outlets or switches, measure care-fully, trace the outline of the switch or outlet box on the panel, and drill pilot holes at opposite corners. Then use a keyhole or saber saw to con-nect the corners with a saw cut.

Home Safety and Security

A house equipped with an expensive burglar alarm won't alert you to a fire, and smoke detectors won't prevent a family member from slipping and falling on the stairs. To create a safe home for your family, you need to take steps to prevent accidents, fires, and theft. You and your family need to know what to do in an emergency. While these measures won't guarantee your family's safety, they will limit your vulnerability. If you have children in your home, be sure to refer to the safety precautions in the "Child Care" chapter. If you have pets, refer to the safety precautions in the "Pet Care" chapter.

ACCIDENT PREVENTION

Home accidents are one of the leading causes of death among children and injuries among adults. In many cases, these accidents could have been avoided by taking simple precautions. Check your house—and your habits—to ensure that your home isn't a danger zone.

■ Wipe up spilled water, grease, and other liquids from your kitchen, bathroom, and garage floors as soon as possible to avoid slips.

■ Secure rugs with nonskid pads or slip-resistant backing. You can also use double-face adhesive carpet tape to keep them in place.

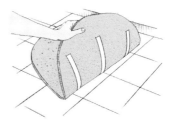

■ Don't put hot tea, coffee, or other hot liquids on a tablecloth that hangs over the side of the table. Someone could trip on the cloth and spill the scalding liquid.

■ Never keep a loaded gun in the house; store ammunition and weaponry separately.

■ If an elderly person or someone who is unsteady on his or her feet lives in your home, install grab bars in bathtubs or showers. A stool with nonskid tips can be used as a seat while showering.

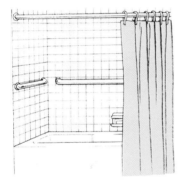

■ Choose a step stool with a handrail to hold when standing on the top step. Always make sure the step stool is fully open and steady before climbing it.

■ Elderly people and children are often at risk of burns from scalding water. By setting the hot-water heater below 120°F, you can avoid this risk. If your hot-water heater does not have a thermostat, use a thermometer to check the water at the faucet.

■ Never place an electric appliance where it can fall in water.

■ Never touch an electric appliance while you are standing in water.

■ Don't place electric heaters near combustible materials.

■ Do you use your basement or garage as a general storage area? If so, there are probably many things you can trip over, including tools and sharp or pointed objects. Look at these areas with an eye toward accident prevention, and remove

STAIR SAFETY

■ Handrails that don't run the full length of a staircase can be dangerous—someone may assume that the stairs end where the handrail ends and miss the last step. If necessary, consider extending or replacing the handrail.

■ If stair carpeting becomes loose, fix it immediately. It's very easy to slip on loose carpeting.

■ Be sure not to use throw rugs at the top or bottom of a flight of stairs.

■ If you intend to paint basement stairs, either add a little sand to the paint for a better grip or install rubber or abrasive treads.

■ If the outside of your house is not well lit, paint the edges of outside steps white so that they are easier to see in the dark or install outdoor lighting.

or rearrange any objects that are potential hazards.

■ Never remove the guards from your power tools. Tools used with the guards removed pose a serious risk of injury.

SAFE USE AND STORAGE OF PESTICIDES

Many pests and insects can be eliminated without the aid of an exterminator, but it's important to know how to safely use and store these poisonous substances. Read the instructions on any pesticide before use, and keep the following in mind:

■ Never spray insecticides near a flame, furnace, lighted stove, or pilot light.

■ Keep insecticide sprays away from children, pets, dishes, food, and cooking utensils.

■ When fumigating, use only the amount of pesticide required for the job.

■ Never flush insecticides down the toilet, sewer, or drains.

■ Never smoke while using pesticide, and thoroughly wash your hands immediately after using the materials.

■ As soon as you have used a space spray (bomb), leave the room. Close the room up tightly for at least ½ hour before ventilating, then air out the room carefully.

■ Follow the manufacturer's instructions for storage. Most pesticides should be tightly sealed and stored in a cool, dark place. Store them in a locked cabinet or on high shelves away from children.

■ Do not reuse insecticide containers. Wrap them in brown paper bags or newspaper and dispose of them properly.

■ Wear rubber gloves when spraying anything poisonous.

FIRE PREVENTION

Fires can strike anywhere at any time. Along with installing smoke detectors in your home, you should have a fire extinguisher in key areas such as the kitchen, bedrooms, workshop, and garage. Walk your family through a fire drill so everyone knows what to do and where to go in case of fire. Every room in the house should have at least two escape exits. If one of these is a window from a second story, install ladders that can be dropped from the windows. Make sure children know where the family will reunite if they have to leave the house in case of fire. The following simple precautions will help minimize the risk of a fire in your home:

■ Assign a special closet for combustible materials and

HOW TO HANDLE A FIRE

- If you smell smoke or your smoke detectors sound, get your family out immediately. Call the fire department from a neighbor's house.

- Never reenter a burning house for any reason. Leave fire fighting to the professionals as soon as they're on the scene.

- Never use water on electric, oil, or grease fires. Turn off the heat immediately, and use a lid or a large piece of metal bakeware to smother the flames.

- If you can't shut off the gas before fighting a gas fire, get out of the house immediately.

- If you can't remove the fuel from a wood, paper, or fabric fire, cut off its air by smothering the fire with a coat or heavy woolen blanket. You might also cool the fire with water or a fire extinguisher.

- Even if a fire is confined to a frying pan or wastebasket, never spend more than 30 seconds fighting the fire. Small fires can grow with frightening speed.

- If someone's clothes are on fire, douse the flames with water or use a heavy blanket to smother the fire.

dangerous tools that you don't want your children to touch. Put a good lock on the door and a heat detector inside to alert you to any fire danger.

- Don't overload electrical circuits with too many appliances. If your fuses are blowing or your circuit breakers are popping, hire an electrician to look at your system.

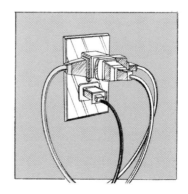

■ Don't run extension cords under rugs or carpets. The cords wear easily and may short out, causing a fire.

■ Nails or staples used to attach electrical cords to the walls or baseboards can damage the cords

SMOKING OUT A FIRE

Smoke detectors won't prevent a fire but they save lives by alerting you to smoke. If you don't have smoke detectors, install them now. In most jurisdictions, landlords are required to have smoke detectors in rental units. For basic protection at minimum expense, place one smoke detector in the hallway near each separate sleeping area. Ask your city or town's fire department for advice on purchasing detectors. And be sure to check the batteries in your smoke detectors at least twice a year. Many people find that they remember to do this if they take care of it when daylight savings time begins in April and ends in October.

Don't mount a smoke detector in areas where the alarm can be triggered inappropriately—such as by smoke from cooking, steam from the shower, or in the garage where combustion products from the car's engine can set it off.

and cause fire or shock hazards. Tape cords to walls or floors instead of using nails or staples.

■ Replace frayed electrical cords before they burn or cause a fire.

■ Keep combustibles away from the furnace, which can emit flames or sparks.

■ Some fire departments supply stickers that can be placed in a window to alert firefighters to the presence of a child or an elderly or physically challenged person. Determine whether such stickers are available in your locality.

■ An electrical outlet or switch that is unusually warm or hot to the touch may indicate a potentially dangerous wiring condition. In such a situation unplug cords, avoid using switches, and call an electrician to check the wiring.

■ Ceiling fixtures and recessed lights trap heat. Since overheating can lead to fire, don't use a high-wattage bulb in such a fixture. If you don't know the correct wattage, use a bulb of 60 or fewer watts.

■ Always extinguish the fire in a wood stove before leaving the house and before going to bed.

■ Unplug your hair dryer or any other small appliance in the bathroom when not in use.

■ An electric blanket should not be tucked in at the sides. It may overheat and start a fire.

SAFETY IN THE KITCHEN

The kitchen is one of the more dangerous rooms in the house. Open flames, sharp knives, hot pots, and scalding liquids can cause serious injuries. Look at your kitchen from the perspective of an accident waiting to happen. Are papers stacked too close to the range or cooktop? Are knives easily accessible to children? Keep the following in mind:

■ Keep the gas cooktop away from open windows where wind could extinguish the cooking flames.

■ Keep the handles of pots and frying pans turned inward on the kitchen range so that they cannot be knocked over by accident.

■ When handing a knife to someone else, always hold the point turned away from the other person.

■ To prevent grease fires, keep the stove clear of anything flammable, including pot holders, napkins, and towels.

■ Keep baking soda on hand for extinguishing kitchen fires.

■ Be sure to turn a heating pad off before you go to sleep. It can cause burns even at a relatively low setting.

■ To make a dry fire extinguisher, pour 6 pounds of fine sand into a large container and add 2 pounds of baking soda. Stir the mixture thoroughly. Keep the container in your shop, garage, or kitchen. This mixture can be sprinkled directly on small oil, grease, and petroleum fires.

■ If you live or work in a high-rise building, locate the fire exits on your floor. If an alarm sounds, remember that you should always use the fire stairs, not the elevator.

STORM SAFETY

■ Always keep a battery-powered radio in your home so that you can tune to radio stations if you lose electricity. Check or change the batteries frequently.

■ Keep a flashlight in an easily accessible spot on every floor of your home. Check the batteries monthly, and replace them as needed.

■ Keep a supply of candles on hand for power failures.

■ As a safety precaution before leaving the house on vacation, unplug all electrical appliances except for those lights connected to automatic timers.

■ If you live in a storm-prone area, nail down roof shingles or use adequate adhesive to keep them from blowing off in a violent wind. For roofs with shingles that are not the seal-down type, apply a little dab of roofing cement under each tab.

■ A lightning-protection system should offer an easy, direct path for the bolt to follow into the ground and thus prevent injury or damage. Grounding rods (at least two for a house) should be placed at opposite corners of the house.

■ Don't go out during a hurricane unless you have to; however, if flooding threatens, seek high ground, and follow the instructions of civil defense personnel.

■ When a major storm is imminent, close shutters, board windows, or tape the inside of larger panes with an "X" along the full length of their diagonals. Even a light material like masking tape may

give the glass the extra margin of strength it needs to resist cracking.

■ When a tornado threatens, leave windows slightly ajar.

■ The basement is not a good shelter during a tornado—it's too close to gas pipes, sewer pipes, drains, and cesspools. A better shelter would be underground, far from the house (in case the roof falls) and away from the gas and sewer systems. Let all family members know where the shelter is.

■ Keep an eye on large trees—even healthy ones—that could damage your house if felled in a storm. Cut them back, if necessary.

Securing Your Property

While it's difficult to protect your home from professional thieves, most home burglaries are done by amateurs. These thieves are more easily thwarted if you employ some of these simple security precautions:

■ Plan to burglarize yourself. You'll discover any weaknesses in your security system that may have previously escaped your notice.

■ Lock up your home, even if you go out only for a short time. Many burglars just walk in through an unlocked door or window.

- Change all the locks and tumblers when you move into a new house.

- For the most effective alarm system, conceal all wiring. A professional burglar looks for places where he or she can disconnect the security system.

- Your house should appear occupied at all times. Use timers to switch lights and radios on and off when you're not at home.

- If you have a faulty alarm that frequently goes off, get it fixed immediately and tell your neighbors that it's been repaired. Many people ignore an alarm that goes off periodically.

- A spring-latch lock is easy prey for burglars who are "loiding" experts.

Loiding is the method of slipping a plastic credit card against the latch tongue to depress it and unlock the door. A deadbolt defies any such attack. It is only vulnerable when there is enough space between the door and its frame to allow an intruder to use power tools or a hacksaw.

- If you lose your keys, change the locks immediately.

- Before turning your house key over to a professional house cleaner for several hours, make sure the person is honest and reputable as well as hardworking. Check all references thoroughly. If the house cleaner is from a firm, call your local Better Business Bureau to check on the firm's reputation.

GARAGE SECURITY

- If you frost or cover your garage windows, burglars won't be able to tell if your car is gone.

- Keep your garage door closed and locked even when your car is not in the garage.

- Install a peephole in the door separating the house from the garage. If you hear suspicious sounds, you can check without opening the door.

- Are you worried about someone entering your house through your attached garage? If the garage door lifts on a track, a C-clamp can provide extra security

since the door cannot be opened if you tighten the C-clamp on the track next to the roller.

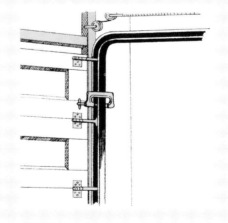

■ Instead of keeping a spare key in a mailbox, under the doormat, or on a nail behind the garage, wrap the key in foil—or put it in a 35mm film can—and bury it where you can easily find it if you need it.

■ Don't leave notes for service people or family members on the door. These act as a welcome mat for a burglar.

■ If the entrances to your home are dark, consider installing lighting with an infrared detector. Most thieves don't want to be observed trying to get in a door.

■ Talk to your neighbors about any suspicious people or strange cars you notice lurking about.

■ To keep your tools from being stolen, paint the handles. Thieves avoid items that are easy to identify.

■ Trees located near windows or shrubbery that might shield a burglar from view can be major flaws in your home-protection plan. Consider your landscaping plan in light of your protection needs.

■ Ask for credentials from any salesperson who requests entry to your home. Ask that their ID be pushed under the door. Many professional burglars use this cover to check out homes. If you're doubtful, check with the person's office before letting him or her in.

■ Do not list your full name on your mailbox or your entry in the telephone book. Use only your initial and your last name.

■ If someone comes to your door asking to use the phone to call a mechanic or the police, keep the door locked and make the call yourself.

■ Dogs are good deterrents to burglars. Even a small, noisy dog can be effective—burglars do not like to have attention drawn to their presence. Be aware, however, that trained guard dogs do not make good pets. Obedience training and attack training are entirely different, and only the former is appropriate for a house pet.

SECURING DOORS

■ To help burglar-proof your home, install 1-inch throw deadbolt locks on all exterior doors.

■ A door with too much space between the door and the frame is an invitation for the burglar to

PROTECTING YOUR VALUABLES

The most obvious way to protect your valuables is to store them in a safe-deposit box or in a secure home safe that is too heavy to be moved. When buying a wall safe, be sure it's fireproof. If you don't want to invest in a safe, other less-expensive alternatives can limit theft potential:

■ A chiseled-out space in the top of a door makes a great "safe" for small valuables.

■ Devise a hiding place in an acoustical ceiling. Remove a tile and restore it afterward with magnetic fasteners or a similar device. Be careful not to leave finger marks.

■ Hollow out the leg of a table or chair for hiding small objects. Drill from the bottom, then cap all the legs with rubber tips.

■ Avoid obvious places such as mattresses, drawers, inside figurines, behind pictures, and under carpets.

■ Many police departments offer a program that includes home inspection, advice on protective measures, and use of an engraving tool to mark a code number that will identify your valuables in case of theft. Call your police department to find out if they offer such a service.

use a jimmy. Reinforce the door with a panel of ¾-inch plywood or a piece of sheet metal.

■ If there are door hinges on the outside of your house, take down the door and reset the hinges inside. Otherwise all a thief has to do to gain entry to your home is knock out the hinge pin.

■ You can burglar-proof your glass patio doors by setting a pipe or metal bar in the middle bottom track of the door slide. The pipe should be the same length as the track.

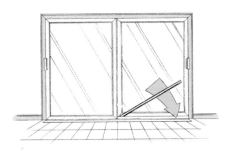

■ It's easy for a burglar to pry through rot. Replace rotted door frames with new, solid wood.

■ It's simple for a thief to break glass panels and then reach in and open a doorknob from the inside. A door with glass panels should be either fortified, replaced, or secured with deadbolts that can only be opened with a key.

SECURING WINDOWS

■ Protect your windows with one or more good locks, an alarm system, burglar-resistant glass, or many small panes instead of one large area of glass.

■ When installing a window lock, drip some solder on the screw heads. It will stop a burglar from unscrewing the lock after cutting a small hole in the windowpane.

WHEN YOU'RE AWAY

■ If your plans to be away from home have been publicized through a funeral, wedding, or similar newspaper notice, hire a house sitter. Burglars often read the newspapers to see who's planning to be away from home all day or for several days.

■ Ask your neighbors to use your garbage cans when you're on vacation so your absence won't be so evident.

■ If you're going to be away from home for several days—or even for just one day—adjust your telephone ring to its lowest volume. An unanswered phone is a quick tip that your home is empty.

Child Care

Parenthood is filled with joys, challenges, rewards, frustrations, surprises—and above all, questions. How can you keep your child safe at home and away? What equipment will your baby need? Do children's clothes need to be specially laundered? Along with the following information about child care, there's a wealth of knowledge about parenting available at bookstores and libraries that will answer your questions.

CREATING A SAFER HOME

Accidents are a leading cause of injury and death in children up to 5 years of age. Most of these accidents occur in and around the home, and many are preventable.

■ Store all poisonous materials on high shelves, out of the reach of children. Never keep poisonous products in containers or bottles used for beverages or food. Toxic products should have safety caps and should be properly closed.

■ The following houseplants are poisonous if swallowed or chewed and should be kept out of the reach of children: poinsettia, mistletoe, dieffenbachia, philodendron, rhubarb, laurel, rhododendron, azalea, and cherry boughs.

■ Make sure that your child cannot accidentally get locked in a closet or other confined space. Check all knobs and locks in the house, and remove any that suggest possible hazards.

■ Set the water heater no higher than 120°F to protect children from being scalded in the bathtub.

■ Make sure all electrical outlets are sealed off with safety caps. Also, check all electrical cords to make sure that the insulation has not become frayed and that the wires are not exposed.

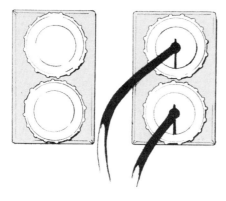

■ All dangling cords should be taped down, unplugged, or moved up out of your baby's reach.

■ Make sure that all windows your child might be able to get to are locked, barred, or adapted with window stops, screens, or grilles so that they will open no more than 6 inches.

■ Keep home workshop tools disconnected, and lock switches and power supplies so a child cannot turn them on.

■ Check all toys to be sure any eyes, noses, buttons, knobs, or other parts will not come off when pulled or chewed. Balloons, in particular, can be dangerous to small children (if a balloon pops, the small pieces are a choking hazard).

■ Keep small unsupervised children away from toys or games with disc batteries. The batteries are small enough to be swallowed and are potentially lethal. Household appliances, watches, and hearing aids containing these batteries should also be kept out of reach.

■ Avoid using caustic drain cleaners. The "metal snake" or standard rubber plunger are more effective in cleaning drains and offer no toxic hazard. Dispose of empty bottles that once contained caustics. Even if rinsed, they may contain crystals which, if ingested by a child, could cause injury.

THE KITCHEN

■ Install childproof latches on all drawers, closets, and cabinets containing poisonous materials and dangerous items.

■ Unplug all small electrical appliances when they are not in use; when they are in use, be sure that the cords are not dangling down where your child can reach them.

■ When using the stove, remember to keep all pot and pan handles turned toward the back of the stove; be careful when handling hot liquids that could spill or splatter; and repeatedly remind your child to stay far away when someone is cooking.

■ When serving or consuming hot foods or beverages, be sure to set them down on the middle of the table—not near the edge where a child could pull them off. Do not use tablecloths that hang over the table and can easily be yanked off.

■ Fold and put away all step stools.

■ Keep knives, forks, graters, and other utensils out of reach of infants and toddlers.

BEDROOMS

■ Do not leave jewelry where children could find it and possibly choke if they put it into their mouths.

■ Perfumes, deodorants, makeup, and other such substances can lead to accidental poisonings.

■ Belts, ties, shoelaces, and especially plastic bags can cause strangulation and suffocation. Keep them out of the reach of infants and children.

■ Never place pillows in an infant's crib, and keep the crib away from the cords of window shades, blinds, or drapes.

BATHROOMS

■ Even if you could manage to secure all the medicines, soaps, shampoos, nail clippers, hair dryers, scissors, and tweezers, the basic materials and equipment that constitute the bathroom would still represent an

unacceptable level of danger to infants and toddlers. There simply are too many slippery surfaces, hard tiles, hot water faucets, and water receptacles. Supervise children in the bathroom.

■ To prevent children from accidentally locking themselves in the bathroom, make sure the door has no fastening—like an inside bolt—that cannot be opened from the outside. You may also remove the lock and instruct everyone in the family to knock when the door is closed.

■ Face your child toward the hot-water faucet in the bathtub to prevent accidentally bumping into the hot metal.

■ If your small child can't distinguish or remember to stay away from the hot-water tap, make it easier by marking it with red tape.

■ Keep electrical appliances, such as shavers, hair dryers, and toothbrushes, away from small children. Teach older children the danger of using such appliances near water or with wet hands.

KEEPING CHILDREN SAFE AWAY FROM HOME

■ A child's fingerprints are a sure means of identification, and many organizations recommend that parents have children fingerprinted. Some police stations offer this service—they make one set of prints that parents keep. Ask if this service is available in your area. Home fingerprinting kits are also available.

■ Make sure your children know your family's rules about talking to or accepting gifts or rides from strangers.

■ Children love T-shirts, backpacks, tote bags, buttons, and other items on which their name is displayed. Unfortunately, such identification makes it easier for a stranger to greet a child by name, thus appearing to be a friend. Teach young children that someone who knows their name can still be a stranger to whom "stranger danger" rules apply. To be on the safe side, avoid having your child wear identity-revealing items.

■ Although it's not wise to have children wear clothing that reveals their name to strangers, they can carry an ID in an inconspicuous place when they go to a zoo, circus, or some other place where they might get lost. Attach a stick-on label listing the child's name and phone number inside a purse, tote bag, or a pocket.

■ When you take older children to a large, crowded place, such as a zoo or a ballpark, decide on a prearranged place where you will meet if you are accidentally separated. Agree to go directly to that location at a prearranged time or if you have failed to meet up after a certain length of time. Be very clear about the location.

■ For your child's safety when bicycling, insist on a helmet and identification including name, address, and phone number.

■ A child with a medical condition, such as diabetes, should always carry identification that includes medical condition, doctor's phone number, and details of medication or emergency treatment.

LIVING AREAS

■ Sofas, coffee tables, desks, and end tables usually have hard edges with sharp corners that pose a hazard to a crawling and climbing baby. Consider placing soft bumpers and round edge protectors on these trouble spots.

■ Remove all unstable furniture (furniture that can be easily pulled or pushed over) to an area that is inaccessible to your child. Also, watch out for rocking chairs and recliners, where a child's fingers or toes can get crushed or caught.

■ Placing a safety gate at the top of every staircase is highly recommended. Placing the lower gate at the third step up from the bottom will give your baby two or three steps on which to practice climbing stairs without risk of serious injury.

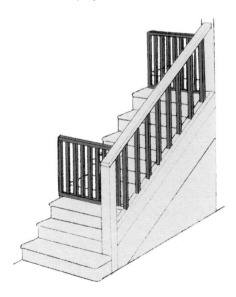

■ If you have a piano in your home, guard against a toddler accidentally dropping the lid on his or her fingers by fastening an upright cork at each end of the keyboard.

■ Make it easy for small children to go up and down your stairs. Add a temporary handrail at child-height on the wall opposite the permanent handrail. Keep stairways well lit and clear of toys, clothes, and debris.

■ Whenever a fire is burning, secure a screen or lock it in place to keep sparks from flying out; use only seasoned wood. A mesh screen is preferable to a glass screen because it won't get as hot.

■ Store pokers, other instruments that are heavy and have sharp points, matches, lighters, and starter fluid out of the reach of infants and young children.

■ Install smoke detectors on every floor of your home.

BUYING BABY EQUIPMENT

Security and stability are the key factors in buying equipment for your infant. First, look for the seal of approval from the Consumer Product Safety Commission (www.cpsc.gov), and examine items carefully to make sure they are stable and without safety hazards. Additional guidelines have been established by the Juvenile Products Manufacturers Association (www.jpma.org), and you may want to see if the product conforms to these voluntary standards.

■ Run your fingers over the equipment, and touch every spot with which the infant is likely to come in contact. Avoid rough surfaces or surfaces that could become dangerously hot if exposed to the sun.

■ Inspect all hinges, springs, or moving parts to make sure there are no places where your baby's hands, feet, fingers, or toes could get caught or pinched.

■ Examine all small parts, straps, and coverings to make sure they are fastened securely.

■ If equipment needs to be assembled, read and follow all manufacturer's directions.

CAR SEATS

■ Car seats for infants and young children are mandatory in all 50 states and must conform to Federal Motor Vehicle Safety Standards. Infants weighing under 20 pounds must be belted into the seat, facing the rear of the car, and in a reclining position. Older children may sit upright facing forward. Except for infant seats, most car seats convert from a reclining position to upright and can be used by children weighing up to 40 pounds. Children between the ages of 4 and 8 and weighing more than 40 pounds should be in a booster seat.

■ Make sure the seat you choose is comfortable for your baby, fits your car, and has a label indicating that it meets all federal requirements.

■ Make sure the seat is not difficult to use or confusing to operate, particularly if you will need to use the seat in more than one car. Incorrect use of car seats is dangerous as well as illegal.

CRIBS

■ Make sure the mattress fits snugly—if you can fit two fingers between the mattress and the side of the crib, your baby's head could become wedged there. A rolled blanket can be used to fill the space between the mattress and end boards. The mattress should be firm.

■ The slats of a crib should be less than 2⅜ inches apart so your baby's head cannot get caught between them. Headboards should not have cutouts or decorations that could trap the head or neck.

■ All hinges and screws should be well set and out of reach, and there should be secure safety latches on the drop side that cannot be tripped, either by your baby or by any curious older children who may have access to the nursery.

■ All finishes should be smooth, and all paints should be nontoxic.

■ Don't use soft pillows or blankets that can become easily bunched; until infants can lift their heads high for long periods of time by themselves, suffocation when lying facedown in soft materials is a possibility.

■ Make sure you can lift a portable crib without too much effort, that it folds and stores easily, and that it is stable.

HIGH CHAIRS AND STROLLERS

■ Anything the infant will be sitting in should have a wide base that keeps the device steady and decreases the chance of tipping.

■ Make sure a high chair or stroller has a good harness. Fasten it firmly to prevent your child from falling or climbing out.

■ Fold a stroller a few times and lift it into the folded position to see whether or not it will fit easily into the trunk of your car.

■ Make sure the mechanism that keeps a collapsible high chair or stroller open is securely locked when in use.

■ Make sure all surfaces are smooth and nontoxic and that all hinges, latches, and other features are in good working order and inaccessible to your baby's hands and fingers.

■ Make sure a stroller has solid wheels; rear wheels should come with shock absorbers.

CLOTHES FOR INFANTS AND CHILDREN

Comfort, convenience, ease of cleaning, and safety factors are important in selecting clothing for infants and children:

■ Try to buy clothing made from flame-retardant fabric. Many manufacturers are now using such materials exclusively, but it is wise to read all labels carefully.

■ Make sure any small items, such as buttons, ribbons, or decorative features attached to your baby's clothing are fastened securely. A button (or whatever is pulled off or falls off) can immediately become a choking hazard. Also check to see that zippers or elastics are stitched strongly into place. If the thread around such features begins to unravel, the article should be fixed or removed before accidental ingestion becomes a possibility.

■ Layettes (a term used to describe the clothing for a newborn) are generally a matter of choice. Along with a plentiful supply of diapers, your baby will also need a couple of changes of clothing daily, such as sleepers, stretch suits, nightgowns, pajamas, and undershirts; a receiving blanket; clothes for warm-weather outings or a knitted cap for cold-weather outings; socks or booties; and sweaters, bunting, or similar clothing for outings in cooler weather.

■ Wash your baby's clothes in mild soap or mild detergent and double-rinse them. Do not wash them with the rest of your laundry, and do not use fabric softeners, since many of them contain chemicals that may irritate your baby's skin. It's best to continue washing your baby's things separately for the first few months until skin becomes less sensitive.

SELECTING TOYS

■ Safety is the most important consideration when selecting toys. Make sure that any item—or any removable part of an item—is no less than 1¼ inches in any dimension so that it cannot be swallowed or produce gagging.

■ Avoid anything with sharp corners, jagged edges, or pointy protrusions.

■ Avoid toys made with straight pins, sharp wires, nails, and other dangerous materials.

■ Check to make sure that all materials and paints used in the production of any item are safe (not glass or brittle plastic) and labeled nontoxic.

■ Stuffed toys should be labeled "nonflammable," "flame resistant," or "flame retardant," as well as "washable."

■ Check for durability and sturdy construction. Don't be shy about

PRECAUTIONS WHEN YOU'RE NOT AT HOME

■ If you have young children and use babysitters, paste a name and address label near (or on) the telephone. Then the babysitter who knows you as "the lady across the road" but doesn't remember the street number of your house will have the full address right there if it's necessary to make an emergency call.

■ Give babysitters a tour of your house, including the location of your first-aid kit.

■ Write down instructions for babysitters; don't expect them to remember verbal instructions.

■ If you will be inaccessible while away, arrange to call and make sure the sitter has the phone number of a nearby friend or relative who can be contacted in case of an emergency.

■ Children should never reveal to callers that they are home alone. Teach them to tell phone callers that you can't come to the phone right now but if they'll give a number you will return their call.

■ Children old enough to answer the door should be able to see who's there, just as you do. Install a second peephole low enough for youngsters to use.

removing a toy from its box and giving it a good going-over. If it can be broken into little pieces, if buttons or other decorations can be torn off without too much effort, or if parts can pinch or trap fingers or catch hair, the toy is potentially dangerous.

■ Regulations go a long way toward protecting your child from unsafe playthings, but they are not an absolute guarantee. It is always possible that a slightly defective item will slip past the safety checks and end up in a store. Moreover, many toys from other countries are not subject to such regulations and many toys that were produced before the regulations went into effect end up on more informal markets, such as garage sales or flea markets. Before purchasing any plaything for your baby, give it a good going-over yourself to make sure that all safety factors are in order.

■ Check toys periodically to make sure they are in good repair. An item that passes all safety checks at the time of purchase can immediately become a serious hazard as soon as it is broken, chipped, or otherwise damaged.

HYGIENE

BATHING INFANTS

■ In the first two to three weeks of life, before the umbilical cord heals, your baby shouldn't have a tub bath. A sponge bath (in which a baby is not actually sitting in water) three to four times a week is usually adequate at this stage.

■ Wash the baby's diaper area, face, and neck whenever necessary.

■ Choose a convenient time for your baby's bath. You'll need to devote all your attention to the process, so aim for a time when you won't be disturbed. It's usually best to give a bath between feedings or before a feeding (although not when a baby is screaming from hunger). Avoid giving baths after a feeding—that's when the baby often sleeps. If the phone rings or someone comes to the door, have someone else answer it or just ignore it. You will not be able to leave, and taking the baby with you could cause your child to get chilled.

■ Be sure to clean the stump of the umbilical cord until it falls off during the second or third week after birth. Until the stump has separated and the area has healed, you'll probably be advised to clean the area with isopropyl (rubbing) alcohol. This should be done three to four times a day (or with every diaper change if that's easier to remember).

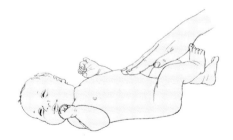

■ Use a baby bathtub to give your baby a bath. It is too difficult to do in a standard bathtub. Be sure that you cover all faucets and that you turn the cold water off last, so that the faucets are not scalding hot should your baby get near them.

■ Support the baby's head and back with one hand as you wash with the other.

■ Make sure the room is warm and that all slippery surfaces are lined with rubber mats or towels.

CARE OF THE GENITALS

Careful skin care in the genital area can help prevent diaper rash and infections.

■ Use a soft washcloth.

■ Use warm water with a small amount of gentle soap, and be sure to rinse thoroughly with clear water.

■ For newborn girls, wash gently in the folds of the genital area; be sure to gently wipe (not rub) from front to back.

■ For newborn boys who have been circumcised, be sure to follow your pediatrician's recommendations for caring for the penis. If you notice bleeding or any sign of infection (pus, redness, or swelling), notify your pediatrician.

■ For newborn boys who have not been circumcised, external washing and rinsing is recommended. Since the natural separation of the foreskin from the glans may not be complete for several years, do not attempt to forcibly retract the foreskin. If you can partially retract the foreskin without using pressure or causing pain, you can clean the part of the glans that is exposed. Otherwise, leave it alone until the foreskin has separated from the glans.

■ If you have questions about the care of your newborn's genitals, contact your pediatrician.

■ Gather everything you will need, including a couple of soft towels, a washcloth, a mild baby soap, a clean diaper, and clean clothes.

■ Fill the baby bathtub with a few inches of water. The water should feel pleasantly warm, not hot, to your elbow. Turn the cold water off last and push the faucets out of the way or cover them.

■ Undress and wrap your baby in a towel. Dip the washcloth in plain warm water, and gently clean the baby's face and ears.

GIVING A NEWBORN A SPONGE BATH

Before you begin, gather your supplies, and then partially fill a container or sink with water that feels gently warm, not hot, to your elbow. Turn the cold water off last and be sure the faucets are pushed out of the way or covered.

■ Keep your newborn wrapped or partially clothed as you wash his or her face and ears with the washcloth dipped in plain warm water.

■ Hold your baby under your arm using the "football carry" with your arm supporting the neck and back and your hand supporting the head. Gently wash baby's head using your fingertips and a small amount of baby soap (or baby shampoo). Keep your baby tilted downward slightly, so the soap does not run into his or her eyes. Rinse thoroughly with plain warm water and pat the head dry.

■ Hold your baby on your lap or on the bathing surface and remove the shirt. Gently wash the chest, arms, and legs using your fingers or the washcloth

and a small amount of soap. Dip the washcloth in plain water, rinse the areas, and pat them dry.

■ Support the neck and head as you gently turn baby to one side. Wash the back, rinse with the washcloth dipped in plain water, and pat the back dry.

■ Remove the diaper. Using the washcloth and a small amount of soap, gently clean the diaper area, especially between the folds for girls and around the penis for boys. Dip the washcloth in plain water, rinse the area, and pat it dry.

■ Diaper and dress your newborn quickly to avoid a chill.

■ Clean your baby's outer ears using a soft, wet cloth. Gently wipe the outer ear and ear folds. Be sure to wipe behind the ears, since this is a good hiding place for cradle cap. The baby's inner ears, or ear canals, are self cleaning. Never use cotton swabs in the baby's ear canals. Not only is it unnecessary, it can be harmful.

■ Remove the towel and gently lower baby, bottom first, into the tub, keeping one hand under the bottom and the other under head and neck. Grasp under the armpit so that the head and back are resting on your arm.

■ Using the other hand, wash the chest, abdomen, arms, and legs. Gently wash the genital area, especially between the folds for girls and around the penis for boys. Be sure to clean in skin creases. Rinse with bathwater.

■ Gently sit baby up, using your free hand to grasp under the armpit from the front, leaning the infant forward so that the head and torso are supported by your arm. Once you have a secure hold on your baby, use the other hand to wash and rinse the back and bottom.

■ Slip your hands under the armpits and carefully lift the baby out of the tub. Wrap the baby in a towel and pat dry.

BATHING TODDLERS

■ Toddlers and preschoolers should be bathed two to three times a week. More frequent bathing can cause dry skin.

■ Sponge-bathe hands, arms, face, and bottom whenever necessary.

■ Avoid using bubble bath in the water, since it can be both drying and irritating to the skin.

■ If your preschooler prefers to take a shower, make sure the child knows how to operate everything.

■ Lightly spread a little lotion over the skin before you towel your child off to help prevent dryness. Avoid lotions with perfumes—they can cause irritation.

■ Dry scalp and dry or damaged hair can result from too much shampooing. Unless your child rolls in dirt every day, daily shampooing is not necessary and not recommended; once or twice a week—or whenever hair looks and smells grimy—should do it.

■ Use a mild shampoo, and only shampoo once. Be sure to rinse hair and scalp thoroughly. Use clean water for rinsing, since using bathwater won't get hair clean enough.

■ If hair is very tangled after shampooing, use a creme rinse or detangling spray to make combing easier.

TRIMMING NAILS

■ Use baby nail scissors with blunt ends to prevent injury if the baby pulls away unexpectedly.

■ You can use a soft emery board to file nails down. It may take two of you to get the job done at first. One can hold the baby while the other grasps one of the baby's fingers at a time and carefully files.

■ Better yet, babies' nails can be cut when they sleep. Try clippers—they make the job easy and quick.

■ Trim the fingernails as often as necessary to keep them short; this may mean once a week or once every other week.

■ A baby's toenails grow more slowly than fingernails, but they require attention too. Trim them as you do the fingernails, just not as often.

DENTAL HYGIENE FOR INFANTS AND TODDLERS

■ Clean your child's teeth at least twice a day and especially after dinner.

■ For infants and young toddlers, use gauze wrapped around your finger to wipe teeth and the gum line. Once your child is willing, introduce a small, soft toothbrush (with or without a small amount of toothpaste). Gently brush a child's teeth using an up-and-down motion.

■ After brushing, floss the teeth by gently sliding the dental floss along the side of each tooth, massaging slightly down and a little bit under the tooth.

■ Let your child watch as you brush your teeth. Make sure to encourage independent brushing, too.

■ Most pediatric dentists suggest that children have their initial visit after the first tooth has erupted or no later than the first birthday.

■ If you have a concern or see a problem before then, consult your pediatrician and/or pediatric dentist. Any problems with baby teeth should be attended to because of the risks of pain and infection.

Moving

Moving a household is never easy, but it doesn't have to be traumatic. The easiest way to handle a move is to divide it into manageable chunks. With thoughtful planning and organization of tasks, you can minimize the work that remains to be accomplished on moving day. Neglecting to take care of chores ahead of time, however, can turn a move into a nightmare.

PLANNING THE MOVE

To effectively organize your move, begin months ahead. Along with making arrangements, you'll want to tend to countless details that can overwhelm anyone if they're left to the last week before the move.

■ Whether you're moving yourself or hiring a mover, don't move unnecessary items. A move is a good time to get rid of things that are no longer useful. For example, don't pay to move paperback books you'll never read again.

■ Make a master checklist of everything that must be done. So that you don't fall behind, schedule a deadline for each task and check off each task when it is done. There's so much involved in a move that you may forget what has already been accomplished.

■ Make reservations well in advance if you plan to rent a moving truck or hire a professional mover.

■ If you plan to ask friends for help, make sure they can make the commitment and ask enough friends to make the job easier.

Don't expect one or two people to move all your belongings.

■ If you plan to rent a truck, get a lesson or two on how to drive one, particularly if you've never driven a truck before or if you will be driving it for a long distance.

■ Get carpets and slipcovers cleaned before you move. They'll come back wrapped and ready to transport, and you won't have to spend time trying to do this at your new location.

■ If you plan to travel by car over long distances, get your car checked out before you leave. Be sure to have a serviceable spare tire.

CHECKLIST FOR MOVING

TWO MONTHS BEFORE MOVE

■ Get estimates from movers
■ Collect boxes
■ Select mover and go over all details of the move
■ Begin packing little-used items
■ Go through your house to find unwanted items
■ Notify correspondents of move
■ Have a yard sale or donate items to a charity
■ Plan menus to use up food in the cupboards
■ Arrange air travel for family, if necessary

ONE MONTH BEFORE MOVE

■ Begin packing
■ Notify post office of change of address
■ Notify utility companies of change in account or disconnections
■ Notify newspaper of address change or stoppage

■ Collect important papers and medical records
■ Make any reservations for lodging

TWO WEEKS BEFORE MOVE

■ Check car; have any necessary repairs done
■ Renew or transfer prescriptions

THE WEEK OF THE MOVE

■ Transfer or close bank accounts if moving long distance
■ Obtain traveler's checks, if needed
■ Defrost refrigerator
■ Tag furniture to identify its location in the new home
■ Prepare survival kit so the family can get along if the moving company is late

THE DAY OF THE MOVE

■ Strip beds
■ Disconnect all appliances

PACKING

■ Take a few hours each day well before your move to begin packing items that you don't need on a daily basis, such as your good china, stemware, books, and seasonal clothes. Put these boxes in an out-of-the-way space until moving day.

■ Save space by not packing the unbreakable contents of tightly loaded drawers. Simply tape the drawers in place with strips of wide masking tape. To minimize tape marks, remove the tape as soon as the furniture arrives at your new home.

■ Get wardrobe boxes to pack clothes. By simply hanging clothes inside these boxes, you'll save time both packing and unpacking.

■ Small linens such as towels, washcloths, and pillowcases can also serve as packing material.

■ Alternate the spines of books when you pack them to save space.

■ To prevent odors from developing in the refrigerator or freezer during the move, put several charcoal briquettes inside the unit to absorb the odors. Alternatively, fill the refrigerator or freezer with crumpled newspapers. The paper will absorb moisture and help prevent odors.

■ Remove furniture casters ahead of time to prevent them from falling off during the move. Tie them together with heavy twine, and tag them so you know which piece of furniture they fit.

■ Pack similar items together. For example, if a box is nearly filled with items from the medicine cabinet, don't add kitchen items to completely fill it. It will just make unpacking more difficult.

■ Plates are less likely to break if they are packed standing on edge. To minimize breakage of glass items, place the heavier ones on the bottom and the more delicate ones on top. Pieces of crumpled newspaper make good packing material for glass.

■ As you tape each packed box, place a piece of string underneath the tape, leaving about an inch sticking out. When it's time to unpack, just pull on the string, which will slit right through the tape.

■ Label each box with clear lettering as to its contents and where it should go. This will help when you unpack because you will be able to quickly sort out the boxes that must be unpacked immediately and those that can wait.

HIRING A PROFESSIONAL MOVER

■ For a local move, get references from friends and be sure to check with the Better Business Bureau about any moving company you are considering.

MANAGING A MOVING SALE

If you're holding a house or garage sale to dispose of items before moving, you'll not only make money, you'll save money by not having to pay for transporting unwanted possessions. Use the following hints to make your sale a success:

■ Organize your sale by categorizing odds and ends in bins. For example, have one bin for kitchen gadgets, another for books, and another for music.

■ To get the best prices at your moving sale, clean and shine the objects you're selling, and display them creatively.

■ Be sure to post signs around the neighborhood in advance to let people know about the sale.

■ If you have a lot of things to sell, take out an ad in the local paper.

■ To display clothes, rig up a clothesline or rent a portable wardrobe hanger.

■ Tag items individually with prices or put items together on a table with a sign for their price. Whether or not you want to negotiate the price further is up to you but it will save you the hassle of trying to come up with a price on the spot.

■ Encourage your children to get rid of old toys and belongings by letting them keep the money from the sale of their possessions. If there are items you do not want sold, pack them away first.

■ Make sure you have plenty of newspapers, boxes, and bags for packing up the items purchased.

■ On interstate moves, charges are based on the weight of the items to be moved, the distance to be moved, packing, and other services. Get two or three estimates well in advance of your move.

■ Make sure the mover is aware of everything to be moved. The cost will increase if anything is added to the shipment that was not included in the estimate.

■ Unless you pay the movers to pack your belongings, it's unlikely that they will be insured against breakage caused by improper packing.

■ The mover will issue you a bill of lading, a legal contract between the customer and the mover. Be sure to hang on to it.

■ Make sure that any contract you enter into covers rates and charges, the mover's liability for your possessions, dates for pickup and delivery, and claims protection.

■ If you have the option to move between October and April, you may be able to receive a better price. If your move is scheduled between June and September, the busiest times for movers, be sure to call well in advance for estimates and to settle on a contract.

■ Once your shipment is picked up, you may incur storage costs if you change the delivery date, so try to make sure you are able to move into your new home on the scheduled date.

■ Movers are responsible for loss or damage to goods caused by the carrier. If anything is missing or if cartons are damaged, this should be noted when you check the inventory sheet at delivery.

MOVING DAY

■ To save time and eliminate confusion, draw a floor plan of your new home ahead of time. Sketch in and number your furnishings the way you want them arranged. Tag furniture pieces to correspond to the floor plan so the movers know where to put each piece.

■ Be sure to be on hand during packing and pickup of your belongings. If you cannot be there, ask a friend or relative to stand in for you. The mover will issue you an inventory of all items. Make sure the inventory is correct and legible before you sign it.

■ If your friends are helping you move, have as much as possible packed ahead of time and ready to be loaded into a truck or van. Don't expect your friends to pack your belongings. Be sure to have plenty of beverages and snacks, and send out for food if the work goes into the lunch or dinner hour.

■ Keep children and pets out of the way of the movers—whether they're your friends or professionals.

IN TRANSIT

■ Keep important papers and documents with you, including

MOVING PLANTS

■ If you are moving to another state, federal and state laws may be affected. In certain areas, plants may have to be quarantined or inspected to be certified that they are pest-free. Some states prohibit bringing any plants into the state. You will have to give them to friends, donate them to a willing institution, or sell them.

■ Professional moving companies usually will move houseplants. Do not expect moving personnel to water your plants during the move or to give them special care.

■ Most indoor houseplants cannot survive temperatures below 30°F or higher than 100°F for more than an hour, particularly if they are not wrapped. If you are moving during the winter over long distances, pack plants in cartons and try to make sure they are moved in a heated vehicle and not left in an unheated car or moving van overnight.

■ Make sure plants are moist when they are packed for moving. They can usually survive for about 10 days without water.

■ If you can't move your plants due to space limitations, consider taking cuttings from your favorite plants. Keep them in a plastic bag with damp vermiculite or peat moss.

birth certificates, marriage license, and deeds.

■ Make sure you allow enough time to get to your destination before the movers.

■ If you are moving over a long distance, keep in touch with the moving company so that they are able to notify you of any delays in delivery.

■ If you drive to your new location and arrive late, spend the first night at a motel rather than trying to "settle in" when everyone's tired. Everything will seem much more manageable in the morning.

■ Take a survival package so you can camp in your new home until the moving van arrives. Include instant coffee, cups, spoons, soap and towels, a can and bottle opener, some light bulbs, a flashlight, toilet paper, cleansing powder, and a first-aid kit. Also be sure that daily medications travel with you.

MOVING WITH PETS

■ Most states have laws regarding the entry of animals. Although most states do not require quarantine, be sure to check on what you will need to move your pet if you are moving interstate.

■ Border inspections of all animals being transported are conducted by some states while others have random inspection. Be prepared with health certificates for dogs and up-to-date rabies inoculations for dogs and cats.

■ Pets cannot be shipped by professional movers. The best alternative is to have your pet travel with you to reduce anxiety. Be sure to have a leash with you because your pet may react oddly to strange surroundings.

■ If you are traveling by air, your pet will have to be in a carrier.

Check with the airline to see if the carrier can be kept in the cabin. Some airlines require that all carriers be stowed in luggage compartments; others allow small carriers to be kept in the cabin.

■ Make sure your pet wears an identification tag with your name, the address of your destination, and the name and phone number of a friend or relative in case the pet is lost during transit.

■ Check ahead of time with the city clerk or county clerk about any local laws about pets before you move. Some communities restrict the number of pets per residence, and most expect pets to be licensed shortly after you move in.

WHEN YOU ARRIVE

■ If you have access to the new home a day or so before the moving van arrives, you could set off a bug bomb or spray. (Even if you don't see bugs, there may be some.) This way, you won't worry about your family, your pets, food, or furnishings during the spraying.

■ If you've hired a professional mover, make sure you have the payment ready for the mover when the truck arrives as specified in the contract.

■ Check your list of contents against the list of what is delivered, and inspect all cartons for damage.

■ Unless you've hired the movers to help unpack, don't try to unpack everything at once. Sort your carefully labeled boxes so that you only have to unpack what is absolutely necessary. This gives you the time to organize your space as you go, instead of being forced to toss things randomly into cupboards and closets.

■ If possible, hire a cleaning service to help you clean the house either before the movers arrive or after they've left.

MAKING THE TRANSITION TO YOUR NEW HOME

■ If you're moving to an unfamiliar location, obtain local maps as soon as possible.

■ Change your address on your driver's license or get a new license, and get your car registered if you move to a new state. Make sure you're aware of local driving regulations and get your car a safety inspection sticker, if required.

■ If your children are moving to a new school, try to find some time to volunteer for school activities. This will help you get to know the school and help you understand any problems your children experience as they get oriented to a new routine.

■ If you're fortunate, your new neighbors will greet you. If they don't, spend some time outside so they have the opportunity to approach you. If all else fails, introduce yourself.

■ Make it a point to get to know your new community. Get library cards, and find out about community-sponsored activities. Subscribe to

MOVING WITH CHILDREN

Whether you're moving out of state or around the block, children and adolescents rarely relish change. Your attitude about the move and your willingness to let your children share in the experience will influence their feelings about the move. Try the following to make the move as anxiety-free as possible:

■ Talk to your children about the move, and encourage them to express their feelings.

■ Sending preschoolers to a sitter or relative during the move may make it easier for you but it could produce anxiety for the children. Involve them in packing and make sure that some of their belongings are with them on the trip.

■ When leaving your previous home, empty the children's rooms last, and restructure their rooms first when you've arrived at your new home. This helps them adjust psychologically.

■ Try to learn as much as possible about the new neighborhood and school so that you can tell older children about them. You don't have to make them sound heavenly; matter-of-fact information will help ease their anxieties about fitting in.

■ Encourage your children to look up facts on your new location at the library, and let them help you plot the most convenient route on a map. If you're moving only a short distance, let children examine the new house and neighborhood before the move.

■ Don't think you have to postpone your move until summer vacation. Some experts believe that summer is the worst time to move children, because they have to wait until school starts again to get involved socially. Of course, if your children have learning problems or aren't doing well in school, it may be advisable to let them finish out the school year in familiar surroundings.

■ Encourage children to exchange addresses and phone numbers with their friends. A few long-distance calls won't break the bank and will help your children make the transition easier.

the local paper so that you get a feel for how the community operates.

■ If your children are having trouble with the move, give them extra attention and don't become impatient. Let them call their old friends, and, if possible, arrange for them to visit them.

■ Make your pet feel at home by putting out its favorite toys, food dishes, or blankets. Don't allow your pet outdoors unleashed. The pet could easily become disoriented and be unable to find its way home.

GETTING THE WORD OUT

The more people you know and correspond with, the more work you'll have to do to let them know about your move. To save money on cards and stamps, send an e-mail or print a page giving your old address and new address. Make copies and then include this with any outgoing correspondence before you move. Going through your address book will help you to avoid leaving out friends and relatives that need notification.

Make sure you notify the following people and institutions of your move:

■ Present and future post offices
■ Associations
■ Banks
■ Book clubs
■ Catalog companies
■ Churches
■ Credit card companies
■ Credit unions
■ Dentists
■ Department stores
■ Doctors

■ Electric company
■ Employers
■ Federal, state, and local government benefits payments
■ Gas company
■ Insurance companies
■ Lawyers
■ Libraries
■ Magazines
■ Motor Vehicle Department

■ Music clubs
■ Newsletters
■ Newspapers
■ Schools
■ Stockbrokers
■ Telephone company
■ Unions
■ Voter registration (both old and new jurisdictions)
■ Water company

Personal Grooming

It takes experience and knowledge to make all the right decisions about personal grooming. But knowing how to care for hair and skin can save you time and money. Use the following tips and techniques to pick the products that will help you look and feel your best.

HAIR CARE

Designer clothing, perfectly applied makeup, and fine jewelry are all wasted if your hair looks greasy, dull, or messy. Fortunately, no one needs a hair salon or expensive hair products to have hair that looks professionally cared for and styled. With the right techniques for shampooing, drying, and styling your hair, it can be among your most attractive features.

BASIC HAIR CARE

■ To minimize breakage, make sure that your hair is thoroughly wet before applying shampoo. Use no more than a quarter-size dollop, and rub the shampoo between your palms first. Lather for no more than 30 seconds.

■ After shampooing, rinse your hair with cool water to seal moisture in the hair shafts.

■ To distribute the natural oils in your hair, bend over and brush your scalp and hair from back to front until the scalp tingles; then massage the scalp with your fingertips.

■ Towel-dry your hair thoroughly before using a blow dryer. You'll save time and avoid damaging your hair with too much heat.

■ To cut down on static electricity, dampen your hairbrush before brushing.

■ Avoid using a brush on wet hair because it is subject to breakage. Comb out snarls.

■ If you suffer from a flaky scalp, try the following treatment every 2 weeks: Section your hair and rub the scalp with a cotton pad saturated with plain rubbing alcohol. Let the alcohol dry, then brush your hair and rinse thoroughly with warm water but don't shampoo.

■ To perk up permed hair between shampoos, lightly mist your hair

HOMEMADE HAIR-CARE AIDS

■ Repair damaged hair by treating it with oil and egg yolk. Massage olive oil into hair. Then beat the yolk of 1 egg and massage it into hair, working from the ends up. Leave on for 10 minutes, then shampoo as usual. Do this once a week for a month, and hair should begin to feel healthier.

■ Condition your hair by applying mayonnaise before shampooing. Apply to dry hair and let sit for ½ hour, then rinse and shampoo as usual.

■ For a lemon rinse, blend ½ cup of strained lemon juice and 1 cup of distilled water in a bottle. Comb the liquid through your hair after each shampoo.

■ For a quick, dry shampoo, rub baby powder into your hair and then brush it out thoroughly.

CLEANING COMBS AND BRUSHES

■ Add shampoo to the water you use to remove hair oil trapped in the teeth or bristles of your combs and brushes.

■ A baking soda solution cleans combs and brushes effectively and inexpensively. Soak them for 10 minutes in a solution of 3 tablespoons of baking soda and 1 quart of warm water. The baking soda loosens oily deposits so they can be easily brushed away.

■ Combs made of bone or hard rubber and brushes with natural bristles can be sanitized with alcohol.

with fresh water and push the curls into place with your fingers.

■ Dull, lifeless hair can be a sign of a poor diet. Try cutting down on cholesterol and fats.

■ Wait at least 48 hours after coloring hair to shampoo it. Every time you wet hair you open the cuticle—so give hair time to seal in the color.

■ Beer can remove residue from your hair. Add 6 tablespoons beer to 1 cup warm water and pour it over your hair as a final rinse.

■ If your hair is prone to buildup from conditioners, styling gel, or hair spray, mix 1 tablespoon baking soda with your regular shampoo once a week. Rinse and dry as usual.

HINTS AND TIPS

■ Use pomade sparingly to remove static, control flyaway ends, and add a glossy sheen to either straight or curly hair. Apply a very small amount to one hand, and liquefy it between your palms. Then run your

MAKING YOUR HAIR SHINE

Whether you have artificial hair color that needs refreshing or you just want to enhance your own shade naturally, customized herbal rinses add highlights or depth and are gentle on your budget. If you want to experiment with customizing herbal rinses, there's no real risk because their effect is subtle. However, avoid acidic fruits and vegetable colors. Do not use lemons or beet juice, for example. These are very unpredictable over time and are greatly affected by sun exposure. Lemon juice and the sun might make you blonder the first time you try it, but after several treatments, your hair color will look like the rings of a tree trunk—in several shades.

Brighten a Blonde: Steep 2 tablespoons dried chamomile and 2 tablespoons dried marigold in 1 quart boiled water for half an hour. Make certain the temperature is comfortable, then pour through wet hair.

Burnish a Brunette: Substitute sage and rosemary for the herbs above. For extra luster, add 1 tablespoon cider vinegar.

Rev Up a Red: Mix 1 tablespoon honey with 2 tablespoons saffron and add 1 quart boiled water. Allow to steep for half an hour, check the temperature, and pour slowly through wet hair as a final rinse.

hands through the hair. If braiding, apply before braiding and use it for small touch-ups.

▪ Use gel after a braid is finished to smooth down loose or uncontrolled hairs. Apply it to your fingertip or to the end of a hairpin, directing it on top of the stray hairs to encourage them back into the braided pattern.

▪ Use hair spray to hold the finished design in place. If you want a soft finish but need to control the hair, spray into the palm of your hand and then smooth over the surface of the hair to control flyaway strands.

▪ Use a coated rubber band or a soft hair tie to secure ponytails and the ends of a braid to reduce the stress on the hair.

▪ Use gel to control hair when you want a "wet" affect. Apply gel sparingly to your hair once styled. To use for braiding, apply it to all of the hair before you braid, or when you want a clean, off-the-face effect, you can apply it to the perimeter hairline where lengths tend to be shorter.

SKIN CARE

Your skin is a bellwether to your overall health. If you're not healthy, it will be reflected in your complexion. But that doesn't mean you should neglect your skin if you're feeling fine.

BASIC SKIN CARE

▪ Always wear a moisturized sunscreen when outdoors, winter and summer. The sun's rays can burn you even if the air feels cool, and sunlight reflected off water or snow can be particularly powerful.

▪ No matter what your skin type is, use a protective sunscreen when you are in the sun; don't expose your skin for more than 15 minutes. Don't forget to use sunscreen on your face and the back of your hands because these are constantly exposed to the sun's rays.

▪ Always remove your makeup before going to bed.

HERB-SCENTED SKIN TONER

Use 1 part vinegar to 3 parts water, and add the following flower or herb petals of your choice. Spray on skin as desired to freshen.

For dry skin: violet, rose, borage, or jasmine

For oily skin: peppermint, marigold, rosemary, or lavender

For sensitive skin: violet, salt burnet, parsley, or borage

For normal skin: lemon balm, rose, spearmint, or chamomile

HOMEMADE SKIN-CARE AIDS

- For an easy weekly facial sauna that unclogs pores, add a few tablespoons of your favorite herbs to water and boil for several minutes. Remove the pot from the heat, and use a bath towel as a tent while you let the steam rise to your face for 3 to 5 minutes. Then rinse your face with very cold water to close the pores.

- This treatment works well for normal to dry skin: Mash ½ of a banana in a bowl. Add 1 tablespoon honey and 2 tablespoons sour cream; mix well. Apply to your face, leave on for 10 minutes, then rinse with warm water.

- For a toning and cleansing mask for normal to oily skin, add 3 tablespoons finely ground oatmeal to 3 table-spoons witch hazel to form a paste. Apply to your face and allow to dry for 20 to 30 minutes, then rinse with warm water.

- To make a toning mask, combine half of a small papaya, 1 egg white, and ½ teaspoon lemon juice and mix in the blender until creamy. Leave the mask on your face for 20 minutes and then rinse with cold water.

- For a cleansing mask for dry skin, mix the yolk of an egg with 2 teaspoons mayonnaise and ½ teaspoon lemon juice. Apply to your face and allow to dry for 20 minutes. Wash off with warm water.

- For a skin-tightening mask for normal and oily skin, whip an egg white, apply to the face, and allow to dry. Rinse off after 20 minutes. Avoid this treatment on dry skin, where it may be too harsh.

- Remove flaky skin by dipping a cotton ball or pad in milk and applying it to the flaky patch. Rinse with cool water.

- For a softener for rough areas, such as your feet, knees, and elbows, mix a paste of 1 tablespoon finely ground oatmeal and cold cream. Apply it several times a week, and rub gently as you wash off the paste with warm water.

- For another softener for rough areas, mix ¼ cup table salt, ¼ cup Epsom salts, and ¼ cup vegetable oil. Stir constantly as you mix the ingredients. Massage the paste into rough skin for several minutes. Remove by bathing or showering.

- Repair cracked and chapped feet or hands by covering them with a thin layer of petroleum jelly, then wearing cotton socks or gloves while you sleep.

SCENTED BUBBLING BATH MIX

2 cups vegetable oil

3 tablespoons shampoo

2 to 3 drops perfume

Pour ingredients into a blender and mix well for 10 seconds. Store in a plastic bottle, and add 2 tablespoons to each bath.

- If you usually wear makeup, give your skin a chance to breathe one day a week by going without.

- If your face tends to be puffy in the mornings, keep skin freshener, astringent, and cotton pads for your eyelids in the refrigerator for a quick pick-me-up.

- Rub moisturizing lotion on your legs before applying shaving cream for a smoother, softer finish when removing leg hair. Men who have normal to dry skin can also benefit from this technique.

- Use a humidifier to lessen the drying effects of indoor heat on your skin in the winter.

- Take baths in the evening to avoid exposing your skin immediately to outdoor air.

CARING FOR YOUR HANDS AND NAILS

- When nails chip excessively, it may be caused by the use of nail polish remover. Leave your nails unpainted for a few days to see if the condition improves.

- When you're preparing anything with lemon and vegetable juices, which contain acids that are hard on your fingernails, rinse your hands often under cool running water.

- To break the habit of nail biting or cuticle chewing, carry a tube of cuticle cream with you. Whenever you start to nibble, put the cream on your cuticles instead. You'll promote healthy nails and possibly break yourself of a bad habit.

- To rescue nail polish that has become hardened or gummy, place the bottle into a pan of boiling water for a few seconds to get the polish flowing smoothly again.

- To soften cuticles, soak hands in a solution of 1 cup warm water and 1 teaspoon of dish-washing liquid.

- For an emergency treatment for dry, chapped hands, soak your hands in a bath of baby oil mixed with sesame oil.

■ Apply hand cream before putting on rubber gloves to prevent your hands from drying.

MAKEUP TIPS

■ In the winter, use oil-base makeup to protect your skin against dry, cold air. In the summer, switch to a water-base foundation to help moisturize your skin.

■ When your mascara begins to dry out, run hot water over the tube for a minute to soften the remaining mascara inside.

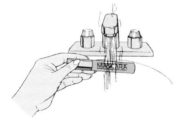

■ After applying mascara, dip a cotton swab in a little baby powder and sweep it over your lashes. Then apply a second coat of mascara. Lashes will appear longer and fuller.

■ Dry milk can be used as a makeup remover. Mix 1 teaspoon milk

BYE-BYE, BLEMISHES

■ After your facial-cleansing routine, apply milk of magnesia with a cotton ball or pad to any acne blemishes. Let dry, then rinse off using cool water.

■ To treat pimples and discourage blemishes, apply a mixture of calamine lotion and 1 percent phenol (available at a drugstore).

■ Apply lemon juice to blackheads using a cotton ball. Leave the juice on overnight. In the morning, rinse your face with cool water. Repeat every night for 1 week.

■ For acne outbreaks, apply lemon juice on a cotton pad several times a day to dry up pimples.

■ Spread mayonnaise over your face, and let it dry for 20 minutes. Rinse off with warm water, then follow with a cold water splash. This treatment will help tighten pores.

■ Honey speeds healing by killing bacteria. For an overnight blemish remedy, dab honey on the spot and cover with a bandage.

powder with warm water and apply to your face using a cotton ball. Rinse clean.

PERFUMES AND COLOGNES

■ Apply perfume and cologne to your skin rather than your clothes. Chemicals in the perfume may weaken fabric or change its color.

■ A dab of petroleum jelly rubbed over your wrist or neck where you've put perfume or cologne will help the scent last longer.

■ Apply perfumes and colognes before putting on your jewelry. The alcohol and oils in your favorite scent can cause a cloudy film on jewelry.

FRESHENERS FOR THE BATH

■ To revive tired muscles, add several handfuls of Epsom salts to your bathwater.

■ To soften skin, toss 2 to 3 teaspoons of baking soda into the tub.

■ For a soothing and fragrant skin massage, mix equal parts of peanut oil, camphor oil, and castor oil and add to the tub as you draw the water.

■ Make yourself a soothing milk bath by adding ½ cup dry milk powder to warm bathwater.

■ To get rid of flaky skin or the remnants of last summer's tan, add 1 cup of cider vinegar or the juice of 3 fresh lemons to your bathwater. Slough off dead skin cells with a dry sponge or brush.

QUICK PICK-ME-UPS FOR YOUR EYES

■ Cover puffy eyes with cotton pads soaked in milk, and relax for 10 minutes. Or dip 2 tea bags in boiling water for 2 minutes, then let the tea bags cool slightly. Meanwhile, heat 1 teaspoon olive oil until it's warm, not hot. Using an absorbent pad, carefully dab the oil around your eyes and on your eyelids. Lie down, and cover each eye with a still-warm tea bag for 10 minutes. Remove the tea bags, and gently wipe off the oil with tissue.

■ Keep an emergency eye-relief kit in the freezer. Dip cotton swabs into cool water and store them in a resealable plastic bag in the freezer. To relieve tired eyes and reduce puffiness, roll the swab under your eyes.

■ Refresh tired eyes by laying cotton pads moistened with witch hazel over closed eyelids for a few minutes.

■ To reduce swelling caused by overexposure to the sun, place thin, freshly cut slices of cucumber over closed eyelids for a few minutes.

Pet Care

People have various reasons for getting a pet. Pets are good company and may reduce the sense of isolation felt by many people, especially those who live alone. Taking responsibility for a pet also expands the owner's interest in the world. But just like anything that's good for you, pets require commitment. Dogs and cats both have average life spans of 14 years, and a parrot can easily outlive you.

PET SELECTION

If you've decided to make the commitment to a pet, keep the following in mind:

■ Monkeys don't make good pets. They tend to be destructive, ill-tempered, and apt to bite because a solitary monkey is always unhappy. Simians crave the company of their own kind.

■ Never try to raise wild animals as pets. They usually can't be tamed; their behavior is unpredictable; and it's cruel to keep a wild animal in captivity unless you have the knowledge, resources, and facilities necessary for its care.

■ Don't buy a pet from an establishment that appears dirty or where the animals seem listless.

■ Don't buy a puppy or kitten before it's 6 weeks old. The ideal age is 8 weeks.

■ Don't buy a puppy or kitten from anyone who says that an animal under 4 months old has "had all its shots." It can't be true.

■ Make sure that you get the necessary papers if you're buying a purebred pet.

■ If possible, spend time alone with the pet you're considering.

■ If you want to get a pet from an animal shelter, ask the attendants about animals that interest you.

ALL ABOUT CATS

CHOOSING A CAT

Cats make delightful pets, even though they are very independent. Before buying or adopting a cat, ask yourself the following questions:

■ Do you want a male or female cat? Generally females are cautious, gentle, and quiet but unless you have your cat spayed, you will have to contend with heat cycles. Males are larger and more outgoing, though unneutered males tend to spray urine to mark their territory, roam, and are prone to fights with other cats.

■ Do you want a long- or short-haired cat? Long-haired cats are glamorous but it will be someone's job to keep it that way. Long-haired cats shed a great deal and tend to get hairballs more frequently.

■ Do you want a purebred or mixed-breed cat? If you want a purebred cat, make sure you buy it only from a reputable breeding establishment and know what you're looking for before you actually buy.

■ Do you want a kitten or a cat? Kittens are cute but they require more time and patience. Older cats require more socialization but generally are easier to care for.

BATHING CATS

■ Cats normally don't require bathing, but if your cat does need a bath, get a friend to assist. Place a small washable rug or towel over the side of the basin or tub for the cat to cling to. A cat gets panicky on a slippery surface where it can't get a foothold. Hold the cat with one hand and lather quickly with the other.

■ Before bathing a cat, put a drop of mineral oil in each eye to prevent irritation from soap.

■ Make certain the water temperature is roughly 100°F. Warmer or cooler water will cause your cat distress and may make it difficult to handle.

■ Wash the head, ears, and neck first. If you don't, any fleas that are on the animal will take refuge there while you clean the rest of its body. Be careful not to get shampoo in the eyes.

- To avoid colds, keep your cat inside for several hours after a bath.

FEEDING CATS

- Never offer your cat bones—they can splinter into sharp pieces and catch in your pet's throat.

- If moist pet food is not eaten within two hours, refrigerate it. Dry food and biscuits are the only foods that can be left out for any length of time.

- Do not feed dog food to a cat.

- If you're going to change your pet's diet, do it gradually. A sudden change may be a shock to the animal's system.

- Don't worry if your cat eats grass; many animals actually graze.

- On a hot day, be vigilant about a cat's water supply. Fill your pet's bowl with cold tap water and freshen it often.

GROOMING AND EXERCISE

- When your cat starts to shed hair, usually after the cold-weather months, massage its coat with your hands, then stroke the animal from head to tail with your palms. You'll have less hair all over the house.

- If you encounter matted or tangled fur when combing a long-haired cat, use your fingers, not a comb, to separate the tangles.

- When brushing short-haired cats, be sure to brush between the shoulders where the cat can't reach to groom itself.

- Your cat's claws will be easier to trim if you press the paw to expose the nails. Use special clippers from the pet supply store—never use human nail clippers on a cat. Cut the nail well clear of the quick—the pink line you can see running through the nail.

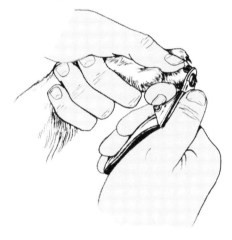

- Your cat's ears should be cleaned monthly. Clean only that part of the ear canal that you can see, using a cotton swab soaked in mineral oil or alcohol.

- Don't leave your cat in a car in hot weather, even if the windows are open. Heat builds up very quickly in a car and can cause collapse or even death.

HEALTH ISSUES FOR CATS

■ Worming medications are dangerous if used incorrectly. Never worm your cat with any medication not prescribed by your vet.

■ If a cat is too sick to clean itself, keep it brushed and rubbed down. Wipe runny eyes often.

■ To give a cat a pill, hold the animal firmly on your lap or between your knees. Grasp the head on either side of the jaw so that the cat has to open its mouth. Place the pill as far back in the throat as possible. Close the cat's mouth, and rub its throat gently to stimulate swallowing.

 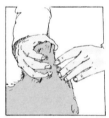

■ Cats are prone to diabetes. If your cat is diabetic, have your vet show you how to give the required insulin injections. If you do this faithfully, diabetes will not shorten your cat's life.

■ If a cat appears malnourished even though well fed, has frequent loose stools, a lackluster coat, and a bloated stomach, you should suspect worms. Consult a veterinarian.

■ Ear mites are a common problem with cats. If you notice black, brown, or gray waxy material in the ear instead of the usual clean pink surface, the cat may have mites. Consult the veterinarian for medicine. If you have more than one cat and one gets ear mites, chances are the others will, too.

■ If a cat's membranous eyelids half-cover its eyes, it's usually a sign of an intestinal illness that should be treated immediately.

■ Constant discharge from your cat's eye can be a symptom of either local infection or systemic disease that should be treated.

■ If a kitten dies suddenly with no sign of illness, it probably had feline distemper. Your other cats should be vaccinated immediately.

■ The easiest way to treat hairballs is to give the cat a preparation that will coat the stomach and combine with the hair so that it can be passed in the stool. White petroleum jelly is an excellent coating agent. Put a teaspoon or two on the cat's mouth and paws, and let the cat lick it off.

- Cats love to play with yarn or string but such games can be fatal. If your cat has swallowed yarn or string, give it white petroleum jelly to ease the passage of the material through the system.

- Keep cats away from the poisonous houseplants, such as dieffenbachia, mistletoe berries, and poinsettia.

ALL ABOUT DOGS

CHOOSING A DOG

Once you've made the commitment to buy a dog, consider what kind of dog is going to fit into your life most satisfactorily. Ask yourself the following questions:

- What size dog will fit into your home? Make sure you know the ultimate size of any puppy you are buying because large dogs require space.

- Who's going to exercise the dog and take care of cleaning up after it? If your space or energy is limited,

choose a dog that's a natural homebody, not an outdoors lover.

- How much dog can you feed? The cost of dog food for large dogs can overstretch an already tight budget.

- What's the temperament of the breed? This is unrelated to size. If you have children, make sure you get a dog that does well with children.

- Do you want a male or female?

- Do you want a purebred or a mutt? You'll know better what you're getting with a purebred but the cost is much higher.

- Do you want a puppy or an adult? Puppies demand a great deal of time, attention, patience, and training but they typically adjust more easily to a new household than adult dogs.

FEEDING DOGS

- In general, dry dog food is more nutritious than moist dog food. Any time you get a new pet, however, check with your veterinarian for dietary recommendations.

- Never offer your dog pork chop bones, chicken bones, or fish bones. These can splinter into sharp pieces and catch in your pet's throat.

- If you must give your dog a bone, give only marrow or knuckle bones that have first been boiled to remove fat and grease that might cause diarrhea. Take the bone away as soon as it starts to splinter.

■ If moist pet food is not eaten within two hours, refrigerate it.

■ If you're going to change your pet's diet, do it gradually. A sudden change may be a shock to the animal's system.

■ Don't feed a dog milk. It will probably give it diarrhea.

■ On a hot day, be vigilant about your dog's water supply. Fill your pet's bowl with cold tap water and freshen it often.

BATHING YOUR DOG

■ Comb a long-haired dog before a bath. Then you won't have to untangle wet hair.

■ Make certain the water temperature is roughly 100°F. Warmer or cooler water will cause your pet distress and may make it difficult to handle.

■ Wash the head, ears, and neck first. If you don't, any fleas that are on the animal will take refuge there while you clean the body.

■ To avoid getting water in your dog's ears during a bath, plug its ears with cotton balls that have been moistened with apple cider vinegar.

■ You can minimize the soap residue that remains after a dog's shampoo by adding some vinegar to the bath's rinse water. Then rinse the dog's coat again thoroughly with plain water.

■ If your dog smells bad but there's no time to give it a bath, rub baking soda or cornstarch into its coat and brush it off.

■ If a skunk sprays your dog, wash the dog with tomato juice, then with shampoo and water.

GROOMING AND EXERCISE

■ Groom short-haired dogs once or twice a week with a grooming comb. Long-haired coats need bristle or wire brushes and pet combs with rounded teeth.

■ Burrs will be easier to comb from your dog's coat if you first crush them with a pair of pliers.

■ Another good burr-remover is vegetable oil worked into the burrs. This also works for tar and other messes the dog may have gotten into. Shampoo to remove the loosened gunk and oil.

■ It's important to wash off your dog's feet in the winter because it will probably pick up salt and chemicals from the street. These substances can injure its feet. If the pads of your dog's feet become dry or cracked, rub a little petroleum jelly into them.

■ To wipe away the rheum that gathers at the corners of your dog's eyes, use a dab of cotton dipped in a boric acid solution.

■ Don't leave your dog in a car in hot weather, even if the windows are open.

■ In hot weather, it's best to exercise your dog early in the morning and late at night. Midday heat could be dangerous.

HEALTH ISSUES FOR DOGS

■ Worming medications are dangerous if used incorrectly. Never worm your dog with any medication not prescribed by your vet.

■ If you have to give a dog liquid medication, have it stand on a towel or bath mat in the tub. Any medication that gets spilled will go in the tub and not on your carpet. Pull out the dog's lower lip at the corner to make a pouch, and use a dropper or a syringe to place the medication in the pouch, a little at a time. Rub its throat to stimulate swallowing.

■ To give a dog a pill, grasp its muzzle in one hand, then gently press the dog's lips over the upper teeth with your thumb on one side and your fingers on the other. Firm pressure will force the dog to open its mouth so that you can place the pill as far back in the mouth as possible with your free hand. Hold the dog's mouth closed, and rub its throat to stimulate swallowing.

■ If your dog won't take a pill readily, try disguising it in a piece of cream cheese, which most dogs will eat without complaint.

■ Don't worry about a young puppy's "garlic breath." This is normal and shows the presence of "good" bacteria in its mouth. The odor will disappear in a few months.

■ Keep puppies away from the droppings of other dogs. A disease known as parvovirus can be fatal to dogs who contract it. (Dogs under 6 months old are most susceptible.) Most puppies contract it through contact with infected feces. See your veterinarian about vaccinations to protect your dog from parvovirus.

OTHER PETS

CHOOSING A BIRD

■ While small birds, such as parakeets and canaries, require minimal care, large birds, such as parrots, cockatoos, and cockateels, can require a great deal of care and demand a lot of affection. Make sure you know about the requirements of the bird you're considering.

■ Avoid buying a canary between July and October, which is the canary's molting season. A sudden environmental change during that period may send it into shock.

■ Before buying a parrot, be prepared for a lifetime relationship—it may live longer than you do. Parrots become extremely attached to their owners.

CARING FOR BIRDS

■ When holding a pet bird, be very gentle. Bird bones are fragile—even the slightest pressure on the wrong spot can cause a fracture.

■ Never let a pet bird loose in the kitchen. It may land on a hot pan or burner.

■ If a pet bird breathes through its open mouth, you know it's sick. Buy a bird antibiotic at the pet store, pulverize it, and add it to your bird's drinking water. If this doesn't help, get it to the veterinarian.

CHOOSING AND CARING FOR OTHER PETS

■ When you buy a fish at a pet shop and bring it home in a plastic bag partially filled with water, float the bag in your home aquarium for 30 minutes before releasing the fish. This helps the fish adjust to the tank's water temperature.

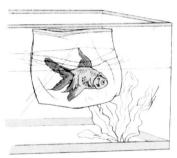

■ If you have a pet reptile, such as a lizard or snake, and need to clean its terrarium, have a duplicate (empty) terrarium handy in which you can place your pet while cleaning. Otherwise it may escape.

■ Handle a pet salamander or newt with wet hands. The rough texture of dry skin may injure it.

- If you have an adult land tortoise as a pet, you needn't confine it in an enclosure. Give it the run of your house or apartment. It will discover cozy places to sleep and warm places to sun itself.

- Feed an adult land tortoise slices of ripe fruit and pieces of leafy vegetables, and provide it with a nontippable pan of water.

- Be careful about moving a small animal's cage from one location to another. An animal has a strong sense of territory and may be seriously upset by relocation.

- Avoid sudden gestures when handling small mammals. They're easily frightened and may bite.

- Don't keep two male rabbits in the same cage or hutch. They'll probably fight like gladiators.

- Never lift a rabbit by its ears. Doing so may damage muscles around the head and make the ears floppy.

- When picking up a pet mouse, lift it by the root of its tail, not the tip. The skin at the tip of the tail is likely to slide right off.

- Make sure pet mice have a piece of unpainted hardwood to gnaw on. If they don't gnaw, their front teeth will grow so long that they'll have difficulty eating.

- Spruce up a horse's coat by adding ½ cup vinegar to 1 quart water. Use this mixture in a spray bottle to apply to the horse's coat before showing.

- Pour ¼ cup apple cider vinegar onto a horse's regular grain feed once a day to deter pesky flies.

HANDLING EMERGENCIES AND INJURIES

- Withhold food and water for 12 hours from a pet that is vomiting, and then give your pet water, a little at a time. Consult your vet if your pet continues to vomit over a 24-hour period.

- Many pets get diarrhea, but the veterinarian should be consulted if it continues more than 24 hours or if it is tinged with blood.

- Lethargy, loss of appetite, or change in your pet's personality are symptoms of disease. See your veterinarian if symptoms worsen or continue after 24 hours.

- If a pet shows the signs of shock after being injured or involved in an accident, keep it warm and don't change its position too suddenly. Sudden movement can cause shock to move to the irreversible stage. Call your veterinarian right away.

PEST CONTROL

■ Ticks can be pulled out with tweezers. If you try to burn them out with a match, you could burn your pet.

■ Never use a flea collar at the same time as flea powder or flea sprays. This constitutes a harmful overdose.

■ Always air out a flea collar for several days before putting it on your pet; otherwise the chemicals may irritate its skin. Keep the collar away from both people and pets while it airs.

■ Check carefully for fleas when brushing or combing your pet, especially around the ears, face, and tail.

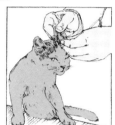

A PET OWNER'S CHECKLIST OF FIRST-AID SUPPLIES

☐ Adhesive tape, 1-inch and 2-inch rolls

☐ Antibacterial skin ointment

☐ Boric acid eye wash

☐ Cotton swabs (for cleaning the ears)

☐ Gauze bandage, 1-inch and 2-inch rolls

☐ Ice bags or chemical ice pack (for use in case of burns or heat prostration)

☐ Petroleum jelly (for treatment of hairballs)

☐ Mineral oil and eyedropper (for use at bath time)

☐ Rectal thermometer (for taking temperature, if recommended by veterinarian)

☐ Plastic or nylon eyedropper or dose syringe

☐ Scissors

☐ Sterile gauze pads

☐ Styptic powder (to stop bleeding from a nail)

☐ Triangular bandage and safety pins (for holding dressings in place)

☐ Tweezers

☐ Wood paint-mixing sticks and cotton batting (for splints)

☐ Wood rule or tongue depressor (for use with a tourniquet)

☐ If you have cats, add cat nail clippers, brush, and cat comb for grooming.

☐ If you have dogs, add dog nail clippers, brush, dog comb for grooming, and a nylon rope (4 to 5 feet long) for restraint.

Index

A

Absorbents, for stains, 88
Accessories, fashion,
    storage, 231
Accidents, prevention,
    262–264, 273–277.
    See also Emergencies.
Acetate, 70
    amyl, 90
Acetic acid, 88
Acetone, 88, 90
Acid stains, 20
Acoustic finish, 43
Acrylic countertops, 54
Acrylic fabric, 70
Address changes, 296
Adhesives, 200–201
Aduki beans, 143
Alabaster, 38–39
Alcohol, isopropyl, 90
Alcoholic beverage stains,
    20, 101
Allspice, 133
Aluminum cookware, 48, 49
Ammonia, 7, 90
Apples, 116
Appliances, kitchen
    large, 47–48, 57–60, 146
    small, 60–62
Apricots, 120
Avocados, 139

B

Baby. *See also* Infant.
    food/formula stains, 101
Babysitter, 281
Backstitch, 97
Baking, 146, 158–172
    ABCs of, 164
    bread
        quick, 160–161
        yeast, 158–160
    cakes, 161–164
    cookies, 164–166
    measuring ingredients,
        158
    pastry, 168–169
    problems/solutions,
        170–171
    substitutions, 172
Baking soda, 7
Bananas, 122
Barbecue grilling, 151–152
Barley, 124

Basil, 132
Basting (sewing), 97
Bath additives, 302, 304
Bathing
    infants, 282–285
    pets, 306–307, 310
    toddlers, 285–286
Bathroom
    childproofing, 275
    cleaning, 7–15
    drains, 13, 14, 196
    faucets, 196
    organization, 236
    toilet, 194–195
Bathtub, cleaning, 10–11
Bay leaf, 132
Beans, 142–143
Bedroom
    childproofing, 275
    organization, 236
Bedspreads, cleaning, 15–16
Beef, 126–127
Berries, 117–118
    stains, 102. *See also* Fruit,
        stains.
Bird, pet, 312
Biscuits, 160–161
Bisque, 154
Black beans, 143
Blackberry, 117
Blackout kit, emergency, 190
Blankets, cleaning, 16
Bleach, 7, 13, 15, 88
    laundry use, 77–78
Blender, 60
Blinds, 63
Blood stains, 20, 102
Blueberry, 117
Boiling foods, 147
Bone objects, 39
Books, cleaning, 34
Brass, cleaning, 35, 36
Brassicas, 136
Bread
    quick, 160–161, 170
    yeast, 170
Brick, 184–185
    floors, 27–28
    walls, 44
Broiling foods, 147
Broth, 154
Buckwheat, 124
Bulb vegetables, 136–137
Burglary prevention,
    268–272
Butter, 111
    stains, 20
Button replacement, 95–97

C

Cabinets, painting, 253
Cakes, 161–164, 171
Candle wax removal, 38
    stains, 20
Cannellini beans, 143
Can opener, electric, 61
Cantaloupes, 120
Capers, 133
Carpet
    burn hole, 23, 199
    cleaning, 19–25, 24
    depressions, 23
Car seats, 278
Cast-iron cookware, 49
Cats
    bathing, 306–307
    choosing, 306
    feeding, 307
    grooming and exercise,
        307
    health, 308–309, 314
Catsup stains, 20
Caulking, 185
Cayenne, 133
Ceiling
    cleaning, 43–44
    painting, 249–250
Cement (adhesive), 200–201
    china and glass, 201
    metal, 201
    plastic, 201
Ceramic-glass cookware, 52
Chalk line, 174
Chandelier, cleaning, 36
Change of address, 296
Cheese, 112–114
Cherries, 120–121
Chewing gum stains, 20
Chicken. *See* Poultry.
Chickpeas, 143
Children. *See also* Infant;
    Toddler.
    clothes, 280
    moving, 295
    safety, 273–282, 276
Chilies, 139–140
Chili powder, 133
Chisels, 173
Chives, 132
Chocolate, 167
    stains, 20, 103
Chowder, 154
Cinnamon, 133
Circuit breakers, 187
Citrus fruit, 118, 119

Clamps, 175
Clay cookware, 49
Cleaning, 5–66
    agents, 7
    bathroom, 7–15
    bedding, 15–19
    carpet, 19–25
    ceiling, 43–44
    combs and brushes, 298
    decorative objects, 37–40
    fireplace, 25–26
    floors, 27–34
    furnishings, 34–42
    grill, 152
    kitchen, 47–62
    metals, 26, 35, 36–37
    schedules, 5, 7, 12
    time-savers, 18
    tools, 5–6
    walls and woodwork,
        44–47
    windows and window
        coverings, 63–66
    wood furniture, 40–42
Closets
    organization, 226–228
    remodeling, 228–236
    systems, 231, 232–234
Clothes, 67–109
    care tips, 87, 99–100
    fabrics, 68–73
    hand-washing, 80
    infants and children, 280
    labels, 67–68, 74–75
    laundry, 67–68, 73–84
    mending, 93–98
    stain removal chart,
        101–109
    storage, 99–100, 229–231
Clove, 133
Coconut, 122
    oil, 90
Coffeemaker, 60–61
Coffee stains, 20, 85, 104
Colognes, 304
Combs and brushes,
    cleaning, 298
Comforters, cleaning, 16–17
    down-filled, 16
Composting, 214
Computer care, 225
Concrete, 184–185
    floors, 28
Consommé, 154
Cookies, 164–166, 170
Cooking. See also Baking;
    Food buying; Food
    storage.
    chocolate, 167
    cranberries, 117
    egg whites, 163
    frozen foods, 149

Cooking (continued)
    legumes, 142
    marinades, 153
    meat, 126, 127
    methods
        baking, 146–147,
            158–172
        barbecue grilling,
            151–152
        boiling, simmering,
            poaching, 147
        broiling, 147
        frying, 148
        microwave, 150–151
        roasting, 141, 146–147
        steaming, 146
        stir-frying, 148
    nuts, 129
    pasta and rice, 149–150
    poultry, 131
    safety. See Food safety.
    salads and salad
        dressings, 153–154
    sauces and gravies, 156
    seafood, 152
    soup stock, 155
    substitutions, 172
    vegetables, 135, 140, 141
Cookware, cleaning, 48–50
Cooling systems. See Heating
    and cooling.
Copper
    cleaning, 37
    cookware, 49–50
    polish, 50
Corn, 124, 138, 142
Cotton, 68
Countertops, 8, 54
    wood, 56
Couscous, 124
Cranberry, 117
Crayon stains, 20, 44, 104
Cream, 111–112
    stains, 105
Cribs, 278–279
Crosscut saw, 174
Cucumbers, 137
Cumin, 133
Cupboards, painting, 253
Currants, 123
Curry powder, 133
Curtains, 63, 65
    shower, 11–13
Cutlery, cleaning, 51

D

Dairy products, 111–115.
    See also individual
    types.
Dates, 121

Decks, 181
Decorative objects,
    cleaning, 37–40
Dental hygiene, infants and
    toddlers, 286
Deodorant stains, 105
Detergents, laundry, 77, 91
Dill, 132
Dinnerware, cleaning, 50
Dirt stains, 21, 107
Dish detergent, 7
Dishwashers, 57
Dogs
    choosing, 309
    feeding, 309–310
    grooming and exercise,
        310–311
    guard, 270
    health, 311, 314
Doorbells, 191
Doors, 197–198
    painting, 252–253
    security, 270, 272
Down-filled bedding, 16,
    17, 19
Downspouts, 179–180
Drains, clogged, 13, 14,
    196
Draperies, 65
Drill, electric, 175
Dryer, clothes, 80
Dry ice, 113
Drywall, 203–204

E

Eggplant, 140
Eggs, 114
    whites, 163
Electricity
    doorbells, 191
    emergency blackout kit,
        190
    fuses and circuit breakers,
        187
    safety, 186–187, 192–193
Emergencies
    blackout kit, 190
    pets, 313
Enamelware (cookware),
    50–51
Endive, 145
Epoxy, 200
Eyes, refreshing, 304

F

Fabric flowers, cleaning,
    37–38

Fabrics
  natural, 68–70
  softeners, 78
  synthetic, 70–73
Facials, 303, 304
Faucets, 196
Fava beans, 138, 143
Fences, 180
Fertilizer, garden, 211, 213
Fiberglass fabric, 70–71
Filing system, 221–223
Fingernail care, 302–303
  infant, 286
Fireplace, cleaning, 25–27
Fire prevention, 264–267
First aid kit, pet, 314
Fish. See Seafood.
Flagstone floors, 29
Flashings, 179–180
Flatware, cleaning, 51
Floor. See also Tile, floor.
  cleaning, 27–34
  repair, 198–199
Food buying
  poultry, 130
  seafood, 134
Food glossary, 111–145
Food processor, 60
Food safety, 127, 130, 153
Food storage. See also
    specific foods.
  baked goods, 161
    bread, 160
    cakes, 163–164
    cookies, 166
    pastry, 169
  cheese, 112–113
  freezer failure, 113
  grains, 124–125
  legumes, 142
  poultry, 130, 132
  seafood, 135
  tips, 110
Freezing foods. See also
    Food storage.
  freezer failure, 113
  soup and stock, 155
Freezing pipes, 196–197
Frozen foods
  cooking, 149
  dairy products, 115
Fruit, 115–124. See also
    individual types.
  soup, 154
  stains, 21, 85, 102
Frying, 148
Furniture
  outdoor, 181–182
  repair, 202
Fuses, 187

G

Garage
  floor, cleaning, 31
  security, 269
  storage, 238
Garage sale, 290
Garbage disposer, 61
Garden, 208–215
  composting, 214
  fertilizing, 211, 213
  herb, 214–215
  maintenance schedule, 212–213
  pest control, 214
  planning, 211
  seeds and seedlings, 213–214
  soil testing and preparation, 209–211
  tools, 207
  vegetable, 215
  watering, 211
Gates, 180–181
Genitals, infant, 283
Ginger, 133
Glass, cleaning, 63, 64
  glassware, 51–52
Glue, 200–201
  stains, 106
Glycerin, 90
Gold, cleaning, 36
Grains, 124–125
Grapefruit, 118
Grapes, 118
Grass stains, 106
Gravy, 156, 158
  stains, 21
Grease stains, 85, 107
Grooming
  personal. See Clothes;
    Hair care; Skin care.
  pet, 307, 310–311
Grout, cleaning, 55
Gutters, 179–180

H

Hacksaw, 174
Hair care, 297–300
  aids, homemade, 298, 299
  tips, 299–300
Hammer, 174
Hand and nail care, 302–303
Hand-washing, 80
Heating and cooling, 187, 190–193
Hemming techniques, 98

Herbs, 132–133
  growing, 214–215
High chairs, 279
Home
  maintenance, 173–220
  new, 294, 296
  office, 224–226
  organization. See
    Organization.
  safety, 273–277
    fire prevention, 264–267
    kitchen, 267
    storms, 267–268
  security, 268–272
House painting. See
    Painting.
Houseplants, 215–219
  fertilizing, 217
  lighting, 216
  moving, 292
  poisonous, 216
  repotting, 218
  seedlings, 219
  time-savers, 219
  vacations, 218
  varieties, 215–216
  watering, 216–217
Hydrogen peroxide, 88
Hydrosulfite, 88

I

Identification, children, 276
Infant, 277–286
  bathing, 282–285
  clothes, 280
  dental hygiene, 286
  equipment, 277–282
  genitals, 283
  nail-trimming, 286
Insecticides, safety, 264
Insects, 219–220
  garden, 214
Ironing, 75, 81–82, 84
Irons, electric, 82, 84
Isopropyl alcohol, 90
Ivory, 39

J

Jade, 39

K

Kidney beans, 143
Kitchen. See also Cooking;
    Food buying; Food
    safety; Food storage.

Kitchen *(continued)*
  appliances, 47–48, 57–62, 146
  cleaning, 47–62
  organization, 236–237
  safety, 267
    childproofing, 274–275
Kiwi, 122

L

Labels, clothing, 67–68, 74–75
Ladders, 183
Lamb, 127
Lamp shades, cleaning, 34–35
Laundry
  basics, 73–84
  clothing labels, 67–68, 74–75
  fabrics, 68–73
  hand-washing, 80
  problems, 83
  stains, 76–77, 84–93
Laundry room, organization, 238
Lawns, 208
  maintenance schedule, 212–213
Leafy vegetables, 137–138
Leather upholstery, cleaning, 42
Legumes, 142–143
Lemons, 119
Lentils, 143
Level, carpenter's, 174
Lima beans, 143
Limes, 119
Linen, 69
Linoleum floors, 29–30
Living areas, childproofing, 277

M

Maintenance and repair, 173–220. *See also* Painting.
  exterior, 179–186
  decks, 181
  gates and fences, 180–181
  gutters, 179–180
  roof, 182–184
  walls, 184–186
  interior, 186–206. *See also* Electricity.
  doorbells, 191

Maintenance and repair *(continued)*
  floor and carpet, 198–199
  heating and cooling, 187, 190–193
  plumbing, 193–197
  stairs, 202–203
  walls, 203–204
  windows and screens, 204–206
  lawn and garden, 207–220
  schedule, 188–189
  time-savers, 178–179
Makeup tips, 303
Mangoes, 122–123
Marble, 30, 39–40, 55
  cultured, 8, 55
Margarine, 111
Marinades, 153
Marjoram, 132
Mattress, cleaning, 17
Measuring tools, 174
Meat, 125–129. *See also* Beef; Lamb; Pork; Veal.
Melons, 120
Metals, cleaning, 26, 35, 36–37
Microwave cooking, 150–151
Microwave ovens, 57–58
Mildew prevention, 100
Milk, 114–115
Mint, 132
Mirrors, cleaning, 9
Modacrylic fabric, 71
Mothproofing, 99–100
Moving, 291–294
  checklist, 288
  children, 295
  day, 291–294
  packing, 289–290
  pets, 293
  planning, 287–288
  plants, 292
  professionals, 290–291
Moving sale, 290
Mud stains, 21, 107
Muffins, 161
Mushrooms, 138

N

Nails. *See* Fingernail care.
Nails, carpenter's, 176, 178
Nectarines, 121
Nonstick cookware, 52
Nutmeg, 133
Nuts (food), 129
Nylon, 71

O

Oats, 124
Office, home, 224–226
Oil stains, 108
Okra, 138, 142
Olives, 121
Oranges, 118
Oregano, 132
Organization
  bathroom, 236
  bedroom, 236
  closets, 228–236
  filing system, 221–223
  garage, 238
  kitchen, 236–237
  laundry room, 238
  sewing supplies, 98
  time-savers, 227
Outdoor furniture, 181–182
Oven, 58–59, 146
  microwave, 57–58
  toaster, 61–62
Overcast stitch, 98
Oxalic acid, 90
Oxygen bleach, 88

P

Packing, 289–290
Paint
  exterior
    application, 242, 244–245
    coverage, 240
    problems, 243
    types, 241
  interior
    color choice, 245–246
    selecting, 245
    types, 246
Paintbrush, 248
Painting, 239–254
  cleanup, 253–254
  exterior, 239–245
    preparation, 240
    tools, 239
  interior, 245–254
    ceilings, 249
    corners, 250
    cupboards, 253
    doors, 252–253
    preparation, 247–249
    safety, 251
    stairways, 253
    taking a break, 247
    tools, 245
    trim, 251
    walls, 250–251
    windows, 251–252

Painting *(continued)*
    tools, 239, 244, 245, 248, 249
Paintings, cleaning, 38
Paint roller, 249
    cleanup, 253–254
Paint sprayer, 244
Paneling, installing, 259–261
Papaya, 123
Paprika, 133
Parsley, 132
Pasta, 149
Pastry, 168–169, 171
Patio furniture, 181–182
Peaches, 121
Pears, 123
Peas, 138, 142
    dried, 143
    split, 143
Peppers, 140–141
Perfumes, 304
Pest control
    garden, 214
    home, 219–220
    pets, 314
Pesticides, safety, 264
Pets, 305–314
    birds, 312
    cats, 306–309
    dogs, 309–311
    emergencies and injuries, 313
    first-aid supplies, 314
    moving, 293
    other pets, 312–313
    pest control, 314
    selecting, 305
Pewter, cleaning, 35
Pianos, 35–36
Pillows, cleaning, 17, 19
Pineapple, 123
Pinto beans, 143
Pipes, plumbing, 196–197
Planes (tool), 175
Planning
    to-do lists, 223
    garden, 211
    home office, 225–226
    moving, 287–288
Plants. *See* Garden;
    Houseplants.
Plaster
    cleaning, 43
    repair, 203
Plastic cookware, 53
Plastic laminate, 8–9, 55–56
Plumbing, 193–197
    drains, 13, 14, 196
    faucets, 196
    pipes, 196–197
    toilet, 194–195
    valves, 197

Plums, 121
Poaching, culinary, 147
Polyester, 71–72
Porcelain, 40
Pork, 127–128
Potato, 145
Potting soil recipe, 215
Poultry, 129–132
    stuffing, 131
    types, 130
Power tools, 175
Priorities, 223–224
Pruning shrubs and trees, 209

Q

Quilts, cleaning, 16–17
Quinoa, 125

R

Raccoons, 220
Raisins, 118–119
Range hoods, 58
Raspberry, 117
Rayon, 72
Refrigerator, 59–60
Repair. *See* Maintenance and repair.
Rhubarb, 124
Rice, 150
Roasting, 146
Rodents, 220
Roof, 182–184
Root vegetables, 142, 144
Rosemary, 132
Router, 175
Rubber cookware, 53
Rule, folding, 174
Running stitch, 97–98
Rust prevention, 176, 177
Rye, 124

S

Safety
    electricity, 186–187, 192–193
    fires, 264–267
    food, 127, 130, 153
    grilling, 152
    home, 13, 15, 178, 262–264
        childproofing, 273–277
    houseplants, poisonous, 216
    kitchen, 267
    ladders, 183

Safety *(continued)*
    painting, 251
    pesticides, 264
    roofs, 184
    stain removal, 89
    stairways, 263
Saffron, 133
Sage, 132
Salad dressings, 153–154
    stains, 21
Salads, 153–154
Sander, electric, 175
Sauces, 156
Saws, 174
Schedule
    cleaning, 12
    home maintenance, 188–189
    lawn and garden maintenance, 212–213
    moving, 288
Scones, 160–161
Screens, window, 206
Screwdrivers, 174
Screws, 177, 178
Seafood, 133–135
    grilling, 152
Seasonings, culinary, 132–133
Security, home, 268–272
Seeds and seedlings, 213–214, 219
Sewing, 93–98
Shades, 65–66
Shellfish, 134
Shelving, between studs, 237
Shoes, care tips, 100
Shower, cleaning, 9–10
Shower curtains, 11–13
Shrubs, 208
    pruning, 209
Shutters, 66
Siding, exterior, 185–186
Silk, 69
Silver, cleaning, 37, 51
Silverware, 51
Simmering, 147
Sinks, 8
    drains, clogged, 13, 14, 196
Skin care, 300–303
    aids, homemade, 300, 301
Slate floor, 29
Sleeping bags, cleaning, 19
Smoke detector, 265, 266
Snow peas, 138, 142
Soap, laundry, 77
Sodium thiosulfate, 90–91
Soft-drink stains, 21, 108
Soil testing, 209–211
Soup, 154–156
    stock, 155

Soybeans, 143
Space organization
    closets, 226–234
    home office, 224–226
    kitchen, 236–237
Spandex, 72–73
Spices, 133
Sponge bath, infant, 284
Squash (vegetable), 137
Stainless-steel cookware, 53
Stains
    carpet, 20–21
    laundry, 83, 84–93,
        101–109
        prewash, 76–77
    removal, chart, 101–109
    tips, 91–93
Stains and paints, 239–245
    applying, 242, 244–245
Stairways, 202–203
    painting, 253
    safety, 263
Starfruit, 123
Steaming foods, 146
Stir-frying, 148
Storage
    clothes, 228–236
    fashion accessories, 231
    garage, 238
    management, 226–228
    maximizing, 235–238
    shelving, between studs,
        237
    tools, 175, 177, 178
Storm safety, 267–268
Stoves, cleaning, 47–48
Strawberries, 117–118
Strollers, 279
Stuffing, poultry, 131
Substitutions
    culinary, 172
    tools, 8
Sweet potatoes, 145

T

Tangerines, 118
Tarragon, 132–133
Terrazzo, 33
Theft prevention, 268–272
Thyme, 133
Tile
    ceiling, 43
    countertops, 55
    floor
        asphalt, 27
        ceramic, 28
        quarry, 30–32
        rubber, 32–33
    wall, 46

Time management,
    221–224
Toaster, 62
Toaster oven, 61–62
Toddler
    bathing, 285–286
    dental hygiene, 286
Toilet
    cleaning, 13, 15
    troubleshooting, 194–195
Tools, 173–175
    cleaning, 5–6, 8
    lawn and garden, 207
    paint, 239, 244, 245, 248,
        249
    rust prevention, 176, 177
    storage and maintenance,
        175, 177, 178
    substitutions, 8
    wallpaper, 254
Toys, safety, 280–282
Trees, 208
    pruning, 209
Triacetate, 73
Trichinosis, 127
Trim, painting, 251
Tubers, 145
Turkey. See Poultry.
Turmeric, 133

U

Upholstery
    cleaning, 42
    furniture, 202
Urine stains, 21, 109

V

Vacation
    home security during,
        272
    houseplants, 218
Valuables, protecting, 271
Valves, water, 197
Veal, 129
Vegetables, 135–145. See
    also individual types.
    cooking, 135, 140, 141
    gardens, 215
Vinegar, 91
    flavored, 157
Vinyl
    floor, 33–34
    upholstery, cleaning, 42
    wallcoverings, 45
Vomit stains, 21, 109

W

Waffle iron, 62
Wallpaper, 254–259
    borders, 258
    choosing, 255–257
    cleaning, 45–46
    coverage, 254–255
    hanging, 257–259
    measuring for, 254–255
    removing, 255
    repair, 205
    time-savers, 260
    tools, 254
Walls
    cleaning, 44–46
    painting, 250–251
Washing machine, 78–80
Water
    conditioners, 79
    pipes, 196–197
    valves, 197
Watering
    garden, 211
    houseplants, 216–217
    lawn, 208
Watermelons, 120
Wheat, 125
Windows, 204–206
    cleaning, 63–64
    painting, 251–252
    security, 272
Wine stains, 21
Wood
    cleaning, 40–42
    countertops, 56
    floors, 32
    glues, 200–201
Woodenware, 53, 54
Woodwork, cleaning, 46–47
Woodworking, 206
Wool, 69–70
Wrenches, 175

Y

Yams, 145
Yeast, 159
Yogurt, 115